Best wishes
Dick Schmedt

More advance praise for
Richard J. Schmeelk's
Mr. Canada

"It has been a pleasure to know Dick Schmeelk for many years, both before and after I served as premier of the province of Ontario. His work with private sector and government agencies was extremely helpful to the economic growth of our province, and his deep commitment to the relationship between our countries has done much to foster better understanding. I wish there were more men like Dick Schmeelk."

> *The Honourable William G. Davis,* P.C., C.C., Q.C.,
> Former Premier of Ontario

"We at Wood Gundy had the pleasure of acting as co-manager with Salomon on several of the underwritings Dick describes in his book. It was always a pleasure to work with Dick and his partners, and I believe that our clients were the beneficiaries of the excellent rapport that existed between the two firms. Dick was very deserving of the title *Mr. Canada.*"

> *Ted Medland,*
> Former Chairman, Wood Gundy Inc.

"Dick Schmeelk has been a good friend of Canada for many years, from his extensive business activities to his philanthropic endeavours. Of all my American friends, Dick's engagement with Canada has been the deepest. His book is a testimony to that."

> *The Honourable Michael H. Wilson,*
> Canadian Ambassador to the United States and
> Former Minister of Finance of Canada

Mr. Canada

Adventures of an Investment Banker
Inside and Outside Business

Richard J. Schmeelk

Twin Dolphin Books
New York

Printed in the United States of America by

Katonah Publishing Corporation.

To Priscilla,

with love

Contents

Foreword

By Henry Kaufman

When I received the manuscript of Dick Schmeelk's book, I expected a quick read. After all, I have known Dick for more than forty years. We were partners at Salomon Brothers and served together on the firm's senior management executive committee. I also consider Dick a close and trusted friend. Admittedly, I therefore do not bring a detached or clinical view. Nevertheless, I learned a lot about my friend from this book—about his personal life and aspirations, and about what made him a very successful investment banker in a highly competitive environment.

No one who knew Dick as a young man could have predicted his remarkable career and achievements. Back then, his ambitions and interests were dominated by sports. He excelled in baseball, basketball, and later, tennis—so much so that, with fewer injuries and a bit more luck, he might have become a prominent professional athlete rather than an investment banker.

Nor did Dick's family background foreshadow his ultimate career path. He was born into a family of humble means. His father made a modest living on the fringes of sports, while his mother was a dutiful housewife. Rockaway Beach, New York, where he was born, was not a breeding ground in the 1940s and early 1950s for future investment bankers, especially those headed for the financial institutions then dominating Wall Street. These were mostly white-shoe institutions that recruited chiefly Anglo-Saxon Protestants from Ivy League schools. That, of course, ruled out Jews, while Catholics like Dick rarely got through the front door.

i

Dick's years of duty in the Navy during World War II and his need to support a wife and growing family prevented him from attending college. Today, the lack of a college degree would at best relegate him to the operations department, or the back office, as it was then known. This is exactly where Dick started at Salomon, but in those days, unlike today, it was not unusual to advance from the back office to trading and sales.

When Dick joined Salomon Brothers, a number of partners held no college degrees but were, like Dick, self-educated men. Ever since I have known Dick, he has read voraciously—mostly non-fiction—and our conversations inevitably gravitate toward whatever book he is reading at the time.

The Salomon Brothers that Dick entered in 1945 was far different from the firm when he left in 1988. At the end of the war, Salomon mainly was a money market and bond house with limited activity in equities and investment banking. The firm operated no offices abroad and conducted little business with foreign institutions. But the makings of a future financial powerhouse were there. Its partners and traders possessed considerable skills, especially when it came to the art and science of pricing securities for purchase or sale.

During Dick's early decades at Salomon, the firm emerged as the leading underwriter of utility company bonds and the obligations of railroads, a challenging market in which underwriting bidding was especially competitive. Salomon also played a leading role in the secondary markets for these securities, and in other key capital markets, all the while honing its skills and burnishing its reputation in the pricing of new issues.

When Dick was advanced from the back office to the trading floor, he—like so many before him—came under the painstaking scrutiny of his supervisors. For many years, Salomon's trading room had no counterpart on Wall Street. Traders, salespeople, and partners of various kinds worked side-by-side in a rabbit warren of frenetic activity. The din in the room rose and fell with changes in the market, punctuated by shouts and waving across the trading floor. The chatter about trades—whether gains or losses—was non-stop. All of this was watched over by the firm's partners, who closely monitored the size and turnover of positions in securities.

In this competitive hothouse, the loss of a trade to a competing firm or client's placement of a sell or buy order with another house always raised the question, "How did we lose that business?" Although newcomers like Dick were watched by partners and peers alike, they were also encouraged to succeed.

In the early 1950s, Dick became the Salomon representative in Canada. The move hardly seemed auspicious. Canada's investment banking business and much of its bond and stock trading long had been controlled by First Boston Corporation, Drexel Harriman, Smith Barney, and four Canadian firms: A.E. Ames, Dominion Securities, McLeod Young & Weir and Wood Gundy. Salomon broke the lock of the establishment and went on to become the leading U.S. investment banker in Canada, catapulting above several American investment banking houses.

Dick started at the bottom, selling commercial paper and covering a variety of insurance companies, a job that took him across the vast nation from Nova Scotia to Alberta, where he called on assistant treasurers, treasurers, and junior institutional portfolio managers. But his tenacity, his considerable knowledge of markets, and his fairness in dealing with clients soon earned him access to senior managers at these leading Canadian institutions, and corporations as well as leading officials in the provincial and national governments.

Dick's indefatigable efforts to become Canada's most successful investment banker—and to make Salomon the nation's leading foreign banker—took their toll. But what ultimately motivated him to leave Salomon Brothers was a growing philosophical difference between him and the firm's senior partners as the 1980s unfolded. Salomon partners never were an especially congenial group, but they always shared an underlying commitment to avoiding conflicts of interest with institutions and corporations and otherwise following industry wide norms. This changed in the 1980s, when the firm's partners began to encourage much greater risk-taking, to leverage Salomon's balance sheet to unprecedented levels, and to divide over how to allocate the firms profits. Dick was among several in senior management—I was another—who were troubled enough by these changes to end our careers at Salomon.

Within a few years, sadly, Salomon Brothers faltered and was taken over by Citigroup. Once a Wall Street powerhouse, it vanished, name and all, into the new corporatized, depersonalized financial markets.

After Salomon, Dick launched a new career and company in finance with his former partner, Peter Gottsegen, called CAI Managers & Co., L.P., a private equity firm, which allowed him to continue his many friendships throughout Canada. His competitive zeal—abundant since his early days on the playing field and throughout his decades at Salomon—continued to carry him forward.

In spite of his drive, Dick is neither overbearing nor arrogant. Easygoing, generous, and warm, he is a man of integrity and forthrightness. It is little wonder, then that he has been so successful in business, and that so many cherish his friendship. All of these qualities come to life in the pages of his enjoyable memoir.

Dr. Henry Kaufman is a former member of the executive committee of Salomon Brothers, Inc., where he was in charge of the firm's four research departments. He is a member of the internal advisory committee of the Federal Reserve Bank of New York and a member (and chairman emeritus) of the board of overseers of the Stern School of Business at New York University. He served or has served on numerous corporate, educational, and non-profit boards.

Mr. Canada

Chapter 1
Out of Belle Harbor

I am flying from Regina to Calgary in a small DeHavilland. The ride is rather bumpy as we have been flying in a heavy snowstorm. The pilot has just announced that we will have to circle the airport in Calgary while they clear the snow from the runways. I spent a bitter cold night in Regina, so cold that I refused to leave the Hotel Saskatchewan despite the fact that the food there was not great. Before that, I'd flown from New York to Toronto to Winnipeg, and after leaving Calgary I'll be heading to Edmonton, which I hear has already used up its entire snow removal budget for the season despite the fact that Canadian Thanksgiving has just passed. That'll make eight different planes I've been on in the past two and a half days (seven of which took off). At each stop I've raced to make connections with my partner Peter Restler, toting a bag in each hand.

Some might call this a strenuous schedule for a man in his seventies. What is wrong with me? Why am I not relaxing on the tennis courts in Florida or enjoying the good life in New York?

I'm writing this book, in part, to figure that out. Maybe the title should be *What Makes Dickie Run?*

I write from the vantage point of what might be called my "unretirement." In 1989, after forty years at Salomon Brothers, I became a founding partner of a private equity fund called CAI Capital. About three quarters of our investments are in Canada. My fellow founding partners (if I may brag for a moment) are a pretty impressive bunch. They include David Culver, the former head of Alcan and a power in the Canadian community; Les Daniels, formerly of First Boston and a private health care investor for twenty years; Peter

3

Gottsegen, my former partner at Salomon, where he ran international corporate finance; and Peter Restler, formerly of Salomon, Wood Gundy, & Lehman Brothers. Having the opportunity to go on working with guys of this caliber is surely one reason I remain on the go, despite the fact that I'm no longer driven by the spur of money-making.

I guess the truth is that I like what I'm doing.

No one could have imagined where I'd be today by looking at my origins. I was born in 1924 and grew up in a little subdivision called Belle Harbor which was part of the New York working-class seaside community known as the Rockaways. We lived on a narrow strip of land about three eighths of a mile wide, dividing the Atlantic Ocean from Jamaica Bay. To the south we could see Sandy Hook, New Jersey, jutting out into the Atlantic, across from the seaside playground of Coney Island in Brooklyn. In between were the Narrows, the great gateway to New York harbor.

The ocean was a constant presence in my early life. We lived through several hurricanes, and on a few occasions the bay and the ocean met. Once the house at the end of my street was destroyed and its garage floated out to sea. I still have occasional dreams of ocean waves rolling up my street.

Access from Brooklyn to the Rockaways was by ferry, which landed near the old Floyd Bennett Field (now part of Gateway National Park). Several miles to the north were the Cross Bay Bridge and a Long Island Railroad trestle that crossed the bay from Broad Channel to the Rockaways.

There were several miles of sand dunes after Neponsit and one road that led to Fort Tilden and the Brooklyn ferry. This was our favored playground. We'd take a lunch and hike through the dunes for several hours, sometimes sneaking into Fort Tilden to see the two big guns (sixteen and fourteen inches) from World War I facing the Atlantic.

Later the Jacob Riis Bridge was built to connect Rockaway and Brooklyn. Today, Jacob Riis Park attracts thousands of summer visitors to its pavilion, its excellent beach, its boardwalk, paddle courts, and children's play area, all of which replaced the miles of dunes of my early youth. Years ago, I found it a wonderful place to take my older children in the winter. Even in January we'd see sun lovers in their bathing suits lying in a little alcove protected against the wind and catching a few rays in shiny reflectors as my tribe and I walked past bundled in our sweaters and coats.

Jamaica Bay at one time was famous for Rockaway oysters, which were served in fine restaurants around the United States. The bay had a strong tide that cleansed the oysters. My grandfather owned oyster beds in the bay in partnership with a man named Lundy, who had a large landmark restaurant in Sheepshead Bay, Brooklyn. (At one time, Lundy's was the largest restaurant in the United States, with seating for 2,400 diners.) Eventually, as the population spread on both sides of the bay, pollution destroyed the oyster beds. In more recent years, sewage plants have cleaned the bay, but the oysters haven't come back.

Although Rockaway is part of New York City, the great events of history that swept through the metropolis rarely affected us. There were a couple of exceptions. In 1933 when I was nine, Italo Balbo, Marshall of the Italian Air Force, led a group of twenty-four flying boats from Rome to Chicago's Lake Michigan and then to Jamaica Bay. I was among the huge crowd that lined both sides of the bay to greet his arrival. Although he was a Fascist, Balbo was given a hero's welcome. A street in New York City was named after him, and President Franklin D. Roosevelt invited him to lunch. (Balbo later became Governor General of Libya, quarreled with Mussolini over which side Italy should support in the Second World War, and died when his plane was shot down by fire from an Italian cruiser—whether by accident or design remains unknown to this day.)

The second famous event in Jamaica Bay was the 1947 speedboat race in which Guy Lombardo, the famous bandleader and restaurateur, sought to defend the International Gold Cup championship he'd won the year before. It was a very windy day and the bay was quite choppy. Early in the race, Lombardo's boat, the *Tempo VI*, hit a log and was knocked out of action. Several other boats suffered the same fate, and that ended speed boat racing in Jamaica Bay.

We lived in a typical Queens row house—two stories high, with a shared driveway. Our family consisted of my mother, the former Mary Smyth (universally known as Mae), my dad Garrett Schmeelk, my older brother Garry, and our great-aunt Kate. I had an older sister whom I never knew—she died of pneumonia when she was six months old—and a younger brother who died shortly after being born. I attended St. Francis de Sales grammar school, just a block from our home.

Our mother Mae was a very steady, outgoing woman, with a good set of values and a friendly personality. Perhaps her strength came from a life of adversity. She had lost her parents at an early age, leaving a large brood of siblings to care for one another. Mom's older sister Jenny was widowed. Her older brothers Eddie and Jack fought in France in World War I. Then there were brothers Joe and Ritchie, whom she took care of when they were growing up, another older sister named Marge, and spinster Aunt Kate who lived with us.

Kate worked for fifty years as a seamstress for DePennas department store in New York City. When she retired with no pension, I wrote to the head of the firm, suggesting it might be the honorable thing to give her a bonus after fifty years. Happily they agreed with me. They sent her $75.00.

Dad was a huge and colorful personality who made a living doing everything he could think of in the then-rudimentary world of professional sports. Along with his brother-in-law, my uncle Dick Smyth, he was one of the best-known professional basketball players in the country. They played originally with the New York Nationals, an early barnstorming team that traveled from New York to San Francisco. On one trip, they lost their first game in Wilkes-Barre, Pennsylvania, then went on to win forty-four straight games—including beating Wilkes-Barre on their way back home.

Also on the team was Elmer Ripley, who later coached Georgetown and is enshrined in the Basketball Hall of Fame. According to Uncle Dick, Ripley had his nose broken in four places during the first half of one game: "Your father took two books and set his nose during halftime. Then Elmer played the second half."

Another time, they were playing in Hazelton, Pennsylvania, where one of the Nationals, a fellow named Walter Grimstead, had shot the winning basket on their last trip. Before the game, a local bully walked into the dressing room, pulled out a gun, and said to Grimstead, "If you go near that basket tonight, I'll blow your brains out." Dad and Uncle Dick had quite a time getting Grimstead out on the court. Grimstead was sandwiched between the two of them taking shots before the game when someone tossed a firecracker out of the balcony. Grimstead turned white. He played the game, but never crossed the midcourt line and didn't take a single shot.

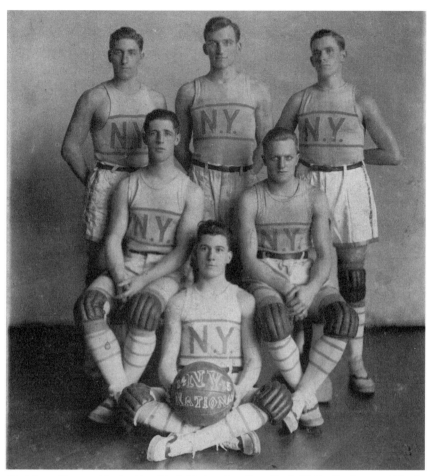

Dad in uniform with the New York Nationals. Top: Dad, Wally Rucker, and Uncle Dick Smyth. Middle: Bill Brunner (later borough president of Queens) and Elmer Ripley (member of the Basketball Hall of Fame). Bottom: Jimmy Bryant.

Years later, in 1942, a bunch of old-time basketball players from the Original Celtics, the Brooklyn Visitations, the Cleveland Rosenblooms, and other early teams held a dinner to honor the New York Nationals. Dad had died after a heart attack the year before, but my brother Garry and I went to the dinner.

We found that the average height of the old-timers was about five foot eight or nine. One of the few tall players there was named Stretch Meenhen. He greeted me and said, "Ask your mother about the time in Wilkes-Barre when she was hitting me over the head with her pocketbook."

I was taken aback—that didn't sound much like my mom. But when I got home, she confirmed the story. "Your father was wrapped in the chicken wire," she explained. (In those days basketball courts were enclosed with chicken wire—that's where we get the slang term *cagers* for basketball players.) "Meenhen was sitting on him, and a couple of women fans were sticking hat pins into your father. So I kept hitting Meenhen till he got off."

Actually, it's understandable that opponents would have wanted to knock my dad out of the game. Dan Parker, the old sports reporter for the New York *Daily Mirror*, called my father the greatest shoot-

Dad, looking every inch the prosperous sports entrepreneur.

8

er he ever saw. He may also have been the first successful one-handed shooter (long before Hank Luisetti of Stanford, who is usually credited with that innovation). It wasn't a deliberate strategy—unbeknownst to my dad and his parents, he'd broken his arm in a fall on the ice as a boy. Ever since then he'd been awkward and unbalanced whenever he tried to take a two-handed shot.

Later my dad had a team called the Brooklyn Nationals. Their stationery boasted, "First team to beat the Original Celtics twice in one year." (Though my uncle Dick used to say that the great black team the Renaissance was every bit as good as the Original Celtics.)

After hanging up the jock, my father managed pro basketball in the old Madison Square Garden. The Original Celtics were the home team, and the legendary Tex Rickard was the promoter. He also managed a Pittsburgh-based hockey team in the old American League, ran a track where midget auto races were held, and with Tim Mara, Sr., was a legal bookmaker at various race tracks. Today he would be considered a sports entrepreneur—and in the high-powered world of professional sports, he would probably be a wealthy man. But there was no money in sports back then, so Dad struggled financially.

Yet he had a ball being part of the sporting scene, and my brother Garry and I were constantly amazed at the wide-ranging friendships he developed. I remember sitting on the Chicago Bears bench for one football game, courtesy of coach George Halas, a good friend of Dad's. Another time we sat behind the Yankee dugout and were greeted by Lou Gehrig and Babe Ruth, two more pals of our dad.

When Garry was in his teens, he had a near-fatal case of double pneumonia. His condition was so grave they even prayed for him in church. To cheer him up, Dad got some of his sports buddies to write him in the hospital. I remember seeing letters from Joe DiMaggio, heavyweight champion Jimmy Braddock (recently portrayed on screen by Russell Crowe in *Cinderella Man*), and Wally Berger, the hard-hitting outfielder of the Boston Braves.

Garry and I both loved and played practically every sport you can think of. Garry played on the St. John's Prep tennis team, which won the Catholic School Championship twice. But he was cut from the football team by coach Herb Hess—unfairly, I still think. (Garry was a good football player. He later played for teams at Manhattan College and Sampson Naval Training Station as well as some good semi-pro teams.) Needless to say, Garry and I tore up several invitations to honor Herb Hess over the years.

I went out for the baseball team at St. John's and ran into the same problem. After several people told me I was a cinch to make the team, I was allowed to pitch to only one batter, who turned out to be almost as tiny as the midget that Bill Veeck, the legendary baseball showman, once inserted into a major league lineup. I walked him and then was cut.

Nonetheless, I was a pretty good pitcher. I established two records in the Rockaways. Once was when I struck out ten Greeks in a row. (I didn't check their nationalities, that was the name of the team.) My other record was hitting a girl player named Pat Finn (we called them tomboys then) in three consecutive plate appearances. On her fourth at-bat, I called my catcher out to the mound. "Let's give her an intentional walk," I said. My first pitch sent her sprawling in the dirt.

Perhaps my most memorable pitch was a fast ball I delivered that hit the batter squarely in the head. (He was leaning over to straighten out home plate, which I hadn't noticed because I'd been checking the runner at second.) When my bean ball failed to kill him, I realized I was not headed for the big leagues.

I didn't even try out for the St. John's football team. Football was my worst sport—probably because I was so good-looking I was afraid of spoiling my chances for Hollywood. (Don't believe me? Hey, I was named the handsomest fellow in the local Catholic Youth Organization after it was discovered that the original winner hadn't paid his dues. It was a hotly-contested election—I believe I got two votes. I never knew who the other voter was.)

Two years later, I got my revenge on St. John's. After Dad died, I switched to Far Rockaway High School, and we upended St John's in basketball on our home court.

Garry and I ended up in the tennis singles finals at the Belle Harbor Yacht Club in Rockaway on several occasions. Overall, he had the edge. But our rivalry was intense. The last time we squared off in the finals was when we were in our forties. (I was working on Wall Street by then.) The final match was played on a sweltering summer day. I won the first set 9-7, and I was up 10-9 in the second set after two and a half hours of exhausting play. At 40-love, I served three times. Each time Garry returned my serve, and I made no attempt to return his shots. Realizing I was out of steam, Garry halted the match.

My heart felt as if it was bursting. I was taken into the club and fed salt and tea with sugar. Later we discovered I'd suffered a heat stroke. As our mother used to say, "You damn fools—you'll kill each other one of these days." This was about as close as we ever came. I suffered occasional dizzy spells for about a year afterward.

A close call like that does something to your competitive juices. You still want to win, but you develop a certain sense of caution. The change in attitude probably cost me a few matches.

There were plenty of open spaces to play in when we were growing up in the Rockaways. We played something we called "block sports"—128th Street against 127th or 129th Street. It wasn't exactly gentlemanly: We'd gather on the sand dunes and scale clam shells or shingles at each other. We also used the beach to play football and baseball, and we played hockey in the street with a wooden puck. One day a woman called the police because we were making noise in front of her house. The police arrived and one of them said, "Why don't you go down to the beach and play?" I offered him my skates, but he declined.

One day a tragedy occurred: A coal truck turned a corner and hit and killed one of our players, a kid named Davey. His older brother Anthony had already lost his arm when his father backed over him in their driveway. Anthony played basketball in the church's senior team with me, and his nickname was Deadeye. He was also a very good outfielder in baseball.

Our father followed the racing seasons to Florida and Saratoga in upstate New York. Usually he'd go down to Florida for eight or nine weeks and have Mother join him for a month or so, leaving Aunt Kate or Aunt Marge in charge of Garry and me. But at least one winter he brought the whole family down south. I remember my first day in school in Miami. Little Johnny sitting behind me tapped me on the shoulder and asked, "What religion are you?"

"Catholic," I replied.

Johnny retorted, "I hates Catholics.'"

Not to be outdone, I asked him, "What religion are *you*?"

"Baptist."

Of course, I had to be smart. I replied, "I hates Baptists." (The truth is that I'd never heard of the Baptists before, and I assure you that anti-Baptist prejudice had nothing to do with my voting against Jimmy Carter many years later. I only wish I could vote against him a couple more times, since I consider him the worst president in my time.) Well, it turned out that every kid in the class was a Baptist. (They also were convinced that the South had won the Civil War.) I ended up having to "constant helm on a zigzag course" (an old Navy term for changing course to avoid torpedoes) to reach school without getting clobbered.

Two other memories from Miami:

Somewhere we got ahold of a picture card showing a group of Seminole Indians. Brother Garry pointed to the card and said, "That little baby is you—that's where we got you." I was fairly dark-skinned, and for a few years I believed him.

Another time a photographer came to the house selling his services. Mom had Garry and me change into our best linen suits and pose on the steps with our tennis rackets. Shortly after the pictures were taken, I found a ripe tomato and bashed Garry with it. Then I took off like a big bird and hid out for a few hours until things calmed down.

Garry got his revenge. We were both altar boys at church, and when I served my first mass with him, he made sure I botched the job by giving me wrong signals about when to ring the bells and when to present the water and wine. Ah, brotherly love.

In the summer, while Dad was in Saratoga for the month of August, Mom, Garry, and I would stay at Aunt Marge's place in the little upstate village of Acre, New York. Garry and I hated it. Neither Mom nor Aunt Marge drove a car. We missed the ocean and found that the most exciting activity was sitting on the porch in the evening counting cars as they passed. Garry would take the north-bound road and I would take the south. Sometimes as many as two or three cars would pass in an hour.

It took all our ingenuity to come up with other forms of entertainment. My Aunt Marge had married a widower named Luke McKeon—a one-time fireman who'd been hit by a train while fighting a fire and was confined to a wheelchair. At the age of twelve, I aspired to be a big-league pitcher like my idol Lefty Grove, and I would hone my fastball by scaling rocks past Uncle Luke as he sat on the porch. Mind you, I never hit him. But for some reason the stones whizzing past his nose upset him. He would call out in a

12

My brother Garry and me, aged about seven and five, one summer in Acre.

cheerful tone to my mother, "Mae, get that little son of a bitch out of here!" I would race away down the hill before my mother could catch me.

Usually my Uncle Joe and my cousin Joe Smyth would come up to Acre for a week. Cousin Joe was like a little brother to me. (Years later he joined me at Salomon Brothers and also became a partner.) One time Mom offered us each a quarter if we could find a four-leaf clover (anything to get us out of the house). After a futile search, we pasted an extra leaf on a three-leaf clover and rushed into the house to claim our reward. In retrospect, this showed that we were clever enough to eventually work on Wall Street. But brother Garry became the original whistle-blower: He uncovered the plot and our payoff was lost.

Uncle Joe always loved Garry dearly. In later years, he would talk and talk about what a terrific person Garry was. Cousin Joe and I agreed, but we got a little tired of the constant testimonials, so finally one of us would say, "Garry may be nicer than us, but at least we've never been sued by a priest!" This would get Uncle Joe all riled up and force him to defend Garry.

(And yes, Garry *was* actually sued by a priest. After the war, Garry and a few of his friends signed to play pro football for a team called the Anthonians, which happened to be managed by a priest. When they jumped their contracts to play for more money elsewhere, they got sued. They finally agreed to play one free game for the Anthonians, and all was forgiven.)

Eventually Dad started taking us all to Saratoga for the month of August. We lived in a rented house on Caroline Street. It was on the main street exiting the track, and our side porch attracted a steady stream of racing fans eager to stop for a drink or two (or three) on the way home.

While waiting for the dinner bell, Garry and I hung out in the back yard playing catch. The balls we used included one signed by the 1924 Washington Senators (who'd won the World Series under Bucky Harris) and another signed by Babe Ruth and Lou Gehrig. Guess what? We lost them both.

Some fifty-five years later, I went into a baseball memorabilia store and asked the proprietor how much a ball signed by Ruth and Gehrig would be worth. He replied, "Twenty-five thousand dollars, if it's in good condition. Let's have a look."

"Sorry, I lost it in a back yard in Saratoga."

"Go back and look for it," he advised me.

The nearby park is where Garry and I learned to play tennis. We played with many of the leading jockeys of the day—Jackie Westrope, Wayne Wright, the Hanford brothers—who wore rubber sweat suits to lose weight prior to the day's races. I also played with a saxophone player from Don Besta's band, who boasted a variety of soft spin shots and uttered a particularly hideous laugh when winning.

Here I must pay tribute to the old Spalding Sporting Goods Company. I owned one of their wood rackets, and when I was frustrated I would fire it high in the air and cry out, "Break, you so-and-so!" It never did.

In the afternoon, we would go to the track. One day Garry, normally much more conservative than I, plunged on a beautiful light brown gelding with a white spot on his head named Barnett who was the odds-on favorite. Barnett refused to break from the starting gate. Evidently he was hard of hearing and didn't notice the starting bell. I believe this was the last bet my brother ever made.

In the evening, Garry and I would go over to the park and watch semi-pro baseball or play ball with the locals. I had a bad habit of jerking my bat back at the plate. On one occasion, the opposing catcher was playing without a face mask and I inadvertently knocked out his two front teeth. This did nothing to make a New York "city slicker" popular with the locals.

Two of the semi-pro teams my brother Garry and I enjoyed watching were the House of David (a team of bearded players originally sponsored by a religious community from Michigan) and the Mohawk Colored Giants (an all-Black team that featured a slugging catcher named Buck Ewing who clearly had big-league talent).

At the track, I had a partner named Solly Piscano. Solly owned horses and also had a restaurant (Libby's) on New York's Fulton Street and a stall in the Fulton Fish Market. Solly figured that, because the bookmakers at the track knew my father, he would get better odds if I placed our bets. This was true, but if you picked the wrong horse the odds didn't matter.

Pretty soon I owed money to everyone in the house, including Aunt Kate and our maid Claudia. Eventually, Dad said to Mom, "Mae, Dick is getting to like horse playing too much. He's barred from the track." But he didn't say anything about the back stretch outside the track, where the grooms and others congregated and bet as little as twenty-five or fifty cents on a horse. Someone would call the order of finish through the trees and invariably got it wrong.

I finally got on a hot streak and pushed my bankroll back to $15.00. My father relented and the last day of the meet allowed me to go to the track. I was standing next to him for the last race. I had ten dollars bet on one horse, and he had a hundred bet on another—a thirty-to-one shot. He couldn't believe I was rooting for my horse against his. Dad's horse finished first, and he won $3,000. But later, all he could say to my mother was, "Can you imagine? I paid for the whole month with my winnings, and my son was rooting against me!"

Race track people tell endless stories, and two of the best are about my father.

One day, he went to the track with twenty dollars. He won six races in a row, betting his winnings on the next race each time, and running his twenty bucks into twenty thousand. Of course, he bet the whole $20,000 on a horse in the seventh race—and the horse came in second. As Dad was leaving the track, a friend approached him and inquired, "How did you do today, Garry?"

His simple answer: "I lost twenty bucks."

Here's the other story. The famous jockey Eddie Arcaro and his wife rented a house in Miami next to my father's. The Arcaros were known to have a very stormy relationship. One day, when my father had a few friends over for a barbecue, Mrs. Arcaro came bursting through the hedges. She had a bloody nose and was wearing a white dress spattered with blood.

Dad took it in stride. "Who are you riding for, kid?" he asked, "The Whitneys?" The Whitney jockey colors were white with red polka dots.

My partner Solly Piscano was quite a character. When I was working on Wall Street, I would go down to see him at the Fulton Fish Market. We would walk around and he would introduce me— never by name, but always as "Garry's boy." One day I met him coming off a fishing boat. He was wearing wet, grimy boots and dirty clothes, and smelled to high heaven. Solly greeted me, took me to his room at the market, grabbed his suit off a nail on the wall, changed into it without washing, ran his hands through his hair, and announced to his buddies, "Well, I'm off to the track."

1941 turned into a very bad year for our family. In August, my father got a telegram telling him that his dad, a big strapping man in his eighties, had died. He was in the clam business in the Great South Bay and lived in Copague, Long Island. The clam business had deteriorated sharply thanks to a combination of reduced water flow, the construction of roads and bridges for the new Jones Beach complex, and the proliferation of duck farms. At one time the price of clams dropped when green spots appeared on them. They tasted all right, but there's only one day when people are willing to eat green clams—St. Patrick's Day.

Much worse news was to come. In October of the same year, Dad had a heart attack. He died soon thereafter from complications of pneumonia. My mother recalled sitting with him in the press box at a baseball game in Philadelphia and hearing Dad complaining about the cold. When they returned to Long Island, he went into Rockaway Beach Hospital and died within the week.

This was a tremendous shock. Dad had never been sick. I took a long walk by myself and cried and cried. It was many years before I shed another tear.

At the time, Garry was a sophomore at Manhattan College. I drove up to the college with Uncle Dick to break the news to Garry. Uncle Dick was too softhearted to do the deed, so I went into the dorm alone to tell Garry his father had died—one of the hardest things I've ever done.

It was thirty-odd years before Garry and I could talk about our father without choking up.

We quickly discovered that our family finances were not in great shape. The house in the Rockaways was mortgaged and now there was no source of income to support it. Because we lived in a summer resort area, we could rent out one floor in the summer. But otherwise, our total assets were five hundred dollars in the bank and a second-hand Buick.

As for the Buick, it proved to be more of a curse than a blessing. One day, Garry was driving along a road in Rockaway often called Suicide Highway, built under elevated subway tracks that created many blind spots. A young cyclist shot out of a side street and crashed into the side of the Buick. Garry picked him up, bleeding badly, and drove him to Rockaway Beach Hospital. The doctors said Garry's quick action saved the boy, but some ambulance chaser convinced the family to sue. My mother was frantic thinking she would lose the house.

A few months later, Garry was driving down 129th Street (the local shopping strip) when a woman stepped out between two cars. He braked, the woman fell backwards, and soon she too had launched a lawsuit.

In the end, my mother got rid of the car, and insurance covered the settlements (which were substantially less than the original suits). Garry dropped out of Manhattan College after Dad's death and went to work to support the family.

There was one blow left for 1941: the attack on Pearl Harbor and the entry of the U.S. into World War II. Garry went to work as a dock builder in Bayonne, New Jersey. He worked long hours (he had to leave in a carpool for work around 5:30 a.m.), but the pay was good. I was going to Far Rockaway High, working as a messenger on

My first wife, Betty, enjoying the sun on the boardwalk at Rockaway.

Wall Street during the summer for $15 a week. I'd begun dating my first wife, Betty Conaghan. And sports continued to be important: I played on the school basketball team and on the St. Francis De Sales Big Five. But already some of our church players were departing for the services. One of our older players, Paulie Esposito, was in the Coast Guard. He would sometimes play the first half of a game and then have to leave for his base in New Jersey.

In 1943, Garry signed with the New York Football Giants and was written up as one of the outstanding rookies in camp. But during one practice session, he was cross-blocked, strained a ligament in his knee, and was released. (In those days, everyone got paid the same $100 for an exhibition game, star players and rookies alike. And if you had an injury, your contract could simply be voided.) Garry went back to dock building. Later he was offered a contract by the Brooklyn team in the American Football League, but as our family's chief breadwinner he felt he couldn't take a chance on another injury.

In September of 1942, I turned eighteen, and four months later, in January of '43, I finished high school. With my family struggling to get by and our nation at war, a serious future loomed. My brother was slated to go in the draft before me, but he was making a lot better money than I could. So unbeknownst to Garry, I went to the draft board and had my draft position moved ahead of his. He was furious until they finally drafted him about eleven months after me.

Here's how the draft worked back then: You showed up at Grand Central Station on the appointed day, had a physical, filled out various forms, and then queued up with hundreds of other young men. Waiting to greet you at the end of the line were representatives of the Army, Navy, Marines, and Coast Guard.

When my day arrived, a friend of mine named Jimmy Dillon was on line with me. Jimmy had an uncle who was a West Point graduate and eventually rose to brigadier general. Jimmy was hell-bent on getting into his uncle's Army, but when he got to the end of the line he was grabbed by a Marine recruiter. All I could make out was Jimmy shaking his head, sweating, and biting his tongue. But as it happened, Jimmy didn't have great teeth. The Marines passed on him, and he ended up in the Army after all. He spent the war in Watertown, New York, and rose to the rank of lieutenant.

As for me, when I reached the end of the line, I chose the Navy. I was following a family tradition—my father was in the Navy during World War I. When asked where he'd served, he would always reply, "I was on the big drive."

The questioner would ask, "What drive?"

My father would reply, "Riverside Drive in New York," which was where he was stationed for the duration.

My own tour of duty would turn out to be a little more adventurous.

Chapter 2
Here Comes the Prowler

As the war ground on, the chief topic of conversation among my gang of buddies in Rockaway was always how and where we might serve when our time came. Our group included a fellow named Jim Donavan who suggested one evening that we should all sign up for the ski troops. The chance of skiers being sent into action was pretty small.

"Hey, stupid," someone responded, "None of us even know how to ski."

"That doesn't matter," Donavan retorted. "All you have to do is fill out an application saying you belong to a ski club and you'll be accepted."

This was enough to convince us. Jim got the applications. But everyone backed out for some reason—one fellow had a trick knee, I had back problems, and so on. In the end, Donavan was the only one to apply. He was pretty put out.

But Donavan had the last laugh. Three of our group landed at Normandy on D-Day, and two were also in the bloody invasion of Anzio in Italy. I spent a couple of years in the Pacific. But Donavan passed the entire war skiing in Colorado; his major action was reported to be throwing a girl through a drum celebrating V-E day. (I didn't start to ski until I was sixty, and I wished I had taken it up much earlier.)

My turn to go to war came in February, 1943. My brother, my mother, and my girl friend Betty saw me off from Penn Station, bound for boot camp at the Sampson Naval Station near Geneva, New York. It was cold, cold country—so cold that most of us sailors slept in our pea coats and hats, except for one weirdo named Strung who slept bare-assed. When he finally came down with a cold, the whole barracks cheered.

I had the fire watch one night. That meant I had to go to four different barracks and make sure the coal fires were going. When I inspected them, the fires were all burning brightly. But no one had warned me that if the coals clung together forming a "clinker," they would eventually go out. In the morning, there were four barracks full of freezing sailors searching for the idiot who'd let their fires go out. I partially redeemed myself by playing on our division basketball team and helping to win the base championship.

By the summer, I was at Diesel School in Richmond, Virginia, which was like going from the North Pole to the Equator. To cool off, we'd stop up the shower drains and lie in the tepid water.

After graduating from Diesel School, I had a choice for further training: landing craft, diving school, PT boats, or submarines. I would have signed up for PT boats, but you had to be twenty-one years old. I didn't realize it at the time, but a lot of PT sailors suffered kidney problems from the pounding those boats took. I think about that today when I see cigarette boats hammering the waves down in Florida.

I opted for submarine school in New London, Connecticut. As I recall, they only took about seven or eight men out of 600 graduates, so my sidekick Charlie Wicker and I were excited when we were accepted. I had one week off before reporting, and I didn't have the guts to tell my mom where I was going. Submarine service was supposed to be dangerous, and I knew she wouldn't be pleased. Finally, on the last day, I said, "Well, Mom, I'm headed for sub school in New London."

Her only comment was, "I thought you'd do something like that." I can imagine what she was really thinking.

Why did I choose submarines? It was partly the money. I'd get twenty percent extra for overseas services and an extra fifty percent for submarine duty. But it was also the sense of challenge. In basketball, I always liked to guard the big scorer on the other team. Anyone who knows about my mechanical skills (or lack thereof) can understand that working in the engine room of a submarine would be quite a stretch for me.

At New London, we started training on O boats of WWI vintage—a little like learning to ride a horse and then being handed a set of car keys. Then we graduated to S boats from the late 20s and early

30s. We also trained in the big tank with our Munson lungs, learning to make an underwater escape from a sunken sub (an unlikely event—only a few such escapes ever occurred). The tank had a depth of 100 feet. We'd sit in a chamber next to the tank as the air pressure was brought up to sea pressure. We'd then adjust the lung and slowly ascend on a rope, stopping every ten feet until we reached the surface.

When I graduated from sub school, I also picked up a new nickname. All of us graduates had our pictures taken, which were sent to our local newspapers—in my case, the Long Island *Daily Press*. Soon my picture appeared with the caption, "While others are sleeping peacefully at home in their beds, young R.J. Schmeelk is out prowling the depths in search of enemy shipping." (The only prowling I was actually doing was in bars around New London.) Unfortunately, this article fell into the hands of some of my comrades, and for a while I would hear, whenever I walked into the room, "Here comes the Prowler."

Mom with me in my navy uniform.

There was no escaping from sports, especially basketball. A group of us from New York City formed the nucleus of a pretty good team. It included my buddy Julie Fuchs, who had played with me for the St. Francis Big Five. Julie is Jewish, and when he was asked to lead us in prayer before a game, he would say, "Hail Mary. I'm sorry, fellows, I don't know the rest." Julie had torn a ligament in a game for St. Francis, so when he tried to enlist in the service at the same time as me, a doctor saw that he couldn't bend and rejected him. Julie was practically in tears. He had his knee operated on, and he was then accepted.

Jackie Wilkenson had also played for the St. Francis Big Five. In the navy, Jackie, Julie, and I teamed together with a fellow we knew from the High School League in Queens—Don Kayden, captain of Richmond Hill—as well as Ushey Cohen, a high scorer at Commerce High in New York, and my friend Charlie Wicker. We played for the Firemen in the base tournament and ended up competing for the base championship against the Machine Shop team.

We played a tough brand of ball, starting with one of our signature plays in the first ten seconds: Wicker jumped center, tapped the ball to me, and cut off me. Then I fed him the ball as he went up for the basket. He was clothes-lined as he went up, and that set the tone for the entire game. (This was the way we were used to playing. Back at Far Rockaway we led the league in fouls two years in a row.)

We won the base championship, and the chief petty officer who refereed the game said afterwards, "Boy, you guys play rough."

Something made me feel like bragging. "What do you expect?" I said. "I was a boxer back in New York. Light heavyweight." In reality, the only fighting I'd ever done was a couple of "Oh, yeahs?" and a few swings in basketball games.)

I'd forgotten that the chief was also in charge of Friday night fights at the base—big affairs attended by a few thousand sailors. He replied, "How about fighting next Friday night?"

I was relieved to be able to say, "Chief, I'd love to, but I'm shipping out on the *Euryale* this week. Why don't you ask Wilkenson? He was one of the classiest club fighters in New York."

I left New London on the *Euryale*. It was a sub tender, a large auxiliary vessel used to provide maintenance and logistical support to submarines. We sailed to Norfork, Virginia, and then to Newport, Rhode Island, picking up torpedoes, ammunition, and spare parts, and then came back to New London for a day. When I visited the gang, Wilkenson buttonholed me. "What the hell did you tell that chief? He won't leave me alone! He keeps trying to get me in the ring." I don't know what happened in the end—I hope poor Wilkenson didn't end up with a broken nose on my account.

The next day we sailed to New York, where we went through a few days of drills and prepared to sail for the Pacific.

Shortly after New Year's day, we departed New York harbor under a light snowfall. As we were passing through the Narrows, our exit was aborted by word of the explosion of a U.S. destroyer off Sandy Hook, New Jersey. At first it was feared that the destroyer had been torpedoed by a German submarine, but later it was found to be an explosion in the magazine. (Many years ago, I recounted this story to my friend Walter Wriston. He remembered it well—he was stationed in Coney Island at the time.)

The following day, we set sail again, this time escorted by a destroyer. I stood watch in the shaft alley deep in the fantail of the ship, a station I reached by climbing down a ladder some thirty or forty feet. My duty was to keep oiling the bearings and make sure they didn't overheat. Originally there was an opening from the shaft alley to the engine room, but this was eventually sealed off to prevent flooding in case a torpedo hit near the fantail. This meant I could no longer converse with the sailors in the engine room, which made for a lonely, boring watch. Every time we went into a port, I was stuck down in the bowels of the ship.

Our first port of call was at Balboa, Panama. It was my initial experience witnessing the behavior of a young group of sailors, many of whom were away from home for the first time. The liberty section had to pass Marine guards to reboard the ship, and many sailors, drunk as skunks, tried to sneak bottles of booze past the Marines. After these attempts failed, a bunch of sailors went to the fantail and tossed ropes overboard to their buddies below. I enjoyed watching the bottles they tied to those ropes slipping the noose or breaking against the hull of the ship.

There are some eighteen-year-olds who are really twenty or twenty-one. Then there are others who are fourteen.

After leaving Panama, we sailed for Bora Bora in the Society Islands—a long way off. I finally got out of the shaft alley as we approached Bora Bora, a volcanic island surrounded by a large reef and an ocean glowing with several beautiful shades of green. (I was so impressed that I returned to Bora Bora for my honeymoon with my second wife, Priscilla.)

It was 7,800 miles from Panama to Australia, and the Japanese controlled all the routes except those in the South Pacific. So Bora

Bora, with its deep, protected harbor, became a vital fueling and staging area. The U.S. got access to it through a treaty with the Free French government in 1942, and stationed some five thousand soldiers and over a thousand sailors there to protect it.

As we pulled into the harbor, we were approached by several Polynesian canoes. The natives were selling bracelets and necklaces made of shells as well as bananas (priced quite a bit higher than bananas in any New York grocery store). We went ashore eager to see the beautiful Polynesian girls. But it appeared as if Fletcher Christian had taken most of the beauties with him to Pitcairn Island. As for the few remaining lookers, it was apparent that the U.S. Army had secured its beachhead. Soldiers and native girls sped by in jeeps, the girls wrinkling their pretty noses in disdain whenever a sailor passed.

What's worse, the sun was unbelievably hot, producing many cases of serious sunburn that required several days' confinement in sick bay. After two days, we weren't disappointed to leave Bora Bora.

We set our course for Brisbane, a 29-day journey across the Pacific for our limping vessel (top speed eight knots). One of the few highlights of this trip was the ship's band, whose repertoire seemed to be limited to "California, Here We Come." Twenty-nine days of the same tune can be a bit wearing.

The *Euryale* reached Brisbane on a Sunday. For a change, I wasn't on duty—in fact, I was in the liberty section. We sailed up the picturesque Thames River (white houses dotting the landscape) and docked at New Farm Wharf. I pulled out my dress blues, showered, and excitedly headed into town.

Much to my dismay, the city was shut down (it *was* the sabbath). The only action was a Salvation Army band playing on a street corner. When I returned to the ship, everyone asked me what was my liberty in Brisbane had been like. I was speechless. Maybe my buddies assumed that my adventures had been too wild even to describe.

Brisbane was where General McArthur had set up his headquarters after leaving Corregidor under orders from President Roosevelt. He had taken over a hotel called Leonard's, which was off limits for army enlisted men. But as a former sailor in the Australian navy, the owner of Leonard's insisted that the navy be allowed to use one pub in the hotel. That became one of our hangouts during my time in Brisbane.

Mingling with the Australian troops, nicknamed diggers, was pretty entertaining. An Aussie soldier would approach a Yank and ask for a cigarette. When the pack was offered, he'd then ask, "Would you mind if I give one to my cobber?" (*Cobber* means mate or buddy.) Of course, he would usually have fifteen or sixteen cobbers with him. When the pack was returned, it would be down to one or two cigarettes. The usual thank-you was, "Good on you, Yank. You should have been a digger."

I would reply with a smile. Discretion, as they say, is the better part of valor.

Our favorite pub was in the Queen Elizabeth Hotel on King Street. It would open for an hour or so in the afternoon and another hour in the evening. In anticipation, crowds of service men congregated outside on the sidewalk, and when the doors opened, a mad rush to the bar would occur. Beer would be served until it ran out, which might take half an hour or so. This meant strategy was in order. If you were with three other sailors, each man had his assignment. You could order up to twelve beers, which would go into a pool to be split evenly. There was a dutch shelf around the bar room where the extra beers were deposited.

The kicker was that Australian beer had a much higher alcohol content than American brews. A full allotment of drinks together with the blazing Australian sun usually led to a snooze in the Botanical Garden or a movie house.

After departing from the *Euryale*, I normally would have been assigned to overhauling submarines returning from combat patrols. But because of a surplus of submarine personnel, I was transferred into the seaman guards—the worst bunch I ran into in my three years in the navy.

One sailor accused another of stealing clothes from him and demanded that his locker be searched. The accused man retaliated with the same charge. When the lockers were opened, it was found that the original accuser had an array of clothes belonging to me and several other sailors. Both men ended up being thrown in the brig.

Another sailor got tired during a night of brig guard duty and decided to nap in an empty cell. The officer of the day discovered the sleeping guard. He tiptoed into the cell, removed the guard's discarded rifle, and locked the cell door. The guard woke up to find himself a prisoner.

Once again, sports was my salvation. Our basketball team won the Brisbane Championship; we were awarded medals that read "Southwest Pacific Champions." I also pitched on our top-notch baseball team, coached by a big leaguer named Don Padgett. Don spent what would have been the most productive years of his career in the navy. He returned briefly to the National League after the war and actually batted .316 for the Phillies in 1947, but he was in his late thirties by then and his career soon petered out.

There were big leaguers playing with other navy teams, including Phil Rizzuto from the Yankees, "the Little Professor" Dom DiMaggio from the Red Sox, and Benny "Babe" McCoy, the original bonus baby, from the Tigers. We ended up playing the army for the championship before a crowd of six or seven thousand American servicemen. Broadway Charlie Wagner of the Red Sox pitched for us, striking out seventeen batters. But the army won 1-0, scoring the game's only run on a couple of back-to-back banjo hits in the fourth

Runners-up in the 1944 Army-Navy Baseball Championship—in Brisbane, not New Guinea (sorry, Phil Rizzuto). I'm the fifth man in uniform in the top row. That's Broadway Charlie Wagner at the far right, and Rizzuto kneeling in his navy blues at the bottom right.

or fifth inning.

I have a picture of our team in full uniform, with Rizzuto along-side dressed in his navy blues. When Rizzuto became a Yankee broadcaster, I sent him a copy. He called me and asked, "I don't understand—why didn't I have a baseball uniform on?"

"Phil," I explained, "We'd eliminated your team in the playoffs."

The Yankees showed the picture on television during rain delays a few times and each time Phil got confused about it: "I think it was in New Guinea or wherever."

By now I was working as a captain's orderly, which I hated with a passion. Making coffee for Lieutenant George Wilson and his staff was not my idea of stimulating work. Looking for a way out, I took the test for third class motor machinist. I passed it, but Lieutenant Wilson called me in and informed me that I had to be on the base for sixty days before I could take the test. I had taken it on my fifty-ninth day, so I was stuck making coffee.

I finally got out of the job through a combination of incompetence and sheer nerve. One morning, I put on a pot of coffee as usual. Early in the afternoon, a commodore came to see the captain and they ordered two coffees, which I delivered from that morning's pot. Within one minute the commodore emerged from the captain's office growling like a bear. The buzzer rang for me, and I confronted the furious captain. "What the hell did you put in that coffee? It was like mud."

I couldn't take it any longer. "Sir," I replied, "with all due respect, I came out here as a submariner to help fight a war, not to be a captain's orderly."

That tore it. I was reassigned to the submarine relief crew. However, submarine rates were frozen on the base. The only way one could advance was being assigned to a submarine and becoming a qualified submariner. This required doing a host of drawings and learning a whole set of skills—how to fire torpedoes, how to escape underwater, how to operate the bow and stern planes, how to pump oil aboard, how to operate the high-pressure air system and, most important of all, how to blow the crew's head (toilet). This last job required turning on a high-pressure line and keeping one hand on the line, one foot on the flap that closed the left-hand toilet bowl, and the other hand on the right-hand bowl. If the flaps weren't kept securely closed, it would wipe the smile off your face.

Meeting all these qualification took a great deal of work, all of which was in addition to standing one's regular watch.

Well, I got back to overhauling subs. It was hard, dirty work overhauling the diesel engines eight hours to twelve hours a day, six days a week. When I came off watch, it would take between thirty and forty-five minutes in the shower to remove the oil and carbon from my hands—not to mention the dozens of small cuts I invariably discovered on them.

One of the advantages of being in the relief crew was the brown-bagging of food off the boats coming in. We use to make pub call with the garbage man on the base. In return, he'd drop off ample food supplies at the house in the hills overlooking Brisbane I'd rented with three other sailors—Henry Prati, whose family had a famous restaurant in Washington, D.C. called Aldo's; Sam Nerponie from the Boston area; and a guy known as Pinky Bad News whose last name I can't recall.

One night we had a party at the house—mostly Pinky's friends. I got bored and turned in early. The next morning I found out that Pinky had almost killed us all. Three quarters of his mattress was burned and Pinky had a badly burned back. Our landlord kicked us out.

Shortly afterwards, Pinky was assigned to a departing submarine. I happened to be standing on the dock when Pinky and his shipments were returning from some outing. Pinky was bare-chested, his back still heavily bandaged from the fire, and thoroughly soused. As he started down the steeply slanted gang plank, he toppled over the side and landed on the deck of the submarine. But thinking he had landed in the water, he lay on his stomach kicking and stroking like mad until two sailors rescued him, just before he fell into the water for real.

One of my closest buddies was J. G. Harris, from Vincennes, Indiana. J.G. was working overhauling the engines on the *Sea Wolf*, an older boat scheduled to make one more patrol and return to the United States. J.G. heard a chief petty officer mention that the *Sea Wolf* needed a fireman. He volunteered and was accepted. What a lucky break—one more patrol and back to the States! Our congratulations to J.G. were tinged with envy.

Sam Nerponie and I threw a farewell party for J.G. and watched as the *Sea Wolf* set sail, only to run into heavy seas and return to port.

It departed again the following day. The ship's mission was to land US Army troops and Phillippine guerrillas on one of the Phillippine islands.

Within a week or so, rumors started to circulate that the *Sea Wolf* had gone down. 1944 was a year of devastating losses for the submarine service, with nineteen U.S. subs sunk (surpassing 1943's toll of seventeen). What's worse, it's believed that the *Sea Wolf* was killed by friendly fire. A U.S. destroyer, the *Rowell,* was on the hunt for a Japanese submarine. It picked up a contact on the *Sea Wolf* and apparently sank the sub with a depth charge.

J.G. was one of 79 submariners killed in this tragic mishap, along with several Phillippine guerrillas and Army personnel. He also had a brother who died in the infamous Bataan Death March (their father was a Sea Bee in Europe). J.G.'s mom was informed that her son's boat was missing in action. Anguished and grief-stricken, she wrote to our friend Sam Nerpounie. Sam asked me what he should write back. I had no answers.

While in Brisbane, I saw many of our subs taking guerrillas to the Philippines. I also saw the *Argonaut*, one of the three large, clumsy subs come in with around 80 men, women, and children they had taken out of the Philippines. The *Argonaut*, along with her sister subs, the *Narwhal* and the *Nautilus*, had two six-inch guns and was mainly used to land guerrillas and Merrill's Marauders, a famous ranger-type outfit charged with destroying supply chains and otherwise disrupting operations behind the Japanese battle lines..

The most memorable sailor I ran into was Motor Machinist First Class George Soldier, a big Indian from Idaho who had been in the navy for many moons. George was in charge of our engine room relief crew. Built like a sumo wrestler, George sported a great smile and a wonderful twinkle in his eyes (when he was sober, which wasn't often). George would stumble into the barracks after a night of drinking and start waking everyone up. My routine way of handling him was to say, "Okay, you big Indian, you want to fight, let's go!" I'd dance him around the barracks twice, ending up at his bunk, and then flip him into the sack with one hand.

We had many memorable evenings with George. One night in the King Edward Hotel Bar on Queens Street, George had me cornered. He kept waving his huge fist in my face and repeating, "Do you know what the white man did to my people, Smyth?" (I have no idea why he called me that. Smyth was my mother's maiden name, but George had never heard it.)

I kept responding, "George, I never did anything to your people. You're the first Indian I ever met. Besides, I've never been to Idaho." He finally let me out of the corner.

As the war moved up the island chains towards Japan, Brisbane was no longer a strategic submarine base. All submarine relief crew personnel were being moved to Fremantle on the Indian Ocean, outside Perth in Western Australia. The small contingent left behind in Brisbane were eventually moved to Subic Bay in the Philippines, where the brave defenders of Corregidor had so valiantly held out, upsetting the Japanese timetable for taking the Philippines and buying precious time for the American forces to regroup from a series of disasters.

A large body of U.S. army, navy, and Australian troops traveled to Perth via the Australian railroad, which left much to be desired. There were five different track gauges, meaning we had to change trains five times. Our first stop was Sydney, where a four-hour liberty was granted. Hundreds of servicemen got drunk in town. Some were escorted back by Australian police, army MPs, or navy shore patrol. Others didn't make it back in time to leave. As a result, there was no more liberty as we crawled around Australia—on to Melbourne, then Adelaide, always confined to railroad stations. The Australian rail system ran along the coast, with the major cities all along the eastern, southern, and western coasts of the island continent (the only city in the north was Darwin).

If the Japanese had taken Port Moresby in New Guinea, the first line of defense in Australia would have been just north of Brisbane. The battle of the Coral Sea was a victory only in the sense that it forced Japanese troop ships heading towards Port Moresby to turn back. The Japanese made a second attempt to cross the Owen Stanley range to reach Port Moresby via a treacherous trail high in the jungle. Many Japanese troops died from disease and starvation before they were beaten back by Australian and American forces.

Then we headed for the great Australian desert. We were in cattle cars the last five days. All day long we played hearts except when it was time to set up mess for breakfast, lunch, and dinner—twenty-one meals of mutton supplied by our Australian hosts. (It's a little-known bit of World War II trivia that the Australians fed all the U.S.

troops stationed in their country.) It was almost impossible to sleep lying on the wooden floor of a boxcar. As we sat in complete darkness, I would watch the glow of cigarettes around the car and listen to the oaths of sleepless sailors.

Whenever we got off the train to stretch our legs in the desert, the aboriginals would suddenly appear, offering to barter crude woodcarvings for cigarettes and food.

The day before we arrived in Perth, the train stopped at a whistle stop in the desert. where several sailors were able to obtain a supply of Penfold wine. They were prostrate the next day. In the days to come, they shuddered at the mere mention of the name Penfold.

Finally we departed the troop train and were assigned to buses for the trip from Perth to Fremantle. As I sat by the window of my bus, a taxi came alongside beeping its horn. The passenger was the big Indian George Soldier, who had obtained a supply of juice and was flying inside the cab. "Hey, Smyth!" he greeted me.

George's alcohol-fueled mishaps continued in Fremantle. One night he fell off the submarine tender *Euryale* and bounced head-first off the pressure hull of a submarine tied up alongside. A couple of sailors from the sub dove in and pulled George aboard.

The first reports were grave—George had a fractured skull and was not expected to live—but gradually his condition improved. When I visited George, I said to him, "I hope you've learned your lesson."

He responded, "No more drinking for me, Smyth. I am through."

A few days later, I was on the basketball court playing my usual charitable game (giving more than I received—fouls, that is), when someone hit me in the back of the head. I didn't black out but temporarily lost my hearing. (Years later, after a car accident, X-rays showed I had chips in my vertebrae, probably from this incident.) That night, I was overhauling an engine when a chain fall came loose and hit me in the forehead. The following day, I had severe headaches and turned into the sickbay with a concussion.

It was quite warm in Fremantle, and after lights-out the windows and door were left open. I was just about to go to sleep when I saw a huge figure looming at the door. I grew increasingly nervous as he started towards me. Finally, as he was about to collapse across the foot of my bed, I recognized him. It was George Soldier. I screamed, "Orderly, get this big Indian out of here."

George's vow of sobriety had had a short life.

A few days later I was back at work. But I suffered severe headaches for several years afterward.

I was getting itchy to go to sea and said as much to the chief petty officer in charge of the relief crew. He said, "Schmeelk, I don't want to lose you. You're the best fireman I have." This was a little like being told you are the best toll-taker on the George Washington Bridge. It taught me a valuable lesson: Never be so valuable in any job that you can't get promoted.

Eventually two incidents led to my escape from the relief crew.

One night I was at a bar in Perth with a sailor named McGuire. He had quite a bit to drink, suddenly got nasty, and smashed some glasses on the bar. I grabbed him by the arm and escorted him out of the bar. As we walked down the street, he swung away from me and pulled a fire alarm. An Australian policeman appeared and held McGuire despite my appeal. The shore patrol arrived. McGuire continued to misbehave and they were ready to club him. I intervened, got him in the paddy wagon, escorted him to the brig, and went back to the base.

A few days later, one of my friends from the USS *Sea Lion* persuaded me and another sailor to take a weekend with him and visit the town of Meriden, where few Americans had ever gone. We arrived Friday night around midnight. We walked several blocks on a dirt road and arrived at the local banker's house, where my sailor friend had stayed on a previous trip. The banker greeted us like family (I remember he had a strange habit of sticking his cigarettes in his ear while using his hands), fixed us a drink, and then walked us several more blocks to the home of Jimmy Hughes.

Jimmy was a local butcher whose son had toured the United States with an Australian band. The people had treated them so kindly that Jimmy had sworn that if he ever had the opportunity to repay that kindness to the Americans, he would do so. Jimmy got out of bed and fixed us a couple of shots of scotch, and we talked till around 3:00 a.m., when we all turned in. I slept on a small couch with a chair at the end to hold my feet.

(An aside: Jimmy introduced us to his granddaughter Vera, a cute little blond of seventeen. I swear I never even kissed her, but when I got home, I received a handmade card from her that read, "Fate divides but love abides." Try as I might, I could never explain this to my first wife or anyone else. The Australians do have some slang expressions that shocked us Yanks. One girl told me, "I got screwed," meaning she'd received her paycheck. Another responded to an invitation to dance by saying, "No thanks, Yank, I'm all knocked up," meaning she was tired. However, I don't think any of this explains Vera.)

Anyway, to get back to my story: The next day we were taken to the local men's club, where, after a hearty breakfast, we were made honorary members. Someone supplied us with a horse and buggy and we drove up and down the streets as the people of Meriden waved to us and cheered as if we were General McArthur and Admiral Nimitz.

On Saturday night we had many invitations to dinner. We chose an Italian refugee who had followed us around all day who served us a wonderful dinner with a couple of glasses of red wine (on top of several beers we'd enjoyed earlier in the day).

We arrived at the train station Sunday night full of good cheer and about an hour early for the train back to Perth. We asked the stationmaster to please wake us up when the train arrived. But he didn't, and we missed the train.

Meanwhile, back in Fremantle, a captain's mast (a navy-style disciplinary hearing, less formal than a court martial) had been arranged for Seaman McGuire that Monday morning, and I was scheduled to be a witness. But since I was in Meriden, I was officially AWOL.

When I returned, I learned that the captain's mast had been rescheduled. I testified for McGuire, and he received a sentence of thirty days confined to base. The next case was mine—for being AWOL. And I too was sentenced to thirty days confined to base.

At the end of my confinement, I put in for a three-day pass and returned to the delightful town of Meriden. On Monday evening, my pass nearly expired, I went down to the railroad station and to my horror discovered that the train didn't run on Monday nights. Now I was AWOL again, and this time I might face a summary court marshal.

Upon my belated return to Fremantle, I went to the chief petty officer—the same fellow who'd rated me his number-one fireman. "Look Chief," I said, "I've been in the navy for two years and I never got into any trouble. You've *got* to get me assigned to a boat."

Reluctantly, he got me a berth on the USS *Blackfin,* which in the end allowed me to earn my good conduct medal when I was discharged. Unlike John Kerry, I never threw my medals away—because I never put in for them in the first place.

Chapter 3
On the Blackfin

The U.S.S. *Blackfin* had been badly depth-charged on its previous patrol. It was making a run at a heavily-protected convoy with its forward torpedo doors open when a Japanese escort spotted it and ran in for the kill. They dove deeper with three hot torpedoes running that could have exploded at any time. The boat took a terrific pounding, which cracked the crank cases in the engine room and threw the engine shaft out of alignment, among other damage.

This is an actual excerpt from the *Blackfin* log of March 29, 1944:

Convoy composed of 8 escorts and 2 freighters, action takes place between Hon Trauman and Hongan Peninsula. We picked the lead freighter, rigged for silent running, all four torpedo doors opened. Escort spots periscope, closes to attack, too close for Blackfin to fire.

Blackfin attempts to dive to 200 feet. Escort passes over, sucks Blackfin back to 90 feet, seven depth charges close by accelerating the descent. Damaged bow planes jammed, power lost on stern planes, 56 light bulbs blow out, gauge faces blown out. Air leaks making a great deal of noise, water coming in the forward torpedo room. The outer doors on three torpedo tubes partly opened and stuck, four torpedoes running hot, water in other areas and numerous other damage.

The boat stuck in the mud at a depth of 156 feet. It's a miracle it survived.

When I joined the crew of the *Blackfin*, the destination for our

36

next patrol was Singapore, then occupied by the Japanese. We departed from Fremantle as the Navy band played "Anchors Aweigh," "The Stars and Stripes Forever," and other suitable martial tunes, the docks crowded with Navy brass and our enlisted friends.

The chief of the boat was from Ozone Park in Queens, about eight miles from my old stomping grounds in Rockaway Beach. He asked me what I'd like to do on my first patrol. "What are my options?" I asked.

The first possibility was to serve as fireman in the engine room. This was a great way to lose weight, far better than the Atkins or South Beach diets, because the engine room was like a constant sauna bath.

Another option was look-out duty. Here you would get to see flying fish and perhaps enemy ships. You would also have the opportunity to get your teeth kicked out, a broken nose, or broken fingers as your ship mates swarmed down the hatch when the diving alarm sounded.

Then there was working in the mess, which was even worse—setting up three shifts a day for breakfast, lunch, and dinner. The job took some fourteen to sixteen hours a day, and in your spare time you were expected to do drawings and learn to operate the systems in all compartments of the boat.

Then the chief gave me the final option—taking care of the laundry for seventy-nine enlisted men and eight officers. Each man paid you a dollar a month, and you washed clothes between one a.m. and three a.m. This was the only occupation I could see myself returning to after my navy career. And the money was pretty good for those days—twenty percent for overseas duty, fifty percent more for submarine duty, and then $86 a month on top of that. Without hesitation, I chose the laundry.

The washing machine was squeezed into the crew's head, which measured about four by six. Water was severely rationed. You could take one brief shower a week. Otherwise, you could put just enough water into the sink—about two inches deep—to shave and brush your teeth. If there was any water in the condensation tank, you could use it to soap up and rinse off.

The first night at sea, I stayed up late playing cards and ended up oversleeping. The chief came in and shook me rather aggressively. I was accustomed to my mother waking me with an affectionate, "Get up, darling boy. It's time for school." I reacted badly, and we had words.

The second day at sea, the washing machine malfunctioned. The third day at sea, the electricians failed in their effort to repair the machine and the executive officer ordered it deep-sixed. I was reassigned to mess cooking.

Submarine food was the best in the navy—at least at the start of a patrol. During the early days we had plenty of steak and lots of fresh vegetables. (Later we'd get into the canned stuff.) Unfortunately, the good food wasn't enough to create harmony between me and the chief.

One night, while eating his steak, the chief requested ketchup. There wasn't any, as we'd forgotten to put it out. Furious, the chief threw his steak in the garbage and stormed out.

A few nights later, the chief was sitting in his favorite seat near the cook's corner. He had his back to me and he was wearing his usual dining attire of dungarees and no shirt. I was struggling with a rubber ice tray when bingo! Out popped several pieces of ice and landed on the chief's back. Again he cursed me out and left the mess.

Now for the third and final incident. This time I was standing behind the chief smoking a cigarette, his bare back facing me as usual. A shipmate bumped into me, and the burning end of my cigarette honed in on the chief's back like a guided missile. It didn't just touch him, either—it clung there somehow as he screamed and fled.

Somehow our relationship never warmed up after that.

We headed through the Indian Ocean to patrol off Singapore. To save time, we headed for the Lombok Strait between Java and Bornea, which was controlled by the Japanese and could be traveled only at night. By now I'd been expelled from the mess and transferred to lookout duty. I did two four-hour watches each day, rotating between the bridge, the conning tower, and the control room.

I was in the control room one rather wild evening as we tried to navigate the Lombok Strait. Reports came down from the bridge about a sighting of Japanese patrol boats, and for a while we chased a large rock formation that was supposedly doing four knots. We then pursued a target that turned out to be a British submarine on the wrong identification wavelength. We figured out who they were at the last minute before we attacked.

Shortly after we exited Lombok, we had an engine malfunction, forcing us to dive and spend about eight hours wrenching the engines. When we surfaced, we got a report that another U.S. sub had sunk three Japanese ships about one hundred miles ahead of us. We headed there only to experience more engine trouble—the ship had never fully recovered from the pounding it had received on its previous patrol.

We were ordered to abort our patrol and head for Subic Bay in the Philippines for repairs. As we approached the bay, lookouts reported contact with a Japanese destroyer. The diving alarm sounded and we went to battle stations. I was a loader in the forward torpedo room. Feeling jittery, I glanced at a hardened veteran nearby, hoping to get a little encouragement, only to find that he was shaking worse than me. I started reciting a Hail Mary but couldn't recall the words.

Suddenly, the "destroyer" dove into the depths. It was actually another American submarine. Battle stations secured—on to Subic.

Two of our sub tenders were in the harbor at Subic—the *Orion* and my old ship the *Euryale*. The crew of the *Blackfin* was assigned to a rest camp, and we all took off in various directions. My engine room companion Closey Edwards, another sailor and I hitched a ride up the Bataan Peninsula to Manila.

The city had been devastated in street-to-street fighting between the Allies and the Japanese resistance. The Japanese still controlled the dam above the city, and U.S. fighter planes were bombing and strafing their position.

Closey had money, but the other sailor and I had been wiped out in a card game. We implored Closey to lend us some money, promising to pay him back as soon as we got paid. But Closey was unyielding. In two days, he bought us each one coke and one ice cream cone. Not the kind of guy you'd pick to spend eight hours on watch with.

While we were in Subic Bay, the notorious Japanese radio propagandist Tokyo Rose broadcast the names of the two tenders in the harbor, the *Orion* and the *Euryale*, and announced that the Japanese were going to sink them the following night. In response, there was a total blackout. The only attack was on a poor AWOL sailor who'd hired a Filipino to row him back to his ship. The small boat was spotted and tracer bullets filled the air. Fortunately our marksmen's aim was poor, and the sailor survived to spend a little brig time.

Now we headed to Saipan, a volcanic island honey-combed with caves. I remember the many thousands of white crosses, most representing young Americans of eighteen or twenty who'd died on this God-forsaken island. The purpose of their sacrifice had been to secure airfields for use in striking the Japanese mainland and to provide emergency landing for returning B29s and fighter planes. In fact, the airfield in Saipan looked like the Long Island Expressway at rush hour, with planes parked shoulder to shoulder. If Japanese fighters had ever gotten through, they would have had a field day.

Meanwhile, rumors circulated as to where we'd be headed next. Gradually a consensus emerged that, because of our constant engine problems, we were headed for the West Coast of the U.S. for a general overhaul. Several sailors even loaded up on cigarettes and other black market goods to sell at a hefty profit when they arrived in the U.S. Bolstering this rumor was the fact that we had unloaded our spare torpedoes and had extra room for storage. We also had aboard a handful of submarine sailors who'd made enough war patrols to be returned to the States. One sailor had been on four subs that had been sunk right *after* he was transferred off them. (Later we got very nervous when he transferred off our boat.)

As is usual in the service, the rumors turned out to be completely wrong. Instead of the West Coast, we were ordered to Pearl Harbor in Hawaii.

Even more surprising was what happened to my former close friend, the chief of the boat. When I asked about his whereabouts one day, I was told that he'd gone to the captain and declared, "I want out. This boat is doomed." He didn't even care if he was disqualified from submarine service. He got his wish and ended up being stationed at the base in Saipan.

I felt a little bad about it all. I even wondered if I'd been partially responsible for the chief staying on Saipan, what with the ice cubes and the burning cigarette and all. If I'd only known how he felt I could at least have bought him some suntan lotion as a sign of my goodwill and to help shield him against the powerful South China Sea sun. Sixty years later I'm tempted to return, see if he is still playing in the sand, and offer a belated apology.

We arrived in Pearl Harbor after an uneventful crossing. Now, submariners are not great believers in dress codes. On the *Blackfin,* shorts, bathing trunks, and T-shirts (or no shirt at all) was the norm.

As we lolled in the shallow waters off Pearl Harbor, various members of our crew were sunning themselves on the deck when Admiral Fife and his aide appeared. The admiral planned to address our crew, but first his aide put a dozen or so sailors on report for being out of uniform. The next few minutes looked like a scene from some old silent movie as sailors hastened down the hatch and then raced back up, properly dressed, and lined up at attention.

Finally, the admiral spoke. "Men, I have good news for you," he began.

We were all smiling. "He's going to tell us we're heading for the good old U.S.A. for a major overhaul. It'll be liberty for all!"

But no. "Men, we are going to give you a general overhaul right here in Pearl Harbor. Then we'll send you out as soon as possible to engage the enemy."

A low grumble could be heard from the fighting crew of the *Blackfin*.

It transpired that we weren't going back to the West Coast because the shipyards there were already full of badly damaged surface craft that had been hit by Japanese suicide planes at Okinawa and Iwo Jima.

Now the hopeful black marketers of cigarettes and other contraband tried desperately to unload their goods, but supply and demand were badly out of whack. The market kept sinking as they tried to dispose of their inventory.

Things weren't all bad. We spent three weeks at the Royal Hawaiian Hotel—the famous Pink Palace on the sands of Waikiki Beach—which we shared with a group of marines who'd fought at Saipan, Okinawa, and Iwo Jima. Each morning we awoke to the navy band playing "The Trolley Song" (you know the one—"Clang, clang, clang went the trolley") and spent our days in softball and swimming competitions against our fellow submariners.

We had a cook on our boat named Troast from New Jersey. He was a really good cook, but a little contrary. I loved his scrambled eggs, and one day I told him, "Now, Troast, when I walk into the crew's mess in the morning, I'll just tell you, 'The usual,' and you scramble me a couple of eggs."

"Sure, Schmeelk," he replied.

The next day, I walked in and ordered, 'The usual.'" Troast replied, "I don't know what you're talking about." I patiently explained and tried ordering that way the next day and the day after that. Every time he said the same thing: "I have no idea what you're talking about."

One day we were having swimming races against the crew of another sub. We had to swim out from shore, pass around a boat anchored some one hundred and fifty yards away, and then back to shore. I told Troast, "You go out in the lead. Then I'll catch you and finish first." I'd never seen Troast swim, and I was just joking with him as usual.

"Okay," Troast replied, "I got you, Schmeelk."

The race started with some twenty sailors plunging into the water with plenty of contact among thrashing arms and legs. I had no idea where Troast was, but I could see one swimmer about fifteen yards ahead, rounding the boat. I said to myself, "You better start going all out," so I started hammering the water, stroking for all I was worth.

I made it back to shore gasping and barely able to stand. Who was there, casually smoking a cigarette, but Troast. He said, "I kept waiting for you, but when you didn't show up, I thought I should make sure the *Blackfin* got first place."

I'd finished a distant second. Exhausted, I went back to bed for a few hours. I shared a large suite at the Royal Hawaiian with two other crew members, and a large contingent would congregate in our room for nightly card games. I was wiped out by the second night and spent the next ten nights as a spectator (I couldn't sleep anyway with all the noise in our room).

Our third week in Honolulu, I attended gunnery school with the gun crew on the new short-barreled 5.25 deck gun. The ensign who served as our instructor started his first lecture by saying, "Men, you don't know what a thrill it is to see your first Japanese ship heading for the bottom." This convinced us all that he had never been to sea other than the ride over from the States.

We spent the first five days learning the mechanics of naval gunnery, and on the last day we were to rapid-fire twenty-five or thirty shells. The ensign was assuring us how safe it would be when we saw the ambulance pulling up—to be ready, just in case. I wasn't surprised; one of our cooks had told how a shipmate on his previous submarine had been killed by a recoiling shell.

The ammunition—huge 100-pound shells—was stored on the right side of the gun and loaded on the left. The ensign urged me not to wait for the gun to recoil but to just dash across with the shell. I hadn't gotten to be the best fireman in our relief crew by taking such risks. I preferred being a fireman for three years to being killed by a recoiling shell after two. I ignored the ensign and moved at my own pace, and I'm here to tell the tale all these years later.

After three weeks, we were scheduled to set sail for Midway, where we would train for a few days in preparation for our next patrol. The day before, we threw a ship's party at Diamond Head. We hired a bunch of Hawaiian dancers, played a little softball, and drank a fair amount of beer. One sailor (out of a crew of seventy-nine) brought a date. When the festivities came to an end, a score of us sailors loaded a truck with beer and took off for Honolulu. Knowing the city was closely monitored by the Shore Patrol, the truck driver got nervous and dropped us off behind a gas station.

We had just opened our first beer when someone shouted, "Here comes the Shore Patrol!" Tailed by another sailor looking for a way out, I took off, spotted a hole in a fence, and dashed through. I was in the backyard of a church. As I ran towards the front of the church, I could hear music and spotted a wedding procession exiting the building. I dashed right through them, beer in hand, trailed by my companion who'd also refused to leave his beer behind. I imagine we gave the members of that wedding party something to talk about for years afterward.

He and I were the only ones to escape. Nine members of the *Blackfin* crew, including one chief petty officer, spent the night in the brig. The captain arrived at the brig in the morning and obtained their release on the ground that we were going to sea and he needed his crew. The next morning, we were off to Midway.

The Battle of Midway (June 5, 1942) was best recounted in Walter Lord's great book *Incredible Victory*. After several unsuccessful attacks by squadron after squadron of antiquated torpedo bombers and other planes, the U.S. navy finally caught three Japanese carriers with their planes on the deck. Within five minutes, they destroyed the carriers, changing the course of the war in the Pacific. One U.S. carrier, the *Yorktown*, already badly damaged from a previous battle, was sunk by a final Japanese submarine torpedo. The battle ended the Japanese plan to take Midway and then Pearl Harbor, and from then on the Japanese fleet was on the defensive.

The other two things for which Midway was noted were huge

43

card games culminating (so the rumors had it) in violent attacks against the biggest winners, and the hundreds of thousands of gooney birds that nested on the island—big, fat birds that rarely flew but gave out a gawking sound that drove the sailors stationed on the island to the brink of insanity. Eventually stern measures had to be threatened against any one harming the gooney birds. Today the island is a sanctuary for the species (technically known as the Laysan albatross), with strict limits on visitors.

We spent several days on Midway practicing shooting, diving, and surfacing, and coordinating operations with the air force and surface craft. I was the second loader on the 5.25 deck gun. We were operating in a very rough sea and it was hard to see the target. I started out cradling the shell standing upright. Then I found myself on one knee and eventually on both knees, praying for a firing position.

After leaving Midway, we headed for Saipan. As we approached the harbor, one of our famous U.S. submarines was exiting—the *Silversides*, veteran of many successful war patrols and the fifth leading submarine in tonnage sunk (90,080). We were there to top off our fuel supply before a patrol that was to take us into the Yellow Sea between the Chinese and Korean coasts. By this time, most Japanese ships had disappeared from the sea. Our patrol was to be mostly lifeguard duty, picking up U.S. flyers who'd been forced to ditch at sea and watching out for Sampans who might try to radio our aircraft positions. Everywhere we went we were accompanied by the steady drone of B29s flying overhead towards the Japanese mainland.

As we left Saipan, we heard rumors that something big was happening on the nearby island of Tinian. As we were approaching our station, we received word that a U.S. plane had gone down, and we were instructed to proceed to rescue the flyers. But once again our rear engines conked out. After working on them for six or seven hours, we finally got them back on line. We were about one hour away from where the plane had gone down when we received word that a PBY (a flying boat, so-called because of its designation as Patrol Bomber, Y Type) had landed and retrieved the plane's crew. We were happy for the flyboys, but we cursed our bad luck and our worse engines.

Next we came upon a Korean junk. According to the rules of engagement, if they had a radio and tried to send a message they would quickly be destroyed by our deck guns. The Koreans looked terrified when we approached. But after we boarded and searched the junk, and found no weapons or other contraband, we departed, leaving behind cigarettes and other goodies. The Korean sailors smiled and waved as we pulled away.

On August 13, we spotted a submarine periscope and dove. According to rumors on board, a torpedo was fired at us, but when I later scrutinized the *Blackfin*'s log, I noted that the sonar operator said merely that it *sounded* like a torpedo, so I'll never know what actually happened.

Two days later, August 15, was a beautiful day. I was in the conning tower when the captain's voice came over the loudspeaker: "Men, the war against Japan has ended. Our instructions are not to fire unless fired upon."

I remember saying to myself that August day, "Some time I would like to take a cruise and see what sailing on this beautiful ocean can really be like—with no pressure, no fear, just relaxing." It never happened. I booked a cruise forty years ago, but the crew went on strike and it was cancelled.

The drone of the B29s now fell silent, and the *Blackfin* became a minesweeper. The Japanese had cut loose a large number of mines and we were assigned to pick them off as they floated down from the Sea of Japan and into the Yellow Sea. We spent two weeks disposing mines, our twenty-millimeter guns constantly popping away as they fired at the mines to detonate them. Occasionally I had the misfortune of standing under the main induction, where our air supply entered the engine room, as a mine blew up. The noise was painfully loud. In the space of two weeks we blew up sixty-three mines. We would go through an area during the day, clean it out, and stay there at night.

Finally, we were instructed to proceed to Guam. En route, we ran into one of the notorious Pacific typhoons. Two U.S. destroyers, the *Monaghan* and the *Hoe*, had capsized in a previous typhoon with a tremendous loss of life. And even Admiral Halsey had supposedly been threatened with court marshal for taking his fleet into a typhoon where hundreds of planes had been lost. So these typhoons were nothing to laugh at.

I made the mistake of going to the bridge to see the unbelievable swells. During my time at sea I'd been in two hurricanes, but a

The Blackfin *in one of the great Pacific Typhoons*

typhoon is even more impressive. The experience can best be described as one of peaks and valleys—you ride to the peak of a towering wave and suddenly you're at the bottom of a valley, looking up. At least half of our crew was seasick as we wallowed through the ocean like a pig. (Maybe that's where submarines got the nickname *pig boats*.)

Finally we arrived in Guam, where we found eight or nine other subs tied up alongside each other in the harbor. It was like old home week. We knew a lot of sailors from the other boats as we'd worked in relief crews together, and we visited back and forth long into the night, swapping movies from our meager on-board supplies and sharing snacks.

While in Guam, I played a dirty trick on a sailor from another sub. In the Yellow Sea, we picked up a life preserver emblazoned with the name *Shornhorst*. Serious students of World War II may remember that there were two ships known as the *Shornhorst*. One was a German luxury liner that was converted into a transport and sunk in the Yellow Sea, the other a pocket battleship. Our life preserver, which we strapped as a trophy to our conning tower, was from the transport, but I told the sailor in Guam that we had sunk the battleship. I even had him pose for a photo with his head through the life preserver and told him, "When you get home, you can tell your girlfriend you were on the sub that sank the battleship *Shornhorst*."

Fortunately, I didn't give him my address. Sooner or later that story would blow up in his face.

One by one, the subs began receiving instructions to report to home bases in the U.S. I knew a few sailors on the USS *Boarfish*, and I asked them, "Where are you guys heading—east coast or west coast?"

The answer was Neither. The *Boarfish* was not returning. They told me the story that explained why.

One day, some of the crew had returned from liberty in Perth, Australia, having consumed a fair bit of juice. Rather than play cards or Scrabble, they decided to entertain themselves by simulating a torpedo attack on a British freighter across the narrow harbor in Fremantle. Now, when in port, it was normal to remove four of the six forward torpedos, leaving two live torpedoes in the forward tubes. The four empty tubes, filled with water to compensate for the loss of weight, were referred to as water slugs.

Maybe you've already guessed what happened. Somehow the wrong button got pushed, and a live fish sped on its way toward the British freighter. You can imagine the feelings of the British sailor on lookout: "First the Revolutionary War, then the War of 1812. Now the Yanks are at it again."

Fortunately, the attack didn't become an international incident. The torpedo hit the dock in front of the freighter without having run far enough to arm itself and explode.
Nonetheless, a score of officers and enlisted men were reduced in rank. As further punishment, the *Boarfish* was not to return to the United States for many, many months.

Many years later I discovered where the *Boarfish* was sent to do penance. In a book recounting the story of the U.S.S. *Nautilus,* I learned that the first submarine to penetrate the waters three miles under the northern ice pack was the USS *Boarfish.*

While on Guam, I received a letter from my brother Garry. He was on a landing craft in Okinawa and had also experienced the typhoon I mentioned. They'd circled the harbor for twenty-four hours until the storm abated, when they dropped the anchor and promptly fell asleep, on the deck or wherever they happened to be.

Garry's next letter informed me he was in Shanghai to play for the navy against the army in the China Bowl football game. He was the only enlisted man on the navy team, which sported some star professional and college players. I wrote Garry back: "You mean to tell me we risked our lives blowing up mines so a group of football players could get through to Shanghai?!"

Garry returned with many beautiful silk kimonos and impressive stories about the lavish banquet a Chinese general had hosted for the players. I just sent home two trays with pictures of submarines— C.O.D., two dollars down and eight to pay.

We left Guam and headed back to Pearl Harbor, where we were tied up alongside the submarine *Plunger*, whose conning tower was painted with Japanese flags representing the many ships they'd sunk. Who should pop out of the hatch but an old teammate from the New London Firemen and former Commerce High School ace, Hushy Cohen. I greeted him on the dock: "Hushy, how are you?"

His reply, "I don't care about anything, I'm Asiatic." This was how he referred to someone who'd been on Asiatic duty and had mentally lost contact with the U.S. I saw Hushy a few times after that at parties in New York, and he was definitely odd.

After departing Pearl, we headed for San Diego, a journey of around twenty days. We arrived on a foggy morning. No rousing greetings for the returning warriors—the usual band was nowhere to be seen. We crept into harbor as quietly as a teenager sneaking home late at night. Navy discipline was enforced—regulation blues, no tailor-made outfits, and regulation haircuts. We looked like a group just out of boot camp.

We soon began losing parts of our crew. There was a point system based on how long you'd been in the navy, and I would be in the third shift to go home. Meanwhile, we had to hang out in San Diego.

One night I was just about to get off watch and head for the crew's mess when smoke started to drift into the engine room. It seemed our new cook (freshly recruited to replace the veteran who'd already been sent home) was cooking steaks and hadn't bothered to clean the grill. Pretty soon you could hardly see with the smoke, and we poured up the hatch choking and gasping for air. The new cook was returned to his seaman's duties.

Now life on the *Blackfin* became as dangerous in San Diego as it had been on war patrol, what with many of our veterans being discharged, the others overindulging in nightlife, and new officers and enlisted men being brought on board.

Although we hadn't dived the boat since leaving Guam, we were assigned to practice operations with the naval air corps. They were to make practice bombing runs on the *Blackfin*, and we were to dive to as to avoid direct hits.

We were all pretty nervous when the day to begin the games arrived. The executive officer passed the word to secure all compartments to dive, hatches were checked, bulkhead doors were secured between compartments, and bulkhead flappers between compartments were closed. Then the order—"Dive! Dive!"—accompanied by the familiar "Ow-ooga, ow-ooga" of the claxon.

We immediately had an unbelievably steep angle on the bow. My engine-room companion Closey Edwards and I held onto the rail for dear life as anything not secured slid forward. We were both bug-eyed, figuring we were out of control and headed for the bottom of the sea. Then one of us noticed the salt water gauge was not registering any depth. Suddenly we heard the captain on the loud speaker addressing the executive officer: "Mr. Balanst, do you think you can trim the boat properly before our next dive?"

What had happened was this: Our ballast tanks, which controlled the dive along with our extruding bow and stern planes, were out of whack. The bow of the *Blackfin* was underwater while the stern was waving in the air—rather embarrassing for a skipper (a bit like mooning the rest of the fleet), but a huge relief for the crew.

Incident number two occurred a few days later. Before a dive, after each compartment is secured by the ranking enlisted man, an officer checks to make certain the boat is ready. I was off-duty, playing cards in the crew's mess when a young ensign entered. He ascended the ladder to make sure the hatch was dogged down properly and then continued his tour of inspection.

Soon the diving alarm sounded. Suddenly I heard water falling on the deck. I turned and saw water pouring down from the hatch. An alert sailor quickly went up the ladder and dogged down the hatch. Ensign No-Brain had turned the wheel the wrong way and loosened the hatch rather than tightening it. The electric motor batteries were under the deck, and if water had infiltrated them deadly chlorine gas would have been released.

The crew gave Ensign No-Brain the silent treatment for some time afterwards.

Thankfully, that was our last major problem. We worked with the Air Force daily for a few weeks, diving three or four times on each watch. It was a real workout—cranking valves closed, opening pet cocks to release air, and then closing them again. I'd left Australia at 210 pounds, but these dives, combined with the intense heat in the engine room after diving, had me down to 165. After working in the bilge on the engines, I would often doff my shirt and pants off and wring them out as if I'd been swimming in them. At night, we hung out in a saloon by the name of The Cuckoo Club, where the crew of the *Blackfin* established a new record for fighting—a perfect zero for nine.

Our weak record as after-hours warriors made us apprehensive when we visited Monterey for Navy Day. The carrier *Hornet* was also slated for Monterey. We arrived first, and the local paper ran a front-page article headlined, "Fighting Submarine Here For Navy Day." The last paragraph added, "the U.S.S. *Hornet* will also be here." We didn't feel this article would endear us to the 1,500 or so members of the *Hornet*'s crew, and after going zero for nine in The Cuckoo Club the thought of eighty against 1,500 didn't appeal to us. So we found a bar that could just about hold our liberty section and stayed glued together. Spartans we were not.

Back we went in very rough seas to San Diego and the start of my thirty-day leave. After that, I was to report to Pier 92 in New York City for discharge. My days in the service were coming to an end.

Chapter 4
A Civilian Again

Looking back over the past few pages, I see that my stories about the submarine service are mostly light-hearted and comical. That's appropriate—we were young men away from home for the first time, and we made sure we had plenty of fun. I'll never forget the friendships I made in those far-away places. But I wouldn't want to leave you with the impression that war is fun and games—or that the work of the submarine service wasn't extremely important and dangerous. It was both.

Military historians record that, from December 10, 1941, to August 6, 1945, the U.S. submarine service lost fifty-two boats. The first, the USS *Sea Lion*, was in the dry docks at Cavite Naval Base in the Phillippine islands when it came under attack along with the USS *Sea Dragon* from a formation of Japanese planes. Both crews manned their deck guns and returned fire until the *Sea Lion* suffered a direct hit. Explosions of munitions on the dock caused both crews to abandon their ships. But the captain and crew of the *Sea Dragon* and crew returned to their ship and got it underway with the aid of a tug. However, the *Sea Lion* was so badly damaged it was destroyed and the base abandoned.

The last submarine lost in the war was the USS *Bull Head*. It was under the command of a new skipper at the time. Edward Rowell Holt, Jr., was caught on the surface by a Japanese plane which claimed two direct hits and reported gushing water and bubbles rising in the water. This occurred in the notoriously dangerous

Lombok Strait which I referred to earlier.

In a report published after the war, JANAC (the Joint Army-Naval Assessment Committee) claimed that U.S. submarines sank 540,192 tons of Japanese naval vessels and 4,779,902 tons of merchant shipping, representing 54.6 percent of the Japanese merchant fleet. Yet many commanders took exception to this report, claiming that the true figure was much higher. Various ships traveling alone were unaccounted for when they sank and they would forever be a mystery.

So the U.S. submarine fleet played a crucial part in helping the Allies win the war in the Pacific. As I've described it in these pages, my own role was a very small one. I'd never want anyone to call me a hero—that's a word I reserve for much bigger men than myself. But I'm proud that I did my part to serve my country in its hour of need.

I was officially discharged from the navy in New York after four days of cross-country travel by train. A civilian once again, I caught the Long Island Railroad to Rockaway.

Having been away about two years, I arrived home and slipped in through the basement door just as my brother and I always did. There was my mother on her hands and knees scrubbing the steps. She hadn't expected me till the following day, and although she was very happy to see me she was upset that she was wearing an ordinary housedress and hadn't had time to have her hair done. I couldn't care less. She looked like a million bucks to me.

The following day, I was planning to get together with some of my army buddies who had come home from the European theatre. George Cornish, my former catcher and basketball teammate, had served as a medic at Anzio and Salerno and also in the invasion of Europe. Danny Murphy, a basketball teammate, had been in all three campaigns as well, and John Shelley had been a medic in the D-Day invasion.

I wanted to look nice for my first night out, so I put on one of the two suits I'd left behind. I also asked my mother where my favorite topcoat was. She replied, "I gave it to Uncle Jack." He was a veteran of the first war who'd never married and had a serious drinking problem.

When I saw Uncle Jack later, I asked him, "What happened to my coat?"

He replied, "It's hanging." That meant he'd pawned it.

So I had to go out in my second-best coat. We all went down to Danny Maher's drinking hole. When I propped up my right foot on the bar railing and tugged on my trouser leg, my knee popped right through the pants. Oops—I now had just one and a half suits left.

Soon my brother Garry was discharged. He'd weighed about 235 pounds going into the Navy and come home around 210. Meanwhile, starting with my leave in San Diego, I'd been enjoying the post-war life and had gotten back up into the 200-pound range. Since Garry's clothes no longer fit him, he pleaded to borrow my one remaining suit, a light tan Italian glen plaid, one night when he had a heavy date.

At first I turned him down. I was going to the movies with my girlfriend, Betty Conaghan (she later became my first wife), so I needed a suit myself. But Garry was persistent and even started altering the pants of his old 235-pound suit so they'd fit me. I got such a kick out of seeing him with pins in his mouth and a needle and thread in his hand that I said, "Okay, you can have my suit for the evening." I went to the movies in a dark gray glen plaid jacket and Garry's pin-striped black trousers.

Garry wasn't through with me, however. After our movie, Betty and I walked into the local watering hole and spotted my brother with his date, looking very sharp. When we walked over to say hello, Garry looked me up and down and said to his date, "Look how seedy my brother is dressed." Thus was my brotherly sacrifice ridiculed.

It may sound strange to hear me obsessing about a suit, but in the years just after the war it was almost impossible to find decent clothes. I wouldn't even bother going into a men's store—I'd just open the door and yell, "Anything in 42 long?" The answer was almost always No. Finally one day I hit pay dirt at Robert Hall, an old haberdashery that has since gone out of business. It was a dark green suit that I hated—I've never worn that shade again.

Like most of my friends who got out of the service, I took the first job I could get and quickly got married. I returned to Salomon where I'd been working summers before the war, and in November, 1946, Betty and I took advantage of my one hundred percent pay increase (from $15 to $30 a week) to get married.

(In the 1980s, the young MBAs I'd interview used to tell me, "I really like Salomon, Mr. Schmeelk, and I'll get back to you after I visit Morgan Stanley, Goldman Sachs, Merrill Lynch, First Boston, and Lehman Brothers." Shopping around like that would never have occurred to me. There were a lot more apples on the tree for the yuppies than there were for the post-war generation.)

Betty and I started out married life renting the upstairs apartment in my mother's house. Later we lived in a basement apartment on the same street. Children began arriving—first Betty, and then Ricky, Marie, Stephen, Virginia, Garry, and Michael.

I decided to supplement my income from Salomon by playing semi-pro basketball for a team based in Saratoga, New York. The contract called for $100 for two games each weekend. Now, a month or so after I'd signed the contract, Red Dehnert, nephew of the Original Celtic Dutch Dehnert (whose son Bucky I'd played with at Far Rockaway High and the St. Francis Big Five), approached me with an offer to sign with a team in the Southern Conference for $7,500 a year. This was very tempting, but I finally decided it was too risky and passed.

However, after I'd worked out for four weeks at the Sunny Side Garden in Long Island City (at my own expense), the Southern League folded. An athletic contract in those days wasn't worth the paper it was written on. We got the boot without seeing a nickel.

Meanwhile, my brother Garry was playing football for a team called the Cedarhurst Stapes owned by a colorful character named Howie Davis—in Garry's words, a team that was always late arriving and two touchdowns behind before even figuring out what town they were playing it.

Their contracts always stipulated that a certain number of players (let's call it twenty) had to be dressed for the game. One time in Erie, Pennsylvania, it was necessary to dress the pilot and co-pilot of the chartered airplane as well as the team's business manager, a mild-mannered non-athlete. The group drove to the field in several cars, and Garry had decreed that the first eleven men to arrive would line up to receive the opening kick-off. Wouldn't you know it? Among the eleven was the mild-mannered business manager, who received the opening kick-off and was carried off the field with a broken leg.

One season opened with an exhibition game against a Brooklyn team in the old American Football League led by All-American Bob Chapias from Illinois. Garry's team had had one workout and no scrimmage prior to the game. The game started with one of Garry's players throwing a punch on the opening kick-off and getting tossed out of the game. (Garry later said he was the smartest player on the team, since he got paid the same as the rest of the team.) At halftime, all the players from the Stapes lay under the shower trying to revive.

Garry was up against the future AFL all-star tackle Martin Ruby. They scored one touchdown through Ruby, and Buddy Schumm (who'd played for Holy Cross back in the early forties) mouthed off to Ruby, saying, "You should have given us a nickel for that ride we gave you." After that crack, Ruby hit so hard his whole body shook.

Another time (in 1948, I think), the Stapes visited Charlotte to play in a game that the New York *Times* called the first integrated professional football game in the South. The Stapes had three Black players, only one of whom, tailback Willie Wilson, showed up.

The trip south was quite an ordeal. The manager of the airport restaurant refused to serve Wilson until his teammates insisted, "All or none." Finally they were all served. At the ballpark, the fans were segregated and there were many hateful remarks directed Wilson as he ran onto the field.

Garry's football career was actually ended on a return visit to Charlotte. He went to the aid of Buddy Schumm, who'd started a fight. The last thing Garry remembered was throwing a punch, hitting a face mask, and then waking up on the sideline with a broken leg.

My mother had a group of ladies over to play cards when the doorbell rang. I opened it to see my brother leg in a cast being carried in by some players. My mother and her friends were all horrified at the sight, and Mom was confirmed in her lifelong dislike of football.

Garry ended up spending over forty years of his life as a salesman for Balfour, the school ring company. He passed away from colon cancer, a few months after his wife had died of the same disease.

The same Howie Davis who owned the Cedarhurst Stapes also had a basketball team called the Kokomo Clowns, for whom I ended up playing. We were a barnstorming team that might be described as a cheap imitation of the Harlem Globetrotters.

My first game for Howie was a real good performance, and Howie told my brother I was headed for the New York Knicks in a matter of weeks. And the way game two started, it looked as though his prediction might come true. We were playing in the County Center in White Plains and had a comfortable lead at the half. Howie came into the locker room in a jovial mood. He said, "Keep it up—if we win tonight, we play the Renaissance two weeks from now, and that'll mean a good payday." (The Renaissance were the best Black pro team in the country at the time.)

But the halftime lead proved to be our high point. The lead gradually faded until we were ahead by a single point with fifteen seconds to go. There was a loose ball under the other team's basket; I moved to grab it and throw in the bucket that would cement our victory. But as I reached out, the best player on the other team—a fellow named Tony Karpowitz from Fordham—stepped on my foot and grabbed my pants. I felt as if I was stuck in cement. Suddenly a little speed demon grabbed the ball, sped the length of the court, and put it in the basket. My shot at the Knicks disappeared, and I entered Howie's doghouse for a couple of weeks.

The Clowns put on a stupid pre-game show in which we all appeared in masks accompanied by a midget, who would end the act by shooting us with a cap gun. It was a tough way to make a buck, a little like being a freak at the circus. My fondest prayer was that no one in the audience would recognize me.

In January, 1950, the Clowns were touring New England and I didn't go along. (When the Clowns went on a midweek road trip, I couldn't play because it would have kept me from getting to Salomon Brothers in the morning.) During this trip, the news of the great Brinks robbery in Boston broke—the biggest heist in U.S. history at that time, with more than $2.5 million in cash, checks, and securities stolen. When I got on the subway after work one day and unfolded my *Herald Tribune*, what did I see on the first but a story about the Clowns having been stopped at some fifteen roadblocks on suspicion of being the gang that had pulled off the robbery.

The police had good reason to be suspicious. The getaway car had been identified as a Cadillac, which was the same make the Clowns drove; the Clowns had masks and looked reasonably thuggish—and the cap pistols in the trunk didn't help. They were taken into police custody, interrogated, and released, only to be stopped and released again and again. It was so ridiculous I started laughing out loud (the people nearby on the subway must have thought I'd lost my mind).

We also played under various other names, such as the Allentown Miners and the Jersey City Reds. One time we were playing in the

Sunnyside Garden in Queens under the banner of the Miners. I had about seventeen foul shots, and each time I went to the line the public address announcer botched my name: "Now shooting, Smek," or Smulke, Secmald, Smirsch, whatever. Finally, as I was about to take my last shot late in the game, he got it right: "Now shooting, Schmeelk." I couldn't resist—I put the ball down, walked up into the stands, and shook his hand.

Another time, we traveled to Hagerstown, Maryland, for a game after staying overnight in a hotel in Philadelphia. At halftime, we were sitting in the locker room when a new player pulled a towel from the hotel out of his bag and starting wiping his head with it. Looking very hurt, Coach Howie addressed him: "How could you steal a towel from our hotel? Don't you think they know when towels are missing? How do you think it reflects on me?" Shaking his head sadly, Howie departed.

Prince Hal Carovon, the former CCNY player and the team's court jester, took up the theme. "Kid, it's not only a reflection on Howic, but it's also a reflection on the whole team." He went on to berate our new teammate for several minutes, finally concluding, "I don't know where you were brought up, kid, but it was probably in the gutter. You're just no good, kid." And as he finished, he reached into his bag, took out a towel from the hotel, and left to wash up. The whole team was in stitches.

As for the game itself: We were putting on a good show for four thousand fans and looking forward to a big payday and a return engagement. Because we had only seven players, Hagerstown had agreed to waive the personal foul rule, which meant that as the game wore on I was playing double, then triple the limit of fouls. Finally fed up with the thirteenth or fourteenth foul, I told the referee, "You're an idiot!" whereupon he (naturally) ejected me from the game.

A heated discussion ensued, and Prince Hal stuck himself between the official and me. "Dick," he declared, "You should know better than to call this man an idiot. He may be stupid, but he's not an idiot." Result: Not only did I get thrown out, but so did our chance of getting a return game. It seemed the ref had a bum ticker and the promoter was very upset over our conduct.

Another night we were headed to Fairfield, Connecticut, to play a team promoted by Walt Dropo, the ex-Red Sox first basemen. It was a bitter cold night, with a snowstorm steadily getting worse. I was sitting with another player in a rumble seat with a blanket over our heads, trying to keep warm. We went across the George Washington Bridge to meet a sedan that would drive us to Fairfield. In the midst of the storm, we stopped at a diner, Howie ordered soup for everyone, and he rushed us back into the car. The storm continued to get worse, and we had to stop frequently to clear the ice from our windshield. Meanwhile, the hours were passing and we were getting later and later.

Finally, Walt Dropo couldn't hold the crowd any longer and had to cancel the game. He got the message to us by calling the chief of police in a town near Fairfield, who flagged down our car and relayed the message. Amid groans from all of the players, our driver Freddie Gardner turned the car around and began heading back for New York. That was the cue for Prince Hal to start entertaining us. "How do you like *this*?" he began, "We'll be traveling twelve hours and our pay is a bowl of soup. Basketball players are the lowest-paid human beings in the world. Even Chinese coolies make more money."

At this point, Freddie Gardner interrupted. "Well," he said, "If I could get along without food for three days during the war, I guess I can survive on a bowl of soup tonight."

Prince Hal: "Freddie, what are you trying to tell us?"

Freddie: "I was in the Air Corps, and I was shot down over Germany, taken prisoner, and had nothing to eat for three days."

Prince Hal (feigning outrage): "Freddie, what do you think it was like *here* during the war? We were playing in all sorts of band boxes, some with cold showers, some with none, sleeping with all sorts of women and waking up in the morning not knowing what we might have caught—and you're complaining just because you got shot down over Germany?!"

The car erupted with hysterical laughter, and Freddie was silent for the balance of the trip.

Two final basketball stories:

We were playing in Saugerties in upstate New York. Once again, the personal foul rule had been waived, and in this case the referee was definitely on the hometown payroll, as bad a homer as we ever saw. The game was tied with about forty seconds to go. The hometown hero and I leapt into the air for a rebound, and as I tried to swat the ball away from him, I caught him right across the mouth. He went down in a heap on the floor, a little blood dripping from his lip. The crowd roared in anger, sounding like the mob in the Roman Coliseum.

Ever the diplomat, I tried to explain that it wasn't intentional, but the official wasn't buying it—he threw me out of the game. Of course, Coach Howie stormed onto the court to defend me: "You can't do that," he yelled, "We're not playing four fouls and you're out."

As the altercation continued, I suddenly heard the opposing coach say, "We'll send for the chief of police and attach their purse." That changed everything. Howie made a quick decision, "Sit down, Dick. Didn't you hear the nice referee say you were out of the game?"

We lost by one point.

The last game I played for Howie was in a big-bucks tournament in Saratoga. This time I was playing for a team called the College All-Stars under the name of Frank Platamura—who was a real player from St. John's. The opposing team was coached by Dutch Dehnert, a member of the Basketball Hall of Fame and a contemporary of my father's from the original Celtics. The game was being broadcast in upstate New York, and while we were dressing in the locker room, the broadcaster came in to get the starting line-up. He turned to me and asked a simple question, "Platamura, how do you spell your name?"

Normally a college student would respond quickly to a question of that difficulty. But I asked him to repeat the question, which he did. Then I started thinking and spelling, "Platamura, P-L-A . . ." and with that my teammate Jimmy Weston—who'd actually played with Platamura at St. John's—finished the spelling as a bewildered broadcaster looked on.

At half time, the game was tied. As the second half started, Dehnert inserted a former Utah player who was about 6'9". When I had to guard him, I tried all the cute stuff I could think of—grabbing his pants, pushing, shoving, and so on. The referee was kind, and after Mr. Utah could see he was complaining to no avail, he left the bucket and went to the sideline. He had a great set shot, and as I was going up and down like a yo-yo, trying in vain to stop him, he destroyed me and the College All-Stars, too.

I suspect that the plot for the future television and movie series,

The Fugitive might have come from that game. The real Frank Platamura must have searched New York for years trying to find the player who'd ruined his reputation in Saratoga. Fortunately for me, he didn't look on Wall Street.

*   *   *

I'd started my career at Salomon as a messenger during summer vacations. Now age twenty-one and back at Salomon, I had a variety of jobs before I reached the trading floor. Back then, a Wall Street career wasn't considered a road to riches. The financial markets had suffered through the Great Depression, the pay was small, and guys like me from working-class families looked on Wall Street as just another place to earn an honest buck and support our families. My cousin Joe Smyth and I launched our Salomon careers at just around the same time.

My first assignment was working in what was known as the cage, where securities were delivered and received. My tasks were pretty mundane. My boss John Keller would arrive every morning and say, "Dick, it's stuffy in here." I would then get out the long hook-nosed pole and use it to pull open the latches at the top of the high windows. In due course, John would depart from his desk on some mission, and Miss Kennedy, the secretary to the office manager, Clem Gaertner, would arrive, whereupon she would say, "It's too cold in here. Dick, will you please close the windows?" This game of musical windows would go on three or four times a day.

I also had to fetch coffee a couple of times a day for the various women in the department. There were a lot of nice people working in what was then called the back office. (The name was later changed to the more prestigious-sounding *operations*, which I suspect raised the salaries as well.) They included John Brown, Arthur Alteneau, Sid Grobert, Tim Dunn, and Allie Riese, as well as my boss John Keller. They lent a helping hand up the ladder to my cousin Joe and me. (Joe eventually became a partner at Salomon along with me.)

Someone in the cage was always pulling off a trick or two to entertain the troops. On one occasion, an unsuspecting husband arrived home with a dozen hard-boiled eggs instead of the fresh eggs his wife has asked him to buy. On another occasion, one of the men opened a hatbox to show his wife the pretty *chapeau* he'd bought her, only to reveal a beat-up fedora that someone had stuck in its place.

In time, thanks to the support of Clem Gaertner, I was promoted to the trading floor and assigned to the municipal desk as an order clerk. My experience as a diesel mechanic had not prepared me for the world of municipal bonds. It was indeed a strange place, and with the exception of a trader named Frank Sisk, no one seemed too interested in teaching a young recruit about municipal bonds.

Unsuprisingly, I was soon floundering. Gene Marks, the partner in charge, called me into his office and he informed me that I didn't have what it took to make it in municipal bonds. I thanked him, saying I would rather find out sooner than later, and broke the news to my benefactor, Clem. He gave me some good advice: "Don't leave until you have something else."

I proceeded to go to an employment agency, which proved to be the turning point of my career. They sent me to meet an executive at the Topps chewing gum company in Brooklyn. This executive had been a "ninety-day wonder" in the Navy, a phrase used to describe someone who becomes an officer after just three months in the service. It's not a term of endearment. We exchanged greetings and shook hands, after which he commented, "Now, one thing I notice is that you have a very weak shake. When you are calling on our customers, it's important to have a firm handshake. This instills confidence in you and in the company you represent."

That was an interesting idea to ponder. My next question was, "Who will I be calling on?"

"You will be calling on various candy stores in Brooklyn and New York."

The idea of spending my days traveling around the city trying to sell packages of gum to the owners of corner candy stores seemed deeply depressing. Panic overtook me. I raced back to Salomon, sought out Clem Gaertner, and said, "Give me a crack at something else—anything else."

My next job was to figure out our daily profits independently and compare my results with those calculated by the auditor. I also reconciled the firm's numerous bank accounts. It could be maddening, since, if you were out by as little as one penny, you'd have to work your way through the day's pile of checks from the top to the bottom until you found it.

Next I moved to the liaison department as an assistant to a gentleman named Joe Graf. At that time, Joe was making a hundred dollars a week, and I thought to myself, "Wow—if I ever got his job, I'd be set for life." (Like the old gray mare, money ain't what it used to be.) Joe later went on to open the Dallas office for Salomon.

In the liaison department, we sought out situations where exchanging one security for another would be financially advantageous and presented our views to salesmen whose accounts held securities we were looking for. It was a great learning experience. Not only did I begin to grasp how securities markets worked, but some of the senior salesman, like Charlie Simon and Dan Kelly, would at times challenge my assumptions, which forced me to *really* know what I was talking about.

My next step, which I took around 1950, was working in the syndicate department under Ted Von Glahn and Harold Gillespie. Harold worried more about the accounts he covered than anyone I ever met, and I learned a great deal from him. The syndicate department bid on new issues of bonds, primarily public utilities. However, there were long periods of inactivity between new issues which we had to fill in somehow. Ted asked me if I wanted to become a salesman and cover accounts, and I said Yes. My list of clients, Ted explained, would include savings banks, fraternal organizations, corporations, and small insurance companies.

I thought that working with corporations sounded promising, but when I inquired about that, Chet Bardsley, one of the partners, discouraged me. "The only thing we do with corporations," he told me, "is sinking fund business. And when they get active, the trading desks take over." Looking back, when I think of how successful I was covering corporations in Canada, I have often pondering how successful I would have been covering U.S. corporations. In fact, later on, I did cover several big U.S. corporations and had a pretty good success rate.

Chet Bardsley helped me a great deal, but he called this one wrong.

The New York sales force had split up the account list to such a degree that when you asked them who they covered, they would have to go over a long list in their book to refresh their memory. This explains the mishap that arose when I made my first sale ever. The client was the Union Labor Life Insurance Company, and I made the sale through their treasurer, a man by the name of George Holland who had a son in an iron lung due to a case of polio. Naturally I was delighted to make my first trade, but a few days later Dan Kelly approached me and told me it was his account. Dan eventually allowed me to keep the account, admitting he had never called on them.

Like most new salespeople, I had to do my share of cold calling. I made one memorable call on the Barber Steamship Company on Front Street. I asked the receptionist (a Black man) whether the treasurer was in. He replied, "What do you want to see him about?"

I replied, "Investments."

His answer was, "Oh, he wouldn't be interested."

I replied, "How do you know?"

This time, the receptionist responded, "What I meant to say is, we are fully invested at this time." What a great line—a fine way of discouraging any further probing.

When I was in the syndicate department common stock was pretty much foreign to Salomon. One time, however, we happened to be bidding on two bond issues and one stock issue for a company called Middle South Utilities. Ted Von Glahn was attending one bond syndicate meeting and Harold Gillespie the other, so Ted asked me to attend the Middle South meeting. Lehman Brothers was the syndicate manager. I knew nothing about pricing common stock, and I asked Ted what I should do. "Just sit there and look smart," was his reply.

That wasn't satisfactory to me, so I approached our arbitrage partner Ray McGivney and asked how a price was arrived at on a new stock issue. His answer: "It's usually a commission off the last sale of a listed stock." Well, Salomon was in for a participation of 30,000 shares, and our book of interest consisted of one possible order—the U.S. Steel Pension Fund might take a hundred shares if our group won.

So I went to the syndicate meeting, and the manager canvassed the group. I was surrounded by gray hairs. My view was solicited and much to my surprise, it was noted that Salomon was bullish on the issue.

The meeting broke up, and I returned to the office. Our then managing partner Rudy Smutny, called me to his desk and asked me about the meeting and our book of interest. I told him we were in for

30,000 and had one possible sale of 100 shares. His next question was a logical one: "Why are we staying?"

My brilliant reply: "I don't know."

Next morning, we dropped out of the syndicate by phone. My bid topped the winning bid by one penny, and the issue sold out. Ray McGivney had a field day, constantly reminding me not to pass the Lehman Building: "They're on the lookout for the tall dark guy with the gray homburg who didn't have the guts to drop out in person."

Chapter 5
North of the Border

Salomon Brothers traces its history back to 1910, when the three Salomon Brothers, Arthur, Herbert, and Percy, along with a clerk, B.J. Levy (known as Ben), launched the firm with starting capital of $5,000.

When I came along, Bill Salomon, the son of Percy, was just starting his illustrious career with the firm. Bill had joined Salomon soon after finishing prep school, starting as a runner (messenger) in the back office and eventually moving into sales. He was mainly responsible for the large New York banks and insurance companies. In 1944, he entered the service and returned to Salomon in 1946.

In 1956, Bill played a major role in the ouster of Rudy Smutny as managing partner. Smutny, an excellent salesman, lost his position through a combination of reckless positioning of questionable illiquid investment that jeopardized the firm's capital base and running roughshod over many of his partners.

Bill eventually rose to become the managing partner. He created a strict discipline for maintaining and building Salomon's capital, which helped the firm survive the Wall Street crisis of the early sixties. At the time, many Wall Street firms got in trouble because their back offices couldn't keep up with equity trades, absentee ownership, and provisions that capital could be withdrawn on thirty or sixty days' notice. This led to the "fail to receive and fail to deliver" crisis. Over-the-counter securities—unlisted stocks that did not trade on the big board of the New York Stock Exchange—were especially hard-hit, since the paper trail on such a stock might lead through eight or ten firms.

A near-panic developed, with partners withdrawing their capital from firms as the problem spread. Several old firms, including Goodbody, Ira Haupt, and DuPont, vanished from the scene. At Salomon, however, a partner could withdraw his money from the firm only over a period of many years. This staved off panic withdrawals and forced the partners and back-office people to roll up their sleeves and work through the problems.

Here's an example of what was happening on Wall Street in those days. An acquaintance of mine with an account at DuPont was receiving double confirmations on share transactions with the company. When I ran into him walking with our kids on the boardwalk at Riis Park, he would ask my advice. "I think you ought to tell DuPont about the mistakes so they can fix them." Unfortunately, he ignored this advice and instead decided to sell the duplicate share holdings with which he'd been incorrectly credited. Of course, it didn't end well; months later, they caught up with him, and he had to reimburse DuPont.

Bill Salomon's disciplined rules on withdrawals helped our firm survive those troubled times. He was also a prudent risk-taker. At the same time, he catered to the youth movement at the firm, willingly entered new business areas, and was always a gracious host to new and old clients alike. In short, Billy was a calming leader for Salomon during a time of dramatic change.

It's no secret that after he picked John Gutfreund as his successor, their relationship rapidly declined, and Billy went into a self-imposed exile from the firm for many years.

I think Mike Bloomberg hit the nail on the head in his book, *Bloomberg by Bloomberg*, when he wrote, "The real difference between Billy and John was that John was smarter with securities, Bill with people." I'm sure that neither man was happy with that distinction, but I always believed the firm benefited when they ran it together, combining their different strengths. Without John, Billy would have had trouble running the financial engineering side of the company, as the securities world grew more complex with derivatives, swaps, mortgage securities, and so on. On the other hand, Billy was very gracious with clients, while John could be very abrasive at times.

Billy was also a strong decision-maker. When he ran an executive committee meeting, he knew when to cut off the debates before they became rancorous. By contrast, John would let debates run interminably, causing bitterness and hostility. When Billy wanted something, you knew it, but John definitely shied away from strong decisions.

I never understood why John cut Billy out of any role at the firm so quickly after his ascendancy. Bill could have served as an excellent good-will ambassador for Salomon Brothers if he'd been allowed to do so. Perhaps it was insecurity on John's part—a not-uncommon affliction among CEOs.

However, I'm jumping ahead of my story just a bit. Let's go back to the mid-1950s, which is when my involvement in Canada began—a connection that ultimately grew into the hallmark of my business career.

It all started when I was assigned to sell securities to some of the smaller Canadian insurance companies—The Imperial Life Association, The Crown Life Insurance Company, The North American Life Insurance Company, and Confederation Life Insurance—as well as two of the larger companies, The Great West Life Insurance Company and The Canada Life Insurance Company.

I also had on my list a fraternal organization that sold insurance to its members, the Independent Order of Foresters. Lou Probst was the president of the order, Cliff McCreary was the treasurer, and Bud Elder was the secretary—all old timers. They had a wonderful musical group called the Robin Hood Band, which performed for many years in the annual Rose Bowl Parade.

A stop at the Foresters offices in Toronto was always a refreshing way to end the day, since they had a paneled wall in their boardroom that concealed a bar (an illegal amenity in those days). Many years later, the Foresters sold the building to the Toronto Police Department. As they were turning it over, they showed the now-bare former bar to the Police Chief and said, "We discovered this secret panel in the wall just the other day."

When I started covering Canada, Leo Shaw, a partner who was covering our major commercial paper clients, GMAC, CIT, & Commercial Credit, arranged for a reception to introduce me to the Toronto investment community. (Leo had a young foreign stock trader reporting to him who had a bad habit of hiding tickets in his drawer, which created a great deal of embarrassment with customers of the firm and losses as well. This individual later became the trader for Bernie Cornfield's Fund of Funds. I personally refused to contact them knowing they had hired him.)

When the day of the reception neared, Leo fell on his sword, and I was on my own with some seventy-odd guests on their way. To add to my sense of panic, the Foresters called and asked if they could bring their board members as well. Guests started arriving, and I was blanking out on names when Bud Elder, secretary of the Foresters, rode to the rescue. He took over all the introducing, as he was a wonder on names. Over the years, I saw him repeat this performance at many New York dinners that the Foresters hosted for the Wall Street firms that covered them.

One night many years later, Bud, his wife, my first wife Betty, and I were walking in New York after having dinner together. In his late sixties by then, Bud was feeling a bit sorry for himself, saying the company was only keeping him on out of charity. In response, I was building Bud up, telling him he was younger in energy and spirit than a lot of people his age.

Our wives were walking ahead when Bud and I were suddenly propositioned by two ladies of the evening. After politely dismissing them, I turned to Bud. "You see," I told him, "You're not as old as you think you are."

"Just make sure this story gets around Bay Street," Bud answered, referring to the financial center of Toronto.

Lou Probst, president of the Foresters, may have been the greatest salesman I ever knew. He had to be pretty good to recover from his first disaster, which became a legendary tale among his friends and colleagues. It seems that Lou had convinced a certain gentleman to take out a substantial insurance policy. Sitting in the client's living room with the man's wife, Lou had his pen ready for signing when he decided to inject a little humor. "Who would you like to be the beneficiary—your wife or your mistress?" he asked.

The man's wife burst into tears. "See what a fool you've made out of me—everybody knows!" Lou Probst was shown the door, the unsigned policy still sitting on the table.

Several years later, my cousin Joe Smyth and I made the same idiotic mistake at a Salomon Christmas party. A partner—let's call him Fred Jones—introduced us to his wife. Joshingly, Joe replied,

"Come on, Fred, this is the third woman you've introduced us to. Which one is the real Mrs. Jones?"

Shortly thereafter, one of the other partners informed us that "Fred Jones" did indeed have a mistress, and that his wife had recently found out about it. The funny thing is that, if you'd known the man, you'd have agreed he was one of the world's least likely suspects.

At the Great West Life in Winnipeg, I dealt with Frank Buchanan, Stan Susinski, Bob McConkey, and Garry Copeland, as well as Bill Lang (a veteran of the bloody landing at Dieppe), Grant Dominy (a terrific investment man), and Doug Leatherdale (later President of the St. Paul Companies). I always enjoyed visiting Winnipeg and found the people (if not the weather) warm and inviting.

On one occasion, Grant Dominy had me to his home for a party with the investment group. They were mixing up a drink they called Fish Eye Number Three, which contained three different liquors plus juice. I was very cautious with this potent mix, but a young lad from the group downed a few, went into the bathroom, and passed out. Unfortunately, it happened to be the only bathroom in the house. There was a lot of lip biting and leg crossing until the young fellow finally awakened.

Doug Leatherdale was president of the Young Conservatives in Manitoba, and through Doug I met Dufferin Roblin, who was Premier of Manitoba from 1958 to 1967. The Parliament Building was right across the street from the Great West Building, so when Frank Buchanan, head of the investment group, saw me crossing the street, he supposedly inquired, "Where is Dick going?"

Bob McConkey answered, "To see Premier Duff Roblin."

Buchanan said, "I've been trying to get an appointment with him for six months. Dick gets off a plane and sees him an hour later— how come?"

McConkey replied, "You're just not close enough to Doug Leatherdale." Ironically, Doug was then the low man on the totem pole in the investment department—but not in political circles.

At Canada Life, I dealt with Gordon Fleming, Dave Radford, and Don Cooper. At North American Life, it was Dave Pretty, Tom Ingles, and Clive Curtis. At the Imperial Life, Don Purdy, John McMeekin, and Bill Monroe. At the Crown Life, George Wilson and Milt Waters. In Waterloo, the Dominion Life, George Pangman,

Andy Mavor, and Gordon Coyne, and at the Mutual Life, J.B. Hawson and others.

On my first visit to Waterloo I was accompanied by Leo Block, a preferred stock trader at Salomon. It was a very cold January day—probably around ten degrees. We took J.B. Hawson and George Pangman to lunch and then returned to our rented car with our guests. Leo couldn't find the keys to the car. After going through all his pockets several times (while our guests stamped their feet and waved their arms to keep warm), Leo found a hole in his overcoat pocket. The keys had fallen through and were trapped inside the lining. As our guests looked on, I worked the keys up inch by inch and through the hole in Leo's pocket. Not a good first impression created by team Salomon.

One of the interesting things about covering the Dominion Life was that they traded bonds very actively even as George Pangman and Andy Mavor were at different ends of the earth. Mavor would actively buy bonds for a while, then go away on business or on vacation, and Pangman would take over—and immediately start selling out Mavor's positions. I welcomed the business, but feared I would be caught in the middle and accused of talking Pangman into liquidating Mavor's bond portfolio.

George Pangman was a very impressive gentleman and someone with whom I was uncomfortable for a few years, feeling he was way ahead of me. Later on I got to know him better, and we spent a few very pleasant evenings together.

Over the many years I covered the Dominion Life, I always called Andy Mavor *Mister* Mavor. He was perhaps twenty-five or thirty years my senior. After he retired to Peterborough, Ontario, I wrote to thank him for the fine relationship we enjoyed over the years. He wrote me a very nice letter in return, ending with, "P.S. Please do not call me Mr. Mavor anymore. Call me Andy."

I said to myself, "I'll probably never see him again, and now he wants me to call him Andy."

One day when I was walking past the National Life Insurance Company in Toronto, I realized that I had never called upon them. I decided to walk in and ask to see the treasurer. He was Jack Rhind, and we had a pleasant conversation. Jack pointed out that their only bond holding in the United States was 250,000 units of ATT 3 3/8 of 1973. I replied, "You could trade those for ATT 2 3/4 of 1971 and pick up better call protection, a little more yield, and a shorter maturity."

Lo and behold, a week later he called to make the trade.

Some months later, I was back in New York when senior partner Joe Ottens called me to his desk. A.M. Best Company had just issued its annual publication showing the purchase and sale of bonds by insurance companies. The sales force lived in some fear of this, as Joe would call you on the carpet about trades done with other firms. When I saw that Joe had the Best book in his hand, I prepared to take my medicine, but instead Joe reached up and shook my hand. "Dick, you're the only one who did one hundred percent of any insurance company's business last year." My one trade with Jack Rhind and the National Life had created the perfect score.

The other insurance company I covered was the ill-fated Confederation Life, shut down by government regulators in 1994 amid fears of collapsing real estate values. I worked with Ron Malone and Jack Slattery there. Ron suffered from narcolepsy, an affliction that caused him to fall asleep suddenly and unexpectedly. One time he and Joe Foley were in a nightclub together and Ron fell fast asleep at a ringside table. The headwaiter thought Ron was drunk and asked them to leave, but it wasn't true—Ron might fall asleep anywhere or any time.

Ron happened to land in New York the same day a huge hurricane hit Long Island. Fool that I was, instead of staying home like most intelligent people I had gone to work. The news reports were grim: The eye of the hurricane was headed for the Rockaways, where I lived on that narrow peninsula between Jamaica Bay and the Atlantic Ocean.

Increasingly agitated, I made several calls home where my wife was holding down the fort. The water was rising, the bay and the ocean were meeting in the streets. My last report from Betty was that the basement was flooded and the water was about a foot from entering the first floor. She was worried about the new broadloom rug we had just put down. I said, "The hell with the rug. Go up to the second or third floor."

Then the phones went dead.

At this point, I reached over and grabbed a cigarette from my sidekick, Joe Foley. I'd been trying to quit and hadn't smoked in about six months, but this struck me as an emergency that would justify a relapse.

In the midst of all this chaos, I got a call from Ron Malone. He'd landed in New York and was having trouble getting a cab. Could I help him?

Under the circumstances, I advised Ron that he was on his own.

After a few hours, I got back into contact with Betty. The worst of the storm had passed, and the water had stopped short of the first floor. I waited till low tide to go home. When I arrived at my street, I took off my shoes and socks, raised my pants above my knees, and waded inside. In our basement, the electrical system was shot, along with the oil burner motor, a refrigerator, the washer and dryer, and several dressers full of winter clothes.

It took about two weeks for the water to fully recede. It was impossible to get help with the cleanup since everyone was in the same boat. Every evening I would come home from work, change into a bathing suit, and go down to the basement. I used an ax to hack away at the dressers to throw out the clothes. As the water receded and we pumped out our basement, it went into the basement next door—a frustrating variation on musical chairs that we played until the water table went down. The smell of stagnant water permeated the house.

I have a lot more sympathy for flood victims after that experience.

Every year, the investment group from Wall Street hosted a dinner party for the insurance industry in Toronto and Waterloo. Over the years, many friends were made amongst competing firms. Jack Sachau of Blyth and I often hosted luncheons together and became close friends. Once when I got itchy and thought about leaving Salomon, I even interviewed at Blyth. Jack talked me out of it, saying I had a great franchise. Luckily I followed his advice—Blyth eventually went out of business.

On one occasion, I took about eight fellows from various insurance companies to lunch at the King Edward Hotel. After lunch, the waiter presented me with the bill. I signed my name and room number and we left.

The following day, I visited Ron Melone at the Confederation Life and we decided to have lunch together. I asked Ron, "Where would you like to go?"

He answered, "How about the King Edward?"

Then it dawned on me that I was staying at the Park Plaza and had signed my room number at the King Edward the day before.

When I arrived at the King Edward dining room, I approached the maitre d', red-faced, and began, "I'm Mr. Schmeelk, and I was here yesterday."

Before I could finish she said, "Oh, Mr. Schmeelk, you don't know what we went through yesterday looking for you!"

I made it right. Imagine the headlines if I'd really forgotten about it and they'd had me arrested sometime later.

Over time, I began to notice that the insurance companies continually brought new young talent in to handle contacts with the New York salesmen. Looking around, I saw salesmen—some in their mid-sixties—covering these young fellows at the insurance companies. I decided that I didn't want to be in my sixties telling the young investment people all the wonderful things I had done for their companies over the past thirty years. Unlike my days as a fireman first class in the navy, I was determined never to be "too valuable to be promoted." So with Joe Foley gradually replacing me with some of the insurance companies, I began to expand my contacts with corporations and commercial banks.

One new relationship was with the Toronto Dominion Bank through Fred Elliott, their agent in New York. Toronto Dominion at that time showed more imagination than the other Canadian banks in the U.S., which basically restricted themselves to buying U.S. treasury bills and short U.S. government bonds. Fred got permission to buy bonds issued by agencies such as Fannie Mae and Federal Home Loans, which yielded a fair bit more than government bonds at that time. Fred also bought a large number of corporate bonds with high coupons that could be called in three or six months. These paid substantial premiums in yield over short-term governments.

Fred and Ellen Elliott became good friends of mine. I also hired Fred's son Tom at Salomon, and he became a very good salesman in the Canadian department. I was a good deal older than Tom, which didn't stop me from abusing him on the tennis court for a number of years. The last time we played, after reaching ten-all, this aging veteran said, "Let's go have a drink." After that, I consider us all even when it comes to tennis.

One evening, Fred invited me to their apartment for a drink. When I arrived half an hour later, I was told by the doorman that the Elliots had just left. They weren't being rude—Ellen had been tidying up prior to my visit when a Venetian blind fell and gave her a serious gash on the temple. I went over to New York Hospital to keep Fred company. You see the world pass by when you spend the middle of the night in an emergency room in New York. Two elderly spinsters entered having interrupted a dinner out together; one thought she was having a heart attack, which turned out to be indigestion. A drug addict nearly dead from an overdose was followed by a drunk loudly proclaiming, "I am an American citizen!" and demanding free attention.

After several hours of this free education in the vagaries of human nature, Ellen was finally ready to go home, having received twenty-one stitches.

A few weeks later, I was going to Toronto for our annual dinner with the insurance companies of Toronto and Waterloo. Fred suggested I drop in on Alan Lambert, President & CEO of Toronto Dominion Bank. I made a 5:30 appointment, thinking this would give me plenty of time to get to the dinner reception at 6:15.

But what I thought would be a courtesy visit turned out quite differently. Alan started to quiz me on the outlook for interest rates and Salomon's inventory in the one- to five-year range. Several calls to our industrial and utility bond trading desks in New York followed. That evening, Alan cleaned out our inventory, buying millions of General Motors Acceptance notes, World Bank bonds, American Tel & Tel, and others. Most important, we were right on the market—interest rates dropped sharply, just as we'd foretold.

I arrived at the dinner around seven thirty. Several people inquired where I had been. "I was detained," was the simple answer.

Most of my competitors never wandered beyond the insurance companies. I was assigned to place commercial paper for CIT, Commercial Credit, and GMAC in Canada. I had a little black book which listed all our commercial paper customers and when their holdings came due. My job was to call them before the due date, ask whether they wanted to renew their commercial paper, and solicit new buyers.

I started my first sales trip in Hamilton, where I visited our client The Steel Company of Canada (now known as Stelco). Bob Taylor was the treasurer (later Chairman of Ontario Hydro). Bob renewed his CIT notes with us, and I dashed off by bus to Toronto. To my dismay, I lost the little black book, which was the only record anyone at

Salomon had. But I traveled on and managed to continue the business successfully without it. I visited Don McGibbon, treasurer of Imperial Oil and some of our other clients in Toronto, and then J.R. Logan, treasurer of Bell Telephone of Canada in Montreal. and James Eccles, a one-man shop who advised a host of industrial and financial clients in Canada. Eccles suggested I visit John Close of the Royal Trust Company in Montreal and make a call on the Canada Steam Ship Company. The gentleman I visited there bought a half million commercial paper notes. His name? Paul Martin, then company treasurer and later Prime Minister of Canada.

As a commercial paper salesman, I built a host of relationships from which we reaped substantial rewards in the future. J.R. Logan, treasurer of Bell Canada, was my entrée into that corporation and paved the way for our future relationship with Bell. Other important relationships were those with Bob Taylor of Ontario Hydro and with Don McGibbon and his wife Paula. Don was treasurer of Imperial Oil, while Paula later became Governor General of Ontario.

Gradually, however, the commercial paper companies decided they didn't need us and started going directly to our client list.

My first taste of investment banking came about in a strange way. As I've mentioned, I belonged to a small club in the Rockaways called the Belle Harbor Yacht Club. During the summer it was quite active, with tennis, dining, sailing, and a summer show where I attained local fame as a singer and producer (though I never managed to parlay it into the big time). Anyway, to keep the club open on winter weekends, members volunteered to tend the bar, though one had to be brave to face the winter winds off Jamaica Bay during January and February at the club.

Well, one weekend I had bartending duty along with a friend of mine, John Doscher, who worked in the media world. A member named Carl Hitschler whom I'd known casually for quite some time was standing at the bar. We were making small talk when Carl asked me what I did for a living.

"I work for Salomon Brothers," I replied.

"That's interesting," Carl said, "I'm the assistant treasurer at Uniroyal."

Pretty soon, Salomon and I were doing a lucrative business with Carl, buying bonds for Uniroyal's sinking fund. Carl introduced me to Bill Crane, the company treasurer, and Frank McGrath, the VP of finance. Eventually I met George Villa, the CEO.

One night sometime in the late fifties I hosted a dinner for Villa with fifteen or twenty investors. An unintended result was an order the next morning from one of the attendees to sell his position in Uniroyal. Soon thereafter, Uniroyal selected Salomon to be its agent placing commercial paper—a business then dominated by Goldman Sachs. I was told by people at Uniroyal that Goldman's Sidney Weinberg was furious when he heard the news and personally called on Villa to express his displeasure.

Now, I was feeling pretty good about my relationship with Uniroyal. I even went out and bought a hundred shares of their stock to show my support. Uniroyal had a subsidiary in Canada called Dominion Tire that was looking to borrow fifteen million dollars. I was pretty confident that this would be my first investment banking deal. I called Frank McGrath and outlined a price and terms, and worked with their VP of international finance. Everything was in place, including the lead buyer; all that was needed was an okay from the board.

Whoops! John Schiff, Chairman of Kuhn Loeb, an icon in the industry, a major holder of Uniroyal stock, and a director of the company, spoke up. From the playback I got, it went something like this: "Just a minute. I am your investment banker. If you don't have confidence in me, I shouldn't be on the board."

Result: Kuhn Loeb borrowed my terms and lead buyer and did the deal.

It was a humbling experience for a young hotshot, but a lesson well learned. We did a lot of other business with Uniroyal over the years and I enjoyed my relationship with the company immensely.

Another interesting experience with a Belle Harbor Yacht Club twist was Railway Express. This was a freight delivery company dating back to Pony Express days and owned by a consortium of sixteen or eighteen railroad companies; as I recall, Penn Central spoke for the group. The business was a constant money loser, with an unbelievable method of operation. Here's an example: Imagine oranges and chinaware being shipped from Florida to Bangor, Maine via New York and Boston. Both items arrive in the New York office; the fruit is rotten and the chinaware is broken. What do they do? They ship it on to the Boston office and then on to Bangor, Maine, before shipping it back to the starting point in Florida.

Clearly Railway Express needed a significant management over-haul. But with so many owners, it was like a club where you pay your dues every year without paying very close attention to what you get for your money.

Eventually, however, the consortium got tired of losing money and decided to sell. Jim McKay in our Canadian group was assigned to put a bid before the group. Now it just so happened that the night and weekend bartender in the Belle Harbor Yacht Club also worked for Railway Express. His name was Tom King. I started riding him mercilessly, telling him that if Salomon bought Railway Express he would be the first one to leave. In response, he began asking when I was going to retire from tennis—particularly when he saw me limp-ing into the bar after a tough match, sweating profusely and covered with clay.

In due course, Railway Express was sold to the company's own management, following the plan Jim McKay had proposed. Afterward, Tom King told me about the first announcement man-agement made to the employees: "Henceforth, anyone stealing from the company will be discharged immediately." Kind of a fresh start—go and sin no more.

The late fifties and early sixties were an interesting time for me. I moved from being a Man Friday and a salesman through the syn-dicate department to being a investment banker covering provinces, municipalities, corporations, and ultimately Crown Corporations and the Dominion of Canada itself. It was quite a ride. (Naturally, I was well prepared for this ascent by my years as a diesel mechanic in the navy.)

In the early sixties, when I started to pursue investment banking in Canada, Salomon had no corporate finance operation—just a man named Roy Greenfield, who headed the statistical department. It also had no relationship with any industrial client other than Swift, the Chicago meat-packing company. Salomon strictly bid on public utility issues and railroad equipment trusts.

Salomon had two partners responsible for Canada: Joe Ottens, head partner for the utility trading desk, and the colorful Mike Perrin, head of the industrial desk. They hated each other with a passion, which created some awkward moments for me.

As I was fairly young and junior, whenever I had an important Canadian—say, the treasurer of one of the provinces—in our offices at Salomon, I would look for Joe or Mike to say hello to our visitor. On one occasion, I asked Mike to greet the treasurer of Manitoba, Ron Burns. He replied, "I won't. He did his last deal with another firm."

I then approached Joe Ottens. He replied, "I saw you go to Mike first. A flat No." That left me nervously casting about for a kinder, gentler partner to offer the greeting—probably Chet Bardsley.

Mike Perrin did some small private placements, working with Nigel Gunn of Bell Gouinlock and Dudley Dawson of Greenshields. Mike's immigrant father had had a pushcart on New York's Lower East Side. Using the proceeds, he successfully educated three sons. Mike's two brothers were Hollywood agents, and one also wrote scripts for the comedian Jack Benny.

The partners at Salomon had a habit of dropping into the dining room around four P.M. for a little pick-me-up. Invariably Mike would return to his desk afterward and improve his bids by a quarter point. Mike also had a habit of saying, "Bid him one one, but don't let him off the phone," meaning if he won't sell there, he'll probably raise the bid. On a few occasions, the client said No and hung up, leaving a young salesman (me) sitting there and wondering, "What do I do now?"

I covered a small company in Knoxville, Tennessee, called the Southern Fire and Casualty. Its president, Fenton A.S. Gentry, handled the portfolio. He told me he had a substantial buy and sell program and asked me for a list of quotations on various preferred stocks and industrial bonds.

The following day, an agitated Mike Perrin approached me. "Your man is in the street dealing with Asiel." (This was an old-line brokerage firm, known today as Tradition Asiel.) "By going to Asiel instead of us, he's stealing money from his company." Mike was implying that we would pay a higher price. Growing more and more upset, Mike went on to say, "If I knew the president of that company—and I know the presidents of *many* companies—I'd call him and say Bob, Phil—whoever—discharge that man immediately! He's stealing money from your company!"

When Mike finished his tirade, I pointed out that my client *was* the president of the company. The following day, Fenton called and gave me his entire investment program.

Mike finally decided to let me start calling directly on the provincial treasurers. I believe a winter trip to Saskatchewan in 1954 with Dudley Dawson of Greenshields might have forced the decision. Mike had flown to Regina from Palm Springs wearing just a tropical suit and raincoat. It was obvious that the frigid weather he encountered had turned him off when he returned to the office and someone asked him, "How was the trip?"

Mike replied, "Terrible. Don't even go to see the picture." (At the time, Alan Ladd was playing the part of a Canadian mounted policeman in a movie called *Saskatchewan.*)

Several years later, Saskatchewan caused me the greatest grief I ever experienced in my long career in Canada. It all began when representatives of the province came to New York and informed us that we had been chosen to be the lead banker in the U.S. for Saskatchewan bond financing. This was great news—they had a double A rating and were an excellent credit risk.

But all hell broke loose soon afterward when they decided to nationalize the potash industry, following the policy of Allan Blakeney's National Democratic Party. Several of our industrial clients, both in the U.S. and Canada, vented their displeasure on me. John Wiley, my partner at the time, was responsible for the province, and John and I agreed we would never do expropriation financing for the province. Our angry clients responded that money is fungible— you can take it out of one pocket and put it in another. Their treasurer also spoke to us about waging a proxy fight against International Minerals and Chemical, which we managed to talk them out of.

Noranda was one of the companies whose Saskatchewan properties were taken over. Later, when tempers cooled down, I'd call my good friend Adam Zimmerman at Noranda each September and ask whether he'd sent a birthday card to Premier Blakeney (who happened to share my birthday—September seventh).

In the midst of this controversy, I spoke at a dinner in New York attended by several U.S. investors and the Canadian Consul General Bruce Rankin. Among other remarks, I noted, "Bruce Rankin is fond of saying that Americans and Canadians are very different from one another. Well, the people may be different, but the bonds are the same."

I thought this was an uncontroversial, conciliatory observation. But a few days later, I received a blistering letter from the CEO of International Minerals and Chemicals, in which he demanded, "How can you say the bonds are the same when Saskatchewan is national-izing the potash industry?" Shows what happens when politics rears its ugly head. Fortunately, our relationship with Saskatchewan was-n't permanently soured by this controversy—we continued to be their banker on utility debt issues.

Bruce Rankin was an outstanding representative of the Canadian Government in New York. We worked very closely with him to promote a better understanding of Canada in the U.S. investment community, bringing investors to meetings around both countries.

One of my escapes from disaster during the early part of my investment banking career was the Atlantic Acceptance case. Sometime around the end of 1964, John Gutfreund received an invi-tation to lunch at Lambert & Company. Jean Lambert, a Frenchman married to (and later divorced from) Phyllis Bronfman, the daughter of Sam Bronfman of Seagram's, was the banker for Atlantic Acceptance, a Canadian finance corporation. Gutfreund invited me to accompany him because of my Canadian background. Don Mutscheler, our finance company specialist, also attended.

Lambert's headquarters, including the dining room where we lunched, were quite impressive. We listened to their pitch on Atlantic Acceptance commercial paper. They had an impressive list of buyers of their notes, led by the Ford Foundation, J.P. Morgan, and Harvey Mole, head of U.S. Steel's pension fund. But there were hardly any Canadian buyers. They wanted to know whether we would act as agent placing their commercial paper notes—and Lambert hinted that, if we placed commercial paper for Atlantic Acceptance, we would stand a good chance of replacing their then-manager, Kuhn Loeb, on long-term notes. But he wanted an answer fast.

One of the things I learned during my long career in Wall Street is this: Beware of a company that is a marginal credit risk and con-stantly changes its financial managers. This usually indicates that they don't want anyone to learn too much about the *real* state of their affairs. Sure enough, Atlantic Acceptance soon blew up. They'd financed a casino in the Bahamas, among other questionable proj-ects. Fraud was involved, and when it was revealed the company fell apart, creating quite a problem for two other finance companies in Canada, Industrial Acceptance and Trader's Finance, both of whom encountered serious problems raising capital.

A second lesson I learned, which the Lambert story also illustrates, is this: Always do your own due diligence—don't rely on others.

You could add a third lesson: When you are unfamiliar with a company and a fast answer is demanded, the fast answer should always be No. Fortunately, that's exactly what we said to Lambert.

Chapter 6
Getting Into the Game

If Salomon was serious about this investment banking business, our task was to attack the establishment, the so-called group of seven that dominated the Canadian market. They were First Boston Corporation, Drexel Harriman, and Smith Barney in the U.S., and Wood Gundy, A.E. Ames, McLeod Young, and Weir & Dominion Securities in Canada. Morgan Stanley, then the dominant North American underwriter, was nowhere in the provincial business; their major Canadian clients were the Dominion of Canada, Alcan, and International Nickel.

Although Bill Wilder of Wood Gundy was a powerful figure on the Canadian scene in the 1960s and early 70s, probably the single most dominant investment banker in Canada in those days was Doug Chapman of A.E. Ames. In his day (from the end of World War II until 1963), he controlled the business of just about every important corporation in Canada. A giant and noble competitor, he seemed to be everywhere at once. (In that respect, Chapman resembled the great Gus Levy of Goldman Sachs, who also appeared to be every-where, including every business dinner I attended.) Early in our campaign to become a power in the Canadian market, I teamed up with John Wiley, then with Halsey Stuart, to lead a group to go after Hydro Quebec's business. But the first few times we approached them, we found that Doug Chapman had been there with a deal a few hours before us. This was the sort of experience that led me to con-clude there must be more than one Doug Chapman—no single man could be so ubiquitous (or so frustrating).

One cold Sunday night during the pre-Lenten carnival season, John Wiley and I flew to Quebec City to see the provincial premier John Lesage and his Deputy Minister of Finance, Jean Bieler. There was a police chiefs' convention going on at the Chateau Frontinac where we were staying. Unfortunately, the chiefs did not believe in sleeping, and the hall outside our room roared with merry-making all night long. Whom do you complain to when the police are keeping you awake? Answer: No one. We went to our early meeting a little bleary-eyed. But it didn't matter—we learned that Chapman had gotten there first.

On this trip, John Wiley introduced me to some of the young civil servants working for the Quebec government. They included Jacque Parizeau, later premier of Quebec who failed in his attempt to win independence for the province, and Michael Belanger, later chairman of the National Bank of Canada and a director of several other companies.

When we met Premier Lesage and Jean Bieler, the latter made a remark that drove John Wiley up a tree: "Mr. Wiley, I don't believe I have ever heard of your firm, but I know Mr. Schmeelk's firm very well." This was strange, since to my knowledge I was the first visitor to Quebec City from Salomon Brothers. I later discovered that M. Bieler had thought I was with the law firm of Sullivan and Cromwell. I let Wiley suffer a few more months before I came clean.

This was my first major presentation to a client in my new role as an investment banker, and I let John Wiley do ninety-nine percent of the talking. On our way back to the airport, Wiley asked me how I thought it had gone. "Well, John," I replied, "You and I have different styles. You like to talk and I like to listen." He was somewhat taken aback, but over the years to come he would bring this up in a good-natured way. Wiley soon joined me at Salomon and became a lifelong friend from whom I learned a great deal.

I did a lot of traveling with Wiley and soon discovered that he had a couple of odd habits. One was tearing out newspaper articles he thought I might like and throwing them on my lap. Another was racing off the plane as soon as it reached the gate and dashing for the nearest phone (there were no cell phones at the time). After observing these peculiarities for several years, I arranged a small prank to let him know I'd been watching. The next time four of us were flying with John, we all started tearing out articles and throwing them on his lap (he was soon buried under a pile of dozens of clippings). And, of course, when the plane landed, we all dashed for the nearest phones.

Back to the omnipresent Doug Chapman. He had great strengths as a business competitor, but he also had one weakness that I recognized thanks to my fondness for reading military history. Doug Chapman's weakness was an overextended supply line. He hadn't brought along a team to cover his flank, operating instead as a one-man show.

To exploit this weakness, I decided to use some of Salomon's many, many assets—our traders, our sales syndicate, our analysts and economists. I built a team around me starting with John Wiley and Peter Gordon, our first and second Canadian partners. Like a pack of wild dogs attacking some much larger prey, we kept nipping at Doug Chapman's heels until we finally wore him down.

While we were pursuing Hydro Quebec in an effort to jump-start our Canadian business, John Wiley and I met Doug Fullerton of Fullerton, MacKenzie and Associates, who were advising Hydro Quebec.

John Wiley and I, looking a bit bemused by our conversation with Margaret Trudeau, the attractive (and controversial) wife of Prime Minister Pierre Trudeau.

Doug advised many Canadian provinces during his career and built a very successful career despite a serious speech impediment—a very pronounced stutter. This didn't stop him from being a popular public speaker. I remember him calling me one day to say he was going to Toronto to address the investment industry. "And do you know what I'm going to tell them?"

"No, Doug, what are you going to tell them?"

"I'm going to tell them they don't hire enough Je- Je- Je- Jews!"

Another time Doug attended a Salomon reception. As he left, he told me, "Di-Di-Di-Dick, great party! It was the fi-fi-fi-fi-first party I haven't been asked to leave in si-si-si-six months!"

Salomon's first success in Canada came when we teamed up with McLeod, Young, Weir (now owned by the Bank of Nova Scotia and operated as their brokerage division under the name of Scotia McLeod) to seek Bell Canada's U.S. underwriting business. George MacDonald of McLeod (later the company's CEO) and I visited Marcel Vincent, the chairman of Bell Canada, to tell him of our desire to compete for Bell's business. Our first meeting was short and unfriendly. Mr. Vincent told us in no uncertain terms that First Boston and A.E. Ames were Bell's underwriters and then showed us the door. But we persisted and gradually built a strong relationship with Bill Corbett, Bell's treasurer, Arnold Groleau, its vice president of finance, and some of the company directors.

Bill Corbett was a wonderful, down-to-earth guy. One day when I had a pretty good idea they would soon be coming to market in the U.S., I called Bill and said, "George MacDonald and I would like to make a proposal for your U.S. bond issue."

Bill replied, "Okay, Dick. But keep in mind this is an unsolicited proposal." I was puzzled until I figured out what he meant. Bill had a commitment to A.E. Ames and First Boston that Bell would not approach anyone else. To honor that commitment, Bill had to make it clear to us that we were approaching Bell uninvited. Fair enough. We just wanted to get our foot in the door.

It was the practice of the group of seven to approach a few large insurance companies in New York—all major buyers of corporate bonds—to set the price for a bond issue. By contrast, we at Salomon priced deals based strictly on our feel for the market. Our managing partner John Gutfreund and I flew to Montreal, met George MacDonald, and presented to Bill a bought deal which was several basis points better than the A.E. Ames/First Boston syndicate were offering. (A bought deal is an offering in which the underwriter or syndicate buys all the shares and resells them, thereby taking on all the risk. It shows a high degree of confidence in the issue's success.

Salomon and other firms did this for British Petroleum in 1987, which cost them over a billion dollars when the market crashed in October. To my knowledge, our Bell deal was the first bought bond deal in the U.S. market.) Our deal would save Bell a lot of money over the life of the issue. We also suggested a longer non-call feature, but in the eyes of Bill Corbett that meant nothing: "These bonds will never be called, so we aren't giving anything away."

Overall, however, our deal was far superior to the one A.E. Ames and First Boston had proposed. We won the deal and were off and running in Canada.

Flush with success, we offered a similar bought deal to Alberta Municipal Finance. But both deals were based on a misapprehension. We'd mistakenly believed that this counted for a haircut (or spread) of five to ten percent of our capital. However, we soon found out that on a private placement we had to put up one hundred percent capital. This took Salomon out of the bought deal business. (If you're reading this, Elliot Spitzer, forget it! The statute of limitations has expired, and you have a full plate anyway.)

George MacDonald had been the head of McLeod's Montreal office, but the Bell deal wafted him to the head office in Toronto as president of the company. Unfortunately, George's successor in Montreal didn't have the same rapport with Bill Corbett, and soon a new VP of finance named Harry Bowler was appointed at Bell. I suggested to George that he join me in Montreal for a luncheon with Harry Bowler to try to cement their relationship. But about halfway through what appeared to be a pleasant luncheon, Bowler suddenly turned to George and announced that McLeod was being dropped as co-manager on the next Bell U.S. offering.

I felt very bad for George. He was a good partner and friend, and it was rather embarrassing to receive the news that way.

However, I'm getting a little ahead of myself. When our first deal with Bell was made, our managing partner John Gutfreund realized he'd put the prestige of the firm on the line. So we pulled out all the stops to make our word good, blanketing the country to solicit orders. Our competition thought it sinful that we'd given away five additional years of call protection and ridiculed the fact that we were distributing the bonds so broadly. But we were proud of it. (I remember one hectic day during the distribution period, hearing a salesman yell out the good news, "The Salvation Army is buying!"

Another voice responded, "Which corner?")

As I recall, we had sixty-six buyers on the issue—a far cry from the five or six buyers with whom the traditional Canadian underwriting group would have placed the issue.

Our successful completion of the Bell offering put Salomon on the map in Canada. Thus began our great drive towards becoming the top underwriter in Canadian/U.S. pay issues. In addition, for five years in the late seventies and early eighties, we were the number one bond underwriter in the U.S. and among the top three equity underwriters (after years of languishing in the seventh or eighth slot).

Shortly thereafter, Hydro Quebec, whom we'd been actively pursuing, decided to do a competitive bond issue in the U.S. Their traditional bankers were a syndicate led by First Boston Corporation and A.E. Ames and a second group led by Halsey, Stuart and Salomon Brothers that included Greenshields; Harris & Partners; Nesbitt, Thompson; and Morgan, Ostiguy & Hudson.

It's worth looking back on how Quebec Hydro was formed and the wheels that turned towards a competitive bid.

When Liberal Party leader Jean Lesage became premier of Quebec, he and his most prominent minister, René Levesque, set out to nationalize the power generation and transmission assets of the province. It was then a daring and ambitious initiative, intended to create a launching pad for a francophone business elite in a province where the commanding heights had forever been dominated by anglo-Quebecers.

Subsequently, Lesage recruited Eric Kierans for his Cabinet in a by-election. Kierans had been president of the Montreal and Canadian Stock Exchanges, director of the School of Commerce at McGill University and, in the late 1940s and 1950s, a successful entrepreneur, buying small and medium-sized failing companies from the Royal Bank of Canada for cents on the dollar and restoring them. In these endeavors, he was aided by Earle McLaughlin, then Manager of the Royal Bank of Canada's main branch.

Once in the Cabinet, Kierans was an enthusiastic supporter of the completed Quebec Hydro initiative.

In those days, financing in Quebec was dominated by A.E. Ames and Company, headed by the redoubtable Mr. Chapman, in conjunction with the Bank of Montreal. As fiscal agents for the province, Quebec Hydro and many provincial municipalities, Chapman dominated the province's financial decision-making process.

Kierans was determined to break this monopoly and sought the advice of McLaughlin, then chairman and CEO of the Royal Bank; Doug Fullerton, senior partner of Canada's largest bond management counseling business; and Jacques Parizeau, then a brilliant professor of economics and the principal economic advisor to Lesage and his cabinet.

Convinced he could succeed, Kierans incautiously announced his intention to establish competitive bidding for all provincial and provincially-backed bond issues. The reaction was swift and negative. In Canada, in those days, competition to upset established fiscal relationships was considered ungentlemanly. Moreover, Chapman was very powerful and many competitors were loath to antagonize him.

McLaughlin told Kierans that the competition in the United States for municipal and utility financing was brutal and advised him to seek out the advice of Salomon (through me) and Halsey Stuart (through Wiley). In the event, Bill Wilder, then corporate president of Wood Gundy, soon to dominate financing in Canada, did not hesitate and, in conjunction with the Royal Bank of Canada, offered to step forward.

However, such was the tenor of the times in Quebec that a compromise was required. At the urging of Lesage, Kierans and Company grudgingly settled on a revolving syndicate arrangement, whereby Ames would lead and price one issue and Wood Gundy the next. Half a loaf, but better than nons.

Now, to return to my story of Hydro Quebec's U.S. bond issue: Halsey, with strong backing from Nesbitt Thompson, was far too aggressive in their pricing. When we tried unsuccessfully to get them to back off, Joe Wilson, one of the underwriters at Nesbitt Thompson, remarked that if Salomon didn't want to go along, they would take over our position. Finessed, we went along with the pricing, and our group bought the issue. Just as we'd feared, it was a dud—overpriced by twenty-odd basis points. The Halsey group lost hundred of thousands of dollars. But Salomon sold its entire position and then some, coming out with a handsome profit as we swapped clients, including the State of Washington, out of other bonds.

Ed Lemieux, the finance director at Hydro Quebec, cleverly used this experience to strengthen his syndicate. The next time Hydro Quebec came to market, his new syndicate was composed of First Boston; Halsey, Stuart; Salomon; and A.E. Ames. By now, the glory days of Halsey, Stuart were rapidly coming to an end. Percy Stuart, a larger-than-life figure like Doug Chapman, was in his 80s and had not planned well for a successor, so Halsey was down to a few key players—men like Bill Hager, their syndicate manager, and John Wiley, their man in Canada, who would shortly join Salomon Brothers.

Arnold Groleau, Bell Canada's chief financial officer, was elated at the savings from Salomon's bid on their last issue. But despite our tremendous effort, the next issue would be open to competition. (In the meantime, Groleau got kicked upstairs, replaced by George Wallace, who'd been president of Bell's wholly-owned Newfoundland Telephone Company.)

Bell called for bids, and in response First Boston and A.E. Ames submitted a "bid not binding." It was the practice of several Canadian firms to submit such non-binding offers and then back off on the pricing once they had the deal in their pocket—a strategy which Salomon condemned strongly. George MacDonald and I submitted our bid, describing it frankly as "very aggressive" and warning that any bid lower than ours stood a real chance of being renegotiated.

To our disappointment, First Boston and A.E. Ames won the Bell mandate. But just a couple of weeks later, rumors began to fly that the deal was in trouble. Then we heard that the price had been renegotiated to the same level as Salomon/McLeod's original bid.

As you can imagine, I was quite upset. I called Bill Corbett. "Bill," I said, "I told you we'd put in an aggressive bid, and I warned you that you'd end up renegotiating any better deal. Now it's happened just like I said, and I don't think it's very fair to Salomon."

Bill couldn't argue. "What would you like me to do?" he asked.

I expressed the desire for a personal meeting in Montreal, and Bill acquiesced.

When I arrived in Bill's office, I found him chomping on a cigar. "Well, Dick," he began, "What do you want?"

I launched into my carefully rehearsed performance—the lament of a deeply wounded investment banker. Bill listened patiently until I reached my bottom line. "There's no way to make the situation completely right," I said, "But at least we should be brought into the deal as equals with First Boston."

Bill stared at me, chomped a couple more times on his cigar, and slowly replied, "Dick, is that what you *really* want?"

Something about the way he said it told me that maybe it really *wasn't* what I wanted. Maybe I wanted to keep my mouth shut and think a little. "Well, Bill," I finally responded, "Let me think about it."

What Bill was telling me was that the deal was so badly screwed up that Salomon would be nuts to get involved.

Sure enough, the deal failed. First Boston was out and Salomon was back in—no more competitive bids. We continued as Bell's banker as long as I reigned at Salomon.

Over the years, I became close friends with many people at Bell Canada, including Bob Scrivner, John de Grandpre, and Walter Light, all three CEOs of the company. Others I remember well were Harold Harris, Bell's treasurer, and a young fellow who worked for him named Jean Monty. (It must have been the advice I gave young Jean that propelled him to be CEO of Nortel and then of Bell Enterprises. Funny, I can't remember what I said.)

Our relationship with Bell was a wonderful boost for Salomon in Canada, and I can honestly say that the private bond deals we did for them were superior to those of any other client we represented during that period. When we did our first public issue for Bell in the U.S., several Canadian underwriters suggested that we price it based off the company's relationship to other borrowers in the Canadian market. We responded, "No way—the issue is going to be priced the same as a double-A U.S. telephone company." This we did, and saved Bell a considerable amount of money.

Bell also did a wonderful job introducing itself to the European community. Harold Harris was dispatched to Europe during his last two years as treasurer, where he built up solid relations in the financial capitals. He laid the groundwork for a trip by Bell's senior officials to London, Paris, Brussels, and Zurich (accompanied by their favorite investment banker, a handsome fellow bearing a striking resemblance to the author).

Our traveling party learned many interesting facts from Bell's protocol man on this trip. We were informed that in Paris it's proper to take your roll off the plate and put it on the tablecloth. In London, we were told to eat asparagus with a fork, while in Brussels we were instructed to pick it up and eat it with our hands. In England, we were invited by Lord Behrens of Baring Brothers—a very proper Englishman of the old school—to brunch at his country estate. The dress code, we were told, was "informal." This turned out to mean a blue blazer with gray slacks, shirt, and tie—not exactly what my American friends and I would wear to a backyard cookout. It's an interesting world out there.

In gratitude for Lord Behrens' hospitality, Harold Harris invited him and his lady to visit Behrens Island in northern Manitoba, purportedly named after one of his lordship's ancestors. On a subsequent trip to Canada, arrangements were made for the visit. As luck would have it, bad weather cancelled the flight to the island. However, Lord and Lady Behrens did get to meet one of their relatives: The Indian bush pilot who was to take them to the island and shared the name of Behrens.

Incidentally, the (female) flight attendants who accompanied Behrens and the rest of our party on our small private plane as flew across the continent referred to him privately as "Lord Pinch." I can't imagine how he acquired that name.

We certainly had fun on trips like these, but don't assume they were pure boondoggle. Personal relationships count for a lot in the investment banking business. When Bell borrowed in the Eurodollar market, they saved a bundle on interest costs because of the good will and face-to-face contacts they'd established.

I mentioned that our competitive strategy in Canada was built around Salomon's institutional might. Here's an example drawn from our continuing relationship with Bell. One Friday I'd made a luncheon date in Montreal with Bill Corbett and Harold Harris, then Bell's assistant treasurer. Before leaving for Montreal, I conferred with our syndicate department and industrial desk to get their views on the appropriate rate for a Bell U.S. bond financing, even though I had no idea whether they were ready to come to market.

Anyway, when Friday afternoon arrived, Bill, Harold, and I were in the Beaver Club at the Queen Elizabeth Hotel enjoying a couple of their rather large martinis (they served martinis in a decanter, and I swear they had a secret compartment that refilled the decanter automatically) when Bill casually asked about the U.S. market and where Bell might borrow at that time.

I gave him a price. Bill asked, "What size?"
I thought a minute and replied, "Sixty million."
"Okay, Dick," Bill said, "You have a deal."

I excused myself from the table, called our syndicate department with the deal terms, and came back to finish lunch. By 4:30, we had circles on forty-five million and knew the deal would be completed by Monday.

As you can see, the Big Green Machine at Salomon was pretty awesome in its institutional coverage.

The depth of our bench was a huge asset. It allowed me to tell our clients, "Whenever I'm not here, there are four or five other guys at Salomon that can price your issues as well as me." The flow of information, the sales and trading strength were something to behold. Salomon made a lot of us look good. Many talented people left Salomon and prospered at other great firms. Others left and found that, without that support system, they were just more trees in the forest.

After Bell and Hydro Quebec, our next major client was the Canadian Pacific Railway Ltd. Ian David Sinclair, the company's president from 1966 to 1982, was one of the great figures in the history of corporate Canada and someone I fully enjoyed. We drank many a martini together as well as doing a host of mutually-beneficial deals. On several occasions we were joined for drinks or dinner by Paul Desmarais, Sr., the CEO of the great diversified firm Power Corporation of Canada who also held a substantial stake in Canadian Pacific. Paul liked to tease me by asking me whether he should take over Canadian Pacific. I gave the only response I could as the company's banker: "Paul, you know I can't answer that question."

One touchy issue in investment banking is the idea of co-managing a deal—something clients occasionally want but that bankers often resent. One time, Ian Sinclair decided to do a U.S. equity issue for Canadian Pacific and called to tell me that he would like Goldman Sachs to be a co-manager. Both personal and business reasons were involved. Ian was friendly with John L. Weinberg, the venerable senior partner of Goldman Sachs (they were fellow directors of Seagram's), and Goldman was an excellent equity distributor. Some of my partners felt we should rule the world alone and would lament sharing. After letting them vent, I'd do what the client wanted.

Something similar came up with Bell Canada. After several successful private placements, Bell asked us to include a second U.S. manager (along with the Canadian firms Wood, Gundy and A.E. Ames) in a forthcoming public offering. Their reasoning was that Bell was constantly involved in rate hearings, and having broader representation would serve them better politically. Again, some of Salomon's executive committee started the war dance, but in time they settled down, smoked the peace pipe, and agreed to expand the management group.

But which U.S. firm should be chosen? Bell mentioned Morgan Stanley. "That's probably impossible," I told them. "Morgan generally insists on being the sole manager and will probably refuse to share."

In this case, however, Morgan offered to change its policy, but they insisted on running the books and appearing on the left side of the tombstone listing—ahead of Salomon. (Running the books and appearing on the left is the name of the game. The book runner gets prestige, the ability to receive directed orders, and larger management fees.)

This was going too far. I protested vigorously, and justice triumphed—Bell showed its loyalty to Salomon by declining Morgan's offer.

Merrill Lynch was approached next and gladly accepted a position behind Salomon. I overruled our chairman, who wanted to split the management fee evenly. Instead, we took the lion's share, which I felt we deserved.

Back to the Canadian Pacific story. A meeting was arranged to discuss the U.S. equity deal at Canadian Pacific's headquarters in Windsor Station in Montreal. I decided to arrive the night before and have dinner with their financial vice president, Paul Neveau. "Paul," I casually remarked over coffee, "We're pleased to have Goldman as a co-manager. But because of our long relationship with Canadian Pacific, I suggest we appear on the left and run the books."

"Fine," Paul said.

The following morning, John Weinberg arrived. At the critical moment in the meeting, John Weinberg asked, "And who will appear on the left?"

Feeling like the cat that swallowed the canary, I answered, "That's all settled. We'll be on the left. Isn't that right, Paul?"

"Yes," Paul agreed.

John wasn't one to surrender easily. He responded, "Well, sometimes the book is run by the co-manager on the right. Have you decided on that?"

"Yes, John," I said, "That's been decided as well. We will be running the book. Isn't that right, Paul?"

"Yes," Paul agreed again.

The moral of the story is simple: The early cat gets the canary.

For many years, Canadian Pacific held magnificent dinners at the Chateau Champlain in Montreal attended by corporate and financial leaders from throughout Canada. One of those dinners and one that I missed stick out in my mind.

First, the special dinner. One year, Ian Sinclair had had a knee operation and was unable to attend. But his wife Ruth was there and she and I had a lovely time catching up with one another. Sometime around one A.M. Ruth and I were dancing when I remarked how much I missed good old Ian.

"I'm sure he misses you, too," Ruth replied.

"I wish there was some way I could pop in to see him," I said, "But I'm scheduled on a seven A.M. flight to New York."

"Why, that's no problem," Ruth replied, "Ian can never sleep. He's usually up by five a.m., and our home is on the way to the airport at Dorval."

A plan was hatched. I arrived at the Sinclairs at 5:30 A.M. and enjoyed a brief but lively pre-dawn breakfast with Ian, one of my favorite Canadians. In fact, I wanted to name my youngest son Ian, but his mother disagreed. (She suggested Luke. We fought to a draw and settled on Andrew.)

Now for the dinner I missed. I'd agreed to speak one evening at a savings bank meeting at Mount Airy Lodge in the Pocono Mountains in Pennsylvania. To my dismay, I found out later that the date conflicted with the Canadian Pacific dinner. When I tried to wriggle out of the commitment, the head of the committee (an executive from the Brooklyn Savings Bank) told me, "Bill Simon cancelled on us last year. If you pull out, Salomon is finished doing business with us." I resigned myself to missing the Canadian event.

My visit to the Poconos turned out to be memorable in its own way. When my wife Priscilla and I arrived at Mount Airy Lodge, we ordered a snack from room service. It arrived in due course served on paper plates and paper cups with plastic knives and forks. We made our way downstairs for the dinner, which was preceded by a two-hour cocktail party. The results were predictable: As they headed in to the banquet room, many of the guests were listing visibly to port and starboard. I sat next to the dinner organizer, who spent the evening telling me what an idiot his chairman was. Not that strange, except that the chairman was sitting at our table.

As for my speech, it was a fiasco. I'd prepared a long and elaborate text filled with wise insights and provocative observations. But when I rose to speak the room was so noisy you'd have thought it was Times Square at midnight on New Year's Eve. I discarded my speech, thanked every one for the business they'd given Salomon, and told jokes for five minutes before mercifully regaining my seat.

After dinner, we were invited to the honorees room, which sported a heart-shaped bathtub. (Mount Airy Lodge is a famous resort for honeymooners.) One of the other couples at the reception must have weighed a combined five hundred pounds, and the highlight of our evening was picturing the two of them floundering around in that heart-shaped tub.

Several years later, I had a very different experience that revolved around a co-managing arrangement with Goldman Sachs. I was friendly with a couple of people at Northern Natural Gas, including chairman Bill Strauss (a fellow member of the British North America Committee) and Roy Meyerhenry, his CFO. One day, Roy visited me at my office at Salomon. "I have good news," he announced. "We want Salomon to co-manage our upcoming bond issue."

This was a surprise. I knew that Goldman had been Northern's banker for many years. "Well, thanks," I replied, "That *is* good news." And purely as a joke, I added, "Naturally, we'll appear on the left and run the books."

Without cracking a smile, Roy said, "Yes, that's right."

My colleagues and I were stunned and baffled. How the hell had this happened? Later the answer emerged: Goldman had represented a client who'd bid successfully against Northern Natural Gas in an acquisition battle. Giving Salomon the lead position for one deal was Northern's way of sticking Goldman in the penalty box.

The vagaries of business are unpredictable. The Northern Natural Gas Company was headquartered in Omaha, Nebraska. It was quite a blow to the city when Northern was acquired by Houston Natural Gas and moved its headquarters to Houston.

Years later, the worm turned. Houston Natural Gas had changed its name to Enron—and we all know what happened to Enron. When that ill-fated company went bankrupt, one of its subsidiaries, Northern Natural Gas, was purchased by none other than Warren Buffett, the legendary investor and chairman of Berkshire Hathaway, often called "the sage of Omaha."

I guess the old saying is true—what goes around comes around.

Chapter 7
The Big Eskimo

One of my longest and most rewarding Canadian business relationships was with the province of Ontario, whose former treasurer
Darcy McKeough remains a very close friend of mine. We had many
interesting trips together, including one to attend the dedication of a
small hydroelectric plant at a place called Lower Notch.

On a Friday night, I flew up there on a chartered DC3 with
George Gathercole, the chairman of Ontario Hydro, and a group of
guests. Darcy had flown up on a small twin-engine plane with Dick
Dillon, the deputy minister of energy in the government under premier William Grenville Davis. Dick held a variety of other positions
in the Ontario Government and since 1983 had been the secretary of
my Canadian Fellowship.

After the ceremony, Darcy offered Bryce Farrill of McLeod and
me a ride back to Toronto, and I took him up on the offer. Lucky for
me—as I found out later, the engine of our chartered DC3 wouldn't
start, delaying its takeoff by several hours. Meanwhile, however, we
were flying through a bad storm. Darcy had brought along a bottle of
scotch, and all I can remember is our glasses bobbing up and down
as we bounced through the sky. What price glory?

On another occasion, Darcy and I were booked on a flight from
JFK via Concorde to London, where Ontario was launching a
Eurobond issue. We arrived around twenty minutes before flight
time, and as I checked in, the British Airways agent informed me that
my passport had expired and I couldn't board the flight. I did what

any self-respecting investment banker would do: I tried to throw my weight around. When that didn't work, I begged and pleaded. "I'm sorry, sir," said the agent, "But the only way you could board this flight is to have a U.S. diplomat vouch for you."

I quickly dialed my office and got both of my secretaries on the phone. I asked one to dial Ambassador Tom Enders in Ottawa and the other to call an assistant secretary of state in Washington.

A few minutes later, the vital phone call from Ottawa came through. Unfortunately, the airport operator who was trying to page me dialed the wrong extension. I was summoned to the baggage area down at the end of the lower level of the terminal. I raced off to the baggage area, grabbed the phone, and asked the operator to dial the number at the check-in counter, then sprinted back to the agent's desk. There I got the green light and boarded the Concorde with a couple of minutes to spare—drenched in sweat, much to Darcy's amusement.

On another occasion in the 1970s, Darcy and I, along with a group from Ontario Hydro, were spreading the gospel of investing in Canada on a trip through Texas, which included stops in Dallas, Houston, and then Austin, where we met the state treasurer—a man named Warren Harding. (I assume that he was no relation of the scandal-plagued U.S. president of the same name.) Harding had succeeded another treasurer named Jesse James (I kid you not) and was a spitting image of the old actor Sydney Greenstreet.

In our meeting, I expounded on the virtues of Canada—the huge volume of trade between our two countries, our shared electrical systems, and other economic bonds—all to explain why Texas should authorize the purchase of bonds from Ontario and Canada. When I finished, Mr. Harding simply said, "Well, down here, our border is with Mexico. Maybe we should be buying Mexican bonds."

Disappointed, we left the office and found that the limousine that had delivered us was nowhere in sight. This was a problem, since our top coats were in the car and it was darned cold. To make matters worse, our Dallas office had made all the arrangements and I didn't have the limo company's name. Finally, one of our group—Milan Nastich, the president of Ontario Hydro—remembered that the car belonged to a funeral parlor. After a frantic search through the Yellow Pages, we finally found the company, tracked down the number and retrieved the car. (The driver had been instructed to return to the office in case there were other calls.)

To this day, Darcy likes to ask me, "What *was* the name of that funeral parlor in Austin?"

My corporate travels on behalf of the Canadian investment community included many other memorable trips. One time, we traveled from Toronto by rail to Moose Factory in Moosonee on the eastern side of James Bay in Ontario. The history of this region is quite fascinating. It was the home of the Cree Indians and the second fur-trading post set up by the Hudson Bay Company in 1673. It's also the place where Henry Hudson's crew mutinied and set him adrift in a small lifeboat, never to be seen again.

Remarkably, fossils from the area indicate that it enjoyed a subtropical climate millions of years ago during the Devonian period. Conditions had changed by the time we visited Moose Factory in late May, crossing the bay in a small boat. It was so cold that the members of our party huddled together for warmth (I was practically holding hands with the treasurer of the state of Connecticut) under a canvas tarp that shielded us against the spray. All the piping in the area was above ground and wrapped in protective insulation as the permafrost made it impossible to bury them. The walls of the small local church had holes in various spots stopped with wooden pegs. These were used to drain the church when it flooded.

A trip like this illustrates the lengths to which I would go to spread the gospel of Canadian investment. It was later written up in a magazine article that noted (with mild exaggeration), "Dick Schmeelk even visits Eskimo villages in search of business." When my west coast partner Bob Larabie read the piece, he promptly gave me a new nickname: "The Big Eskimo."

At a later date, I flew by helicopter to the Quebec side of the bay to inspect the construction of the magnificent James Bay Project, a colossal (and somewhat controversial) hydroelectric plant backed by Hydro Quebec. The topography of the two sides of the bay was very different: The Ontario side was very flat, while the Quebec side was much higher, which allowed for the flow of water down through the penstocks (conduits) to drive the generators. The complex logistics reminded me of some of the vast construction projects I'd seen during the war in the Pacific. A man-made island had been built to serve as a landing site for the dozens of ships bringing supplies and parts.

Later I was interviewed by the French Canadian paper, *La*

Presse. "James Bay," I declared, "is the ninth wonder of the world"—a rather catchy line, if I say so myself. Unfortunately, the paper described me as a vice president of First Boston Corporation—a big step down from partner at Salomon Brothers. Ah, the media.

Through the 1970s, Salomon built up quite a list of municipal clients in Canada, including Metropolitan Toronto, the City of Montreal, the City of Winnipeg, and Metropolitan Winnipeg.

After one Metropolitan Toronto bond offering, we had a closing dinner at my home. It was a riotous affair, especially after one of my associates, Bob Kenny, learned that Jack Pickard, Toronto's finance director, played the harmonica. After several rounds of drinks and dinner, Bob persuaded Jack to perform for us. As the hours passed, Jack played on, more drinks flowed freely, and no one wanted to leave. The group finally broke up after four A.M., which gave me an hour and a half to sleep before a seven o'clock flight to Montreal and a six-appointment day. I spent it slapping and pinching my face to keep awake through those meetings.

Salomon helped raise money for the City of Montreal for the site of Expo 67, the great world's fair that attracted fifty million visitors. The day of the opening ceremonies was the hottest day I can remember in Montreal. Wiley and I were sitting in the stifling heat just behind the bandstand, watching a performance by the Royal Canadian Mounted Police, when suddenly a strong breeze came in off the St. Lawrence River. Refreshing? Maybe, but with the breeze came thousands of moths that descended on the audience. At the same moment, a fireworks display started. Flares were shot into the air and then started to drop amongst the band members. Instruments were abandoned and the band members ran for cover, fleeing both the flares and the invading moths.

I turned to Wiley and said, "Tell them we'll give the commission back if they let us out alive."

Later that year we planned a closing dinner to celebrate a Bell Canada bond issue. I invited the senior officers of Bell, the trustees of the Royal Trust Company, and the members of Bell's legal firm, along with everyone's spouses. John Gutfreund and I would host. Salomon had taken an apartment at Habitat, the futuristic apartment complex on the St. Lawrence River adjoining the Expo—a very pretty setting. The idea was to enjoy cocktails on the terrace and then take a trip over to the Chateau Champlain for dinner. Two weeks in advance, I approached the manager at Habitat to arrange for a bar, a bartender, and *hors d'oeuvres*. I called again the week before and was assured that everything was in order.

But when I arrived at the apartment around four P.M.—two hours before our guests were due—there was no sign of catering activity. I went down to the manager's apartment and asked his wife where he was.

"It's his day off," she replied.

"He's supposed to be arranging a cocktail party for me!" I told her.

With a shrug, she replied, "If my husband said it would be taken care of, it will be done."

I didn't find this very reassuring. "Get him now," I insisted.

The manager showed up about five o'clock. It seemed he had given the assignment to a cousin who had a drinking problem. Swallowing my rage, I took charge. "Get me all the liquor you have, and quick."

A glance in the kitchen cabinet revealed six regular glasses and four beer glasses. I rushed down to the only store at Habitat, a small grocery, and purchased some cheese, crackers, and styrofoam cups. The manager returned bearing a motley assortment of bottles— Cherry Heering liqueur, brandy, a little gin, and some scotch. To make matters worse, there was a liquor store strike in Montreal and nothing more to be had.

As I chopped away at the cheese, the guests started to arrive. Everyone else seemed to find my predicament hilarious. A large blonde bartender arrived—the one necessity that the manager's cousin had managed to arrange—but of course she had no supplies to work with.

John Gutfreund arrived. I said, "Hello, John. Go down to apartment 3D and ask Mr. Belanger for a bottle of gin." (He was the only neighbor I knew—I'd met him once.) Then I told the manager, "Go over to the Chateau Champlain and pick up three silver trays of canapés." (I'd called the restaurant and frantically begged for their help.) As he was leaving, he turned and said, "Let me get this straight. I go to the Hotel Bonaventure."

"No!" I shouted, "The Chateau Champlain!" Our guests chortled with glee over every exchange, enjoying the show I was putting on.

About a half hour later, the phone rang. It was the manager, sounding puzzled. "I'm at the Hotel Bonaventure and no one knows anything about the canapés."

I shouted into the phone, "No! Not the Bonaventure! The *Chateau Champlain!*" My guests were roaring.

Now we were out of scotch. I raced down to Belanger's apartment. "Hello, we met once before. I'm your neighbor and I need a bottle of scotch."

Belanger replied, "Don't you know there is a liquor strike?" He was staring at me warily, which isn't surprising—I must have had a crazed look in my eyes.

"Yes, yes," I replied. "Please, I need it. I'll make it up to you." He gave me a bottle just to get me to go away.

Naturally the limousines that the manager was supposed to provide to take our guests to the Chateau for dinner never showed up. We managed to order taxis instead. I slept very soundly that night, exhausted by a day more frenzied than any on the trading floor.

Some thirty guests later told me that one of my worst nights ever was one of the best parties they'd ever attended.

Our next conquest was Manitoba Hydro. Halsey and Salomon combined on this, John Wiley's last deal at Halsey. Our Canadian partner on the deal was Greenshields, led by another longtime friend, Dudley Dawson, while Mike Beauford was their man on provincial and government accounts. Mike, John Wiley, and I flew out to Winnipeg to have a closing dinner on the Manitoba financing and to watch the Winnipeg Ballet perform. Wiley was in rare form—he found a Winnipegger who'd been born in my old neighborhood, Rockaway, and had run away from home at age thirteen, never to return.

During the second act of the ballet, Beauford and I gave Wiley the slip and boarded a plane for Edmonton. The next morning, we submitted a bought deal to Fred Stewart, the treasurer of Alberta Municipal Finance. We got the mandate and pulled off another very tough deal. Wiley couldn't believe it—this was the kind of thing that Halsey, then in steep decline, could never have accomplished.

Wiley left Halsey a short time later and joined Salomon. But over the years he kept bringing up that night in Winnipeg: "I couldn't believe what you guys did."

We also did some deals with other provinces, managing for New Brunswick Power and Newfoundland and Labrador Power. At this time, Salomon's Canadian Department consisted of Joe Foley, John Wiley, and me. Joe's father was an old-timer who'd worked in the back office. Joe was a terrific guy, mild-mannered and very well respected by the insurance companies in Canada, which we covered together until I became involved in Canadian underwriting.

Joe also had a quirky side. One time I picked up my pen and found it very sticky. "What the heck happened to my pen?" I said aloud.

Joe said, "Oh, I stirred my coffee with it."

On another occasion, Joe introduced me to one of his clients using the odd phrase, "I would like you to meet my supervisor."

Later I asked him, "Joe, what the hell was that? It sounds like we work for the telephone company." I never did figure that one out.

Joe was a very nervous guy. If you came up behind Joe and gave him a friendly slap on the back, he would jump about a foot out of his chair. Joe's shyness and my big, outgoing personality made it tough for people to realize how good Joe really was.

When John Wiley joined us, he took over British Columbia, Alberta, Saskatchewan, Manitoba, New Brunswick, Nova Scotia, and Newfoundland. This was a new stage in what developed into a long and very rewarding friendship for Wiley and me. We worked jointly on Quebec and the Government of Canada. I was to concentrate on Ontario, Bell Canada Northern Telephone, Crown Corporation's Canadian companies, and several large U.S. corporations.

By now, the traditional group of seven was showing some signs of weakness. Salomon was rising, its distribution on Canadian issues now second to none. I mentioned earlier our leadership position on Manitoba, but perhaps a little color on Ontario and Manitoba would be of interest. Drexel Harriman had long enjoyed that position, but I'd become friendly with Len Farmer, the treasurer of Ontario, and knew that a change was in the wind. The same was true in Manitoba, where John Wiley and I were close to treasurer Stuart Anderson, whom we knew from his days in New York as treasurer of International Nickel. (Stuart wore a black cape, which earned him the name "The Caped Crusader.")

As part of the wooing process, I arranged for Premier Duff Roblin of Manitoba to speak before an audience in New York. Roblin will forever be enshrined in Canadian history as the architect of the spillway that saved Winnipeg from the Red River flood that devastated Grand Forks, North Dakota, in 1997. One Winnipegger told me about seeing Roblin enter a restaurant just after the flood and being greeted with a standing ovation from the grateful diners.

Nailing down the details for Roblin's trip to New York proved trickier than I expected. In one of my most difficult challenges, I managed to get a shipment of Winnipeg goldeye (a much-prized smoked fish from Canada) through U.S. customs just in time for the 21 Club to serve it as an appetizer before our dinner for Mr. Roblin. I'd also arranged for the premier to speak before a luncheon group at the University Club in New York.

Just a few days before this luncheon, I received a call from a female assistant who was going to handle the premier's slide presentation. We discussed a few details, and I hung up. Around 11:00 P.M. the night before the luncheon, it hit me: The University Club did not allow women. (The policy has since been changed.) I called the lady early the next morning at her hotel. The bad news: I'd had to arrange for a male to take over her duties at the University Club. I offered my apologies and then presented the good news: I'd arranged for her to be taken to the 21 Club for lunch as a consolation prize.

As decision time approached concerning the future of the Ontario and Manitoba syndicates, both provinces descended on New York the same day. In the morning, Dave Waldon, the president of Inter Provincial Pipeline, was coming in. At noon, Len Farmer, the treasurer of Ontario Hydro, was arriving with Ian MacDonald, the provincial deputy minister of finance, and around four P.M. Stuart Anderson and the Deputy Minister of Finance of Manitoba were coming. Finally, that evening there was to be a dinner at the Plaza Hotel for Ontario premier John Robarts, attended by various government officials and executives of the present syndicate, along with representatives of Morgan Stanley, First Boston, and Salomon.

Keeping all these comings and goings straight proved a bit hairy. While I was chatting in our offices with Dave Waldon, he mentioned a run-in he'd had with Len Farmer at a social event. "Next time I see him," Waldon announced, "I'm going to punch him in the nose." (I was surprised to hear that Farmer had generated such animosity, but I suppose it demonstrates the truth of one of my favorite sayings—"Everyone's friend is somebody else's son of a bitch.")

Waldon and I finished our conversation and I escorted him to the elevator. Sure enough, just as the elevator doors were closing on him, the opposite elevator opened and Len Farmer and Ian MacDonald stepped out. Bloodshed in the hallowed halls of Salomon had narrowly been averted.

The hectic day continued. Our luncheon meeting at Salomon with MacDonald and Farmer was long and pleasant. We used the time to restate our case as the rising power in Canadian investment banking and the best choice to head the new syndicate. Around four, Stuart Anderson and the rest of the Manitoba delegation arrived. They met with our syndicate people, traders, and others, and then adjoined to the dining room for drinks with Wiley and me shortly after five.

Around six, I excused myself and raced to the washroom to shave, while Wiley continued to entertain the Manitoba officials. I remember inflicting various wounds on my face and then hastening to the cloak room to change for the black-tie dinner—for some reason I felt it would be embarrassing if the Manitoba people found me changing in the washroom to go to dinner with their counterparts from Ontario. I emerged at six fifteen, the receptionist helped me with my cufflinks, and I sprinted for the garage.

The redoubtable Elias Popowitz—a wonderful gentleman who catered to the needs of the partners—was behind the wheel of my car. Noting my agitation, Elias said, "Calm down, Mr. Schmeelk. I'll put on some soft music. You just relax, I'll get you there."

We arrived at the Plaza a little late. The first person I ran into in the lobby was Len Farmer. "Dick!" he announced, "Am I glad to see you. I forgot my cufflinks. Can you get me a pair?"

This I needed. I tried the bell captain—no luck. I was licking my lips and racking my brains over where to find a pair of cufflinks in the next five minutes when a nice old gray-haired gent toddled over. "Excuse me, young man," he said, "I couldn't help hearing your request. I have an extra pair of pearl cufflinks in my room. You're free to borrow them if you like."

I could have kissed him. I just had time for half a drink before dinner.

One of the attendees at the dinner was a fellow from First Boston named Bob Wadds. Not to put too fine a point on it, Wadds was a jerk. He demonstrated this during the dinner by spreading the word that his close friend, Premier John Robarts, had already declared First Boston the winner. In so doing, he violated two important life lessons. First, never refer to the premier of Ontario or any compara-ble luminary as "my good friend John" in a public setting. Show a little respect—call him "the premier." Second, never declare your-self the winner of a fifteen-round boxing match in the fourteenth round. (We oldsters remember that Bill Conn thought he was the winner against Joe Louis in the fourteenth round—and then, bop!)

By the time dinner ended, I was quite exhausted. I turned to Wadds and said, "I was going to stay for one more drink, but you made such a horse's ass out of yourself I've decided to go home." I almost fell asleep three or four times during the hour's drive home.

A few days later, we learned that we had the mandate to lead Manitoba's first U.S. offering as well as the leading position in the Ontario syndicate, composed of Salomon; Wood, Gundy; and McLeod. Hallelujah!

Recently, at a birthday party in Toronto arranged by Darcy McKeough, I learned a little more about the circumstances sur-rounding Salomon's selection as Ontario's lead underwriter. Ian MacDonald, the deputy minister at the time of the decision said that Bob Wadds had told him, "It makes no difference who you prefer. I'll just go over your head to my good friend, John Robarts."

Atta boy, Bob! Thanks again. It's too bad that Wadds eventual-ly left First Boston; the more he talked, the more business Salomon got.

Ontario was a huge boon to Salomon and to me personally. With its large and growing industrial base, Ontario was an excellent cred-it risk (AAA) and the prime provincial borrower off of whom all the other provinces in Canada keyed their rates.

Over the next twenty years, I worked with Premier John Robarts and his successor, Bill Davis, as well as four treasurers: Charles McNaughton, John White, my close friend Darcy McKeogh, and Frank Miller. The three deputy ministers of finance were David Holmes, Ian MacDonald, and Rendell Dick, while the treasurers of Ontario Hydro were Len Farmer and Jim Fullerton. Finally, on the province's financial side I worked with Don McCall and George McIntyre.

As our business grew, I continued to build the Canadian group. Peter Gordon joined us from Royal Securities. Jim McKay became our corporate finance leader and the first person to put together a professional presentation booklet for corporate finance at Salomon.

Two of my closest friends in business: Darcy McKeogh and Citigroup's Walter Wriston.

John Black, Bob Kenny, John Morris, Bob O'Brien, Bill Farrill, Della Oliver, David McCutcheon, and I strove to service and maintain our existing business while at the same time building new relationships. It was a heady and exciting time.

During the 1970s, we helped raise many billions of dollars for Canadian provinces, Crown Corporations, municipalities, and corporations. Ontario and Quebec for several years in this period were among the top five borrowers on the world markets, along with AT&T, GMAC, and the World Bank. In three deals alone, Quebec Hydro borrowed one billion dollars, Ontario Hydro 650 million and British Columbia 600 million. For three consecutive years, Canadian negotiated business was fully one third of Salomon's total negotiated business—a staggering achievement for a country of that size.

From time to time, the ravages of inflation dried up the supply of funds, leading to fierce competition between Ontario and Quebec to meet their borrowing needs. (We were the lead manager on the Ontario account, while the lead manager for Quebec was First Boston—Salomon and Merrill Lynch were the other managers.) Under these circumstances, conflicts were unavoidable.

The first conflict arose when Hydro Quebec was planning a one-billion-dollar private placement. We informed their finance minister, Ed Lemieux, that we were about to enter the market with a large Ontario issue. Lemieux informed us that First Boston had already received indications of interest from the Prudential and Metropolitan Life Insurance companies.

John Gutfreund and I discussed the situation with Lemieux and decided to hold off on marketing Ontario. We did this for two reasons. First, we knew that, if both issues hit simultaneously, the big institutional buyers would play one against the other to get higher interest rates. Second, we guessed that overall interest rates would be coming down soon anyway.

Our strategy was not without risk. If we were wrong, Ontario would not be pleased. Fortunately, we guessed right. Interest rates came down, and Ontario saved millions of dollars. (So did Hydro Quebec, incidentally.)

Another time, when both provinces were about to do public offerings (the prospectuses were literally at the printers at the same time), we were accused of speeding up the Ontario offering to get ahead of Quebec.

Conflicts also arose over continual allegations by other managers that we weren't aggressive enough when it came to pricing Hydro Quebec. Gutfreund and I got tired of this nonsense and decided to teach our fellow managers a lesson.

At the next pricing meeting, Ed Townsend of First Boston announced they had a book of interest for roughly seventy percent of the issue and proceeded to give a very stiff pricing indication. Now, I knew the deal would be a dud at the First Boston price, and normally I wouldn't have hesitated to say so. But this time I answered, "We'll support you."

Several members of the syndicate sitting around the table looked aghast. Bill MacKenzie, who had worked for me at Salomon, was now representing Prudential Bache and sat across from me at the meeting. He looked as appalled as anyone else. I passed him a note saying, "Bill, do you share in the losses as well as the profits?"

When the meeting ended, I walked up to Ed Townsend and said, "I couldn't hear you very well at the other of the table. Did you say the issue was thirty percent spoken for?"

Ed said, "No, I said seventy percent."

I replied, "Hell, if I'd heard that, we would have been a lot more aggressive in our pricing views!"

The syndicate took a bath on this badly overpriced issue. But we still came out with a profit. For that time on, our fellow managers no longer scolded me for being conservative about pricing.

Shortly thereafter, René Lévesque was elected premier of Quebec on a platform that called for taking Quebec out of the confederation. I'd never met Lévesque, but I'd met Jacque Parizeau, his minister of finance, when he was a young civil servant under Premier John Lesage. After the election, market spreads widened dramatically, indicating the sense of unease that investors felt about Lévesque's victory. I was hounded by the media to give an interview interpreting the market reaction. My basic comment was, "It's up to Mr. Lévesque to prove that his policies will benefit the province economically and enable the province to support its large debt burden."

Soon after his election, Lévesque visited New York to speak about his plans and his policies. First Boston hosted a dinner for him at the Links Club attended by the province's lead investment managers as well representatives from Prudential Life, Metropolitan Life, Equitable Life, Morgan Guarantee, and Bankers Trust. All the participants were introduced to the premier, and when it was my turn, Lévesque remarked, "I understand you're one of the people who is nervous about me."

I replied with a variation of my media line: "No, Mr. Premier. It's up to you to prove to the marketplace that your policies work."

Lévesque then gave an impassioned speech likening the struggle for Quebec's independence to the American Revolution. The audience was polite but unreceptive. Americans had many billions of dollars invested in Canada. Any sign of political instability or uncertainty would cause a flight of capital. The next evening at the Economic Club, Mr. Lévesque repeated his speech. Again, it didn't sell.

A week or so later, John Wiley and I flew to Montreal to meet with finance minister Parizeau. It didn't go well. Our plane was delayed, and Parizeau moved our dinner meeting to a small town about thirty miles from Montreal. This put intense time pressure on John and me, since we both had to be on the last flight back to New York. (The next morning, John was involved in a pricing for Atlanta Richfield, later to be known as Arco, and I was involved in pricing a Canadian Pacific issue.)

A limousine drove us to the dinner meeting. It was bitterly cold—ten below zero, I'd guess—and we were so late that we left our coats in the car and told the driver, "Keep the motor running and point the car towards the airport."

We sat down. Mr. Parizeau ordered a bottle of wine and an elaborate dinner. Speaking quickly, John and I forecast dire results for the Montreal economy if Quebec separated from the rest of Canada, including the loss of corporate and financial headquarters, major accounting and legal firms, and all the other services related to major corporate tenants.

The fish dinner arrived. Wiley and I took two or three bites, stood up, apologized profusely, and fled the restaurant, leaving behind an astonished Jacque Parizeau. Our days as managers of Quebec's investment offerings were rapidly drawing to a close. Frankly, if I'd been Mr. Parizeau, I would have been hard pressed to say, "Those are the boys I would like to have representing my interests in the U.S."

Our limo arrived at the airport six or seven minutes before flight time. As we scrambled for our bags, Wiley told the driver "Charge it!" The driver replied, "Oh, no! My instructions are that you guys have to pay cash."

I said, "John, you pay, I'll run and hold the plane." Off I dashed through customs and down to the gate, occasionally turning to watch Wiley's progress. I got to the plane and positioned myself in the doorway so the flight attendant couldn't close the door. Wiley made his last lunge and I pulled him aboard.

The next day I heard my long-time secretary, Laurie Doscher, engaged in several long conversations with the offices of the limo company, Murray Hill. Finally she explained the mixup: "It seems there was a rock group called The Salomons who went through Canada and stiffed Murray Hill for fifteen hundred dollars. I spent all day trying to convince them that you and Wiley are not the rock group but the investment banking Salomons." It was the first and only time I've ever been mistaken for a rock star.

This brought back memories of my first visit to Quebec City when I met Michel Belanger, the distinguished Canadian businessman, president of the Montreal stock exchange, and co-chairman of the Commission on the Political and Constitutional Future of Quebec, known as the Belanger-Campeau Commission. Belanger told me about receiving an angry letter from a woman who'd con-

110

fused him with a plumber by the same name (it's a common one in Quebec) and threatened to sue him for an unsatisfactory job. Michel wrote back explaining the mistake and concluding, "Madam, always remember there is more than one dog called Fido."

Soon after Lévesque's visit to New York, Prime Minister Pierre Trudeau was invited to speak at the Economic Club. I was in Germany involved in a pricing for an Ontario Hydro European issue led by the Deutsche Bank. I arrived late in the afternoon having swallowed six Bufferin for a severe headache. The Canadian Broadcasting System had approached me along with Henry Fowler, the former Secretary of the Treasury and a senior advisor to Goldman Sachs, to make a comment after Trudeau's speech.

At the conclusion of the speech, I tip-toed down from the dais and arrived at the designated area for the television interview. A young lady greeted me: "Oh, I'm sorry, Mr. Schmeelk. We're just about out of time. We're finishing up with Mr. Fowler now and we can't interview you tonight."

Exhausted and aching, I was now thoroughly exasperated. "Try me again some time," I said, which was a polite way of saying, "Go to hell," and left.

The next day, I had a number of calls from Canadian friends, most of them angrily demanding, "Who the hell do you think you are, leaving the dais while the Prime Minister of Canada is still answering questions?" Clearly it was not a great night for me.

Salomon Brothers was now the investment underwriter for a conservative government in Ontario, a separatist government in Quebec, New Democratic Party governments in Manitoba and Saskatchewan, a liberal government in New Brunswick, and a Social Credit government in British Columbia. Believe me, this was no mean trick. Our official position was always, "We represent the province and its people, not any particular party." But politically we felt like the man on the flying trapeze—with no net below.

In the midst of our high-wire act, Ontario's Premier Bill Davis arrived in New York, where he was scheduled to hold a press conference at Salomon Brothers. I cautioned his people that we had always refrained from taking sides in Canadian politics, and they assured me his press conference would not be political. I went to the premier's hotel and met with him and his wife Kathy, a wonderful down-to-earth lady, a Chicago Bears fan (born in the Windy City) and a naturalized Canadian citizen. (The premier, on the other hand, was a strong supporter of the Miami Dolphins.)

We spent a long time chatting at the hotel, and unfortunately this left Peter Gordon alone with several press wolves who started to quiz him about Lévesque's election. Peter commented that there would be a period of uncertainty until the new government spelled out its policies. The next day the Canadian papers headlined Salomon's "lack of confidence" in the Lévesque government.

This was the final straw. George LaFond, who had replaced Ed Lemeuix as the CFO at Hydro Quebec, came to New York and met with John Wiley and me. He suggested that Salomon remain in the syndicate maintaining the same percentage of bonds but not be involved as co-manager or in the pricing of the issue.

John Wiley and I talked it all over. The Quebec relationship meant a great deal to us, we had many friends in the Quebec government and at Hydro Quebec, and we had worked hard to market their bonds in the U.S. Sadly, we concluded that we couldn't continue with a shadow of suspicion hanging over our head. We informed LaFond that we would withdraw from the syndicate. At the same time, we told him we would continue to support Quebec's U.S. offerings. We did this by taking millions of bonds down in the selling group each time they came to market.

Happily, this policy led to Salomon being reinstated as a manager when my career at Salomon was winding down. Tom Enders, John Wiley, and I visited with the Quebec financial team, and the lost sheep were welcomed back into the flock.

Chapter 8
Mergers, Acquisitions, and the World of Big Oil

As the years rolled along, our Canadian business kept growing, and were hard pressed to keep up with it. Peter Gordon started to back me up on various Canadian accounts such as Ontario, Bell Canada, and their new majority-owned subsidiary, Northern Electric.

Ultimately, Bell decided to sell off a portion of their holding in Northern Electric, and we headed the syndicate charged with marketing the issue in the U.S. It was a very tough sell. At the time, no firm in the investment business, to my knowledge, had a telecommunications analyst—an amazing difference from today, when the same industry gobbles up billions and billions of dollars and is tracked by hundreds of analysts. We ended up owning a substantial number of shares for several months after the offering.

John Loeb, then the chairman of Northern, was friendly with the magazine publisher and high-living jet-setter Malcolm Forbes. As we were planning our tombstone ad announcing the Northern offer, Loeb kept adding *Forbes* to the list of magazines where it would run. Each time he did so, Layton Smith, a partner in corporate finance who was in charge of such things, would delete it. An irritated John Loeb finally asked me to intercede, which I did. The ad ran in *Forbes*, making Loeb and his buddy Malcolm happy.

We continued to add to our impressive list of Canadian clients. One was Mitel, an Ottawa-based maker of communications equipment. Our pursuit of Mitel in connection with a U.S. equity issue the company planned around 1975 was the occasion for one of my more memorable business trips.

A group of us rented a small prop plane to fly directly to Ottawa. I was accompanied by Peter Gordon from our Canadian Group; Denis Bovin, a future partner from corporate finance; another young associate whose name I can't recall; and Bob Bernhard, a fellow corporate finance partner.

A word about Bob, whose pedigree was somewhat above the norm at Salomon. Through his mother Dorothy, Bob was a member of the Lehman clan, which had founded the firm of Lehman Brothers in 1850 as a cotton brokerage company. Finance ran in the family veins: Bob's father was a partner in Wertheim, and Bob's uncles, John Loeb and Benjamin Buttenweiser, were at Loeb Rhoades.

Bob himself graduated from Williams College in 1951 and the Harvard Business School in 1953, then served a year as a midshipman at the naval air station in Pensacola, Florida. Bob spent twenty years at Lehman Brothers, becoming a partner in 1962. He joined Salomon in 1972 as a partner and left in 1981. He first headed equity research, then became a corporate finance partner. In addition to running Salomon's international and telephone industry businesses, Bob opened offices in Japan and Hong Kong.

After leaving Salomon, Bob started a money management business, known today (after a merger) as Munn Bernhard. The firm manages in excess of one billion dollars and has an excellent track record. Bob serves as chairman of the board of the Cooper Union for the Advancement of Science and Art, and as vice chairman of Montefiore Medical Center. He's also a trustee of the Robert Lehman Foundation and a member of the executive committees of Vassar College and Temple Emanuel as well as the boards of Lincoln Center Institute and the Albert Einstein College of Medicine.

Back to our trip. The flight up was uneventful, but we arrived in Ottawa during a massive labor rally. As we drove to Mitel's office in our black limousine, we received many angry scowls, which I transformed into smiles by the simple expedient of flashing the demonstrators the peace sign.

We made our presentation and left for the airport with the weather noticeably deteriorating. Our takeoff was rather bumpy, and we were just settling in for the flight when the pilot realized he'd forgotten to file his flight plan, forcing us to return to Ottawa. We took off again, this time into a terrific rainstorm that bounced us through the skies like a yo-yo.

Our problems were just beginning. Partway through the flight, the pilot came on the intercom. "Sorry, folks," he announced, "We don't have enough fuel to make it to Teterboro. I'm going to land in Albany to refuel."

As we huddled in the private terminal in Albany, I was feeling fed up. "This is ridiculous," I told my colleagues. "Let's get a limousine and drive down to the city."

The pilot overheard me. "Did I hear you say you were going to take a limousine to New York?" he demanded. "Don't be silly. The weather's clear at Teterboro. I'll have you there in forty-five minutes."

Sheep that we were, we reboarded the plane. Five minutes in, another heavy rainstorm struck. The plane jolted and bobbed through the air, and inside the cabin we were white-faced, clutching our arm rests in a death grip and praying we'd survive. In an effort to relieve the tension, I turned to Denis Bovin with a challenge. "I'll give you ten bucks if you can name the fifty states in fifteen minutes."

Bob Bernhard said, "You're giving your money away—you know how smart Denis is." But after fifteen minutes, Denis had blanked out with ten states still unnamed. He was understandably distracted: As we jolted through the skies, we could see the pilot and co-pilot anxiously scanning the map, which is not a sight calculated to produce confidence in the passengers. The pilot's announcements didn't help matters. At one point he told us, "We're at two thousand feet and we should be landing in fifteen minutes." Thirty minutes later, we were still aloft, and through the open door to the cockpit we could all see that we were at 3,500 feet.

Finally, the pilot announced we were going to land. "Make sure your seat belts are secure," he added, "Things could get bumpy." I wondered, how much worse can it get?

Finally, we were safely down, and I could have kissed the ground the way the Pope does when he arrives in a new country. (Maybe His Holiness has trouble finding good pilots, too.) Our young associate turned to me. It had been his very first flight. "Is flying always like this?" he wondered.

I replied, "If it were, we'd all take the train."

I got home around 11:30 and climbed into the tub to relax, where my wife found me, dead to the world. When she heard my story and learned that I hadn't had dinner, she brought me up a ham sandwich and a glass of milk. "Priscilla," I told her, "I thought this might be my last flight."

The next morning I was up at 6:00 A.M. to catch a 7:30 plane to Montreal. Such is the life of an investment banker.

At least I can say that our hair-raising mission to Ottawa was successful. Soon thereafter, Mitel gave us the lead underwriting position, along with Wood Gundy, then a dominant player in Canada with whom we worked successfully on many underwritings. Ted Medland, the company chairman, is still a good friend of mine, and I had close relations with a number of other fine bankers at Wood Gundy, including Mike Chapman, Ed King, Jim Black, and two departed friends, Ross LaMesseur and John Abel..

One of our partnerships with Wood Gundy was in underwriting the Export Development Corporation, a Canadian Crown corporation designed to help finance Canadian business abroad (much like the U.S. Export/Import Bank). The relationship worked fine for many years, but then Salomon and Export Development had a falling out. I didn't know the details of how the rupture occurred until much later, when Clare Marshall, the Senior Financial Officer at Export Development, told me the story.

It seems that a small group of Salomonites were visiting Ottawa in an attempt to patch up some differences that had arisen between Salomon and Export Development. Unbeknownst to them, the driver who picked them up at the airport worked for Export Development. They indiscreetly spent the whole trip blasting their hosts, then repeated the performance on the return trip to the airport. When word got back to headquarters, a new lead underwriter was chosen. (Back in the war, we had a slogan, "Loose lips sink ships." They sink business deals, too.)

Our final, greatest triumph in Canada was yet to come. For several years we had worked to build a relationship with the national government. It was a full-court press. John Wiley, David McCutcheon, and I kept in close touch with the Department of Finance and the Bank of Canada, often visiting them with our esteemed economist Henry Kaufman. Joe Foley and our trading desk people posted the Bank's trading desk daily on trends in Canadian US pay markets and the US government bond markets.

We also wooed a long roster of the Bank's leaders. We met with Deputy Governor Ralph McGibbon and with Governors Lou Rasminsky, Gerry Bowey, and John Crow. At finance, we visited the Honorable Donald McDonald and the Honorable Marc Lalonde, as well as Simon Reisman and Mickey Cohen, who were deputy ministers of finance at that time. (Mickey went on to be president of Gulf Canada and later CEO of Molson's.)

We also invited them to attend our dinners at the annual meetings of the World Bank and International Monetary Fund in Washington. To my knowledge, during my career, we always hosted the governors at the IMF meetings in Washington.

During this long pursuit, I put together some ideas that saved Canada a substantial amount of money. For example, during the administration of Lyndon Johnson, Canadian entities were borrowing large quantities of U.S. dollars. There were two main reasons. First, the Canadian market wasn't large enough to accommodate the biggest Canadian borrowers, such as Ontario Hydro, Hydro Quebec, and Bell Canada. Second, borrowing was usually 50 or 60 basis points cheaper in the U.S. The only downside was currency risk, which the large borrowers were willing to accept.

In time, however, the U.S. began to put pressure on Canada to reduce its balance of payments. At an Ottawa luncheon with Bank of Canada officials, we discussed their options.

At that time, the Bank of Canada purchased U.S. government issues exclusively through the Federal Reserve Bank in New York. Buying U.S. government bonds through a dealer to reduce the deficit wasn't recognized as an option. The only other option appeared to be buying long-term Canada 5s, which were placed with the big insurance companies. Yet Canada did this borrowing at the same rate that we felt Manitoba, Alberta, Ontario, and British Columbia all could have borrowed at in the U.S.

(I subsequently proposed such a deal to Premier Duff Roblin of Manitoba and his Treasurer Ron Burns. We weren't well known to Manitoba at that time, but I believe that if I'd been more forceful in my presentation, we would have gotten the mandate to place the bonds of Manitoba at the same rate as the Dominion of Canada—a move unheard of before or since, although Alberta did borrow in the U.S. shortly thereafter at that rate.)

Now, the big five insurance companies would not sell at a loss.

The bonds were worth somewhere in the 80s, and if Canada repurchased them, it would have to pay around 100. The Dominion of Canada bonds had declined sharply as high inflation rates had savaged the bond markets. As we discussed our options, we eventually got around to World Bank bonds, which somehow qualified as a legitimate vehicle. But the Bank of Canada was worried about their liquidity.

However, it so happened that there was a large block of short-term World Bank bonds available, and after consulting with my trading desk, we told the bank we would take them out of any position 1/8 of a point from the offering side of the market. The deal was struck. We traded between 50 million and 75 million World Bank bonds to the bank and traded them out when their balance of payment position changed. It was the first time the bank had dealt with a U.S. dealer rather than with the Federal Reserve, as well as one of the largest bond trades by Salomon's corporate desk up to that time. Most important, it saved Canada from a fifteen point pay-up on their long term bonds.

Later, the bank asked us to buy in several million 3 7/8 of 88, a widely-held issue that traded at a substantial discount. This was an exclusive order, one that we would guard in great secrecy. But while in the process of completing this order, John Wiley and I were in Boston at a lobster dinner hosted by Louis Robichaud, the premier of New Brunswick. (Robichaud would don an apron to crack and serve lobsters, all in an effort to attract sea food lovers to buy New Brunswick bonds.) John and I were chatting with an investor named Andy Carter and a co-manager from a Canadian firm when Carter said, "That was one hell of a price you got for those Canada 3 7/8 of 88." John and I both tried to change the subject, but Carter kept harping on it as the Canadian dealer listened. We both thought the cat was out of the bag, but evidently the dealer's antennae were defective—he never called the bank about it.

We'd been working for years with the government of Canada, always trying to help them save money. We provided the Bank of Canada with intelligence about market developments in the United States and about U.S. investors appropriate for Canadian provincial and corporate bonds.

Finally, our big dream came true. The Dominion of Canada asked that Salomon be made a co-manager on their next financing, scheduled for July of 1985.

As I walked over to the offices of Morgan Stanley, our co-manager on the deal, I couldn't help recalling my first visit to Morgan twelve years earlier. It was a Friday shortly after noon, and I was ducking out to meet my first wife Betty and another couple, Dave and Ann McCauley, at Belmont race track. I was wearing a sports coat and loafers when my syndicate manager, Ted Ottens, got the call from Morgan inviting us to discuss a proposition we had presented to Alcan for a small private placement, ten million or so. I threw up my hands and said, "Morgan Stanley—looking like this?" Ted shrugged, and off we went.

The meeting took place in a room paneled with beautiful dark wood and furnished with handsome old leather chairs and a deep, soft sofa. Across from us sat a phalanx of Morganites, all with snow-white hair and dark suits heavily dusted with dandruff, peering with shocked eyes at the orphans from Salomon.

During the discussion, Alcan had called their bankers at Morgan Stanley for advice. We wanted to make a call of our own to a potential undisclosed buyer. In a haughty tone, the chief negotiator for Morgan replied, "You may make *one* phone call."

Ted and I concluded we didn't care for the rules of Morgan's game and declined. Now here I was, twelve years later, about to be the lead banker on an issue of 900 million Dominion of Canada U.S. Pay Bonds with Morgan Stanley and two other firms. We'd come a long way, baby.

Of course, this triumph was made possible by many people, including Joe Foley, who posted Jacque Clamont daily on the U.S. markets; John Wiley, who covered the government of Canada with David McCucheon after I became responsible for world wide corporate finance following Jim Wolfensohn's departure; and our much-acclaimed economist, Henry Kaufman.

Although being displaced as lead manager on a Canadian government issue must have been a bitter pill for the people at Morgan Stanley to swallow, they were very gracious about it. I chartered a plane and invited their president, Frank Paterno, and their future president, Parker Gilbert, to fly to Ottawa with me to meet with the government's financial people. We enjoyed a dinner together in Hull, across the river from Ottawa, and on our next trip together they chartered the plane.

Later, I arranged a celebratory luncheon in a small restaurant housed in the basement of One New York Plaza. I remember that everyone ordered iced tea. I couldn't help but comment, "Can you imagine what we would have been drinking if this were a few years ago?" Drinking had gone out of style on Wall Street—or perhaps we aging veterans had simply learned to behave ourselves.

*　　*　　*

Many of our most memorable business dealings were with the great Canadian oil firms.

In 1976, Bill Hopper, the first CEO of Petro Canada, called me at Salomon Brothers one morning around 10:00 A.M. Bill was a human dynamo, constantly on the move, looking to build Petro Canada into a large integrated oil company to rival the multi-nationals that dominated Canadian energy.

"Something big has come up," Bill said. "Can you be at my office in Toronto by noon?"

This raised a couple of minor problems, starting with the fact that I wasn't standing on the runway at LaGuardia or JFK and I didn't have a private jet. What's more, I had a luncheon scheduled at 12:15 with the U.S. ambassador to Canada, Tom Enders. After lunch, I was hosting an outing at my club for some forty-odd members of the Canadian department and another group, the Hartford team, that also reported to me. After the outing, they were all coming to my home in Lawrence, Long Island, for refreshments and dinner. As I said, minor problems.

I set to work to solve them. Luckily, John Gutfreund was free for lunch; he pinch hit for me with the ambassador. Then the incredibly efficient Laurie Doscher, my secretary at the time, took over. She checked flights to Toronto and booked me on one around noon. "And what about the party at your home?" she asked. I said,

"You run it," I told her, "See that everyone has a good time. I don't know when I'll get back."

I arrived at Bill Hopper's office around 2:30 P.M. The purpose of the meeting, as it turned out, was to discuss a possible takeover of Husky Oil. Oddly enough, two directors of Husky, Canadian investment bankers, were actually present at the meeting. I figured this must be a peculiarity of the Canadian system. One at least was firmly convinced that Husky's management would be receptive to a takeover bid.

We talked into the early evening. Then I flew back to New York and arrived in Lawrence shortly before 10:00 P.M. The party had been a huge success—Laurie and my cook had performed nobly, and everybody had a great time without the boss looking over their shoulders. I suggest other executives try skipping their own parties—it works great.

The party was a smash. The Husky deal, not so much. The two directors had misjudged the reaction of Husky's CEO. Our mergers and acquisitions team and Salomon's legal advisors told me I should never have had discussions with Petro Canada with the other bankers in the room. Furious, Husky fired the directors and fought against the deal tooth and nail—and won. As far as I know, it's the only battle Bill Hopper ever lost.

For many years, I cultivated a friendship with the leaders of TransCanada Pipe Line, including their chairman Jim Kerr, his successors Rad Latimer and George Woods, and their CFO, Neil Nichols. We all worked together for years on the dream of a proposed polar pipe line that would bring Arctic gas to market, a project for which Salomon was appointed the lead banker. Each time we met, the cost of the pipeline seemed to go up by another billion dollars, reaching some twelve billion dollars by the time of our last meeting. I remember saying to an associate, "You know, when I started in this business I thought it was great to do a fifty-million-dollar deal. Then it was exciting to do a hundred-million-dollar deal. But I'd feel a lot better about *this* deal if it was a two-hundred-million-dollar deal instead of a twelve-billion-dollar deal."

Today the Arctic pipe line is still a dream, awaiting an energy crisis of gigantic proportions to make it economically viable. Perhaps the current boom in energy will revive the dream.

Spend a few years in business, and you eventually discover how closely interconnected the various fields of endeavor really are. A phone call I received during a luncheon back in 1981 vividly illustrates the point.

It was the luncheon that always followed the annual meeting of the TransCanada Pipe Line company. I was sitting at a table with a collection of most of the leading lights of the Canadian oil industry, including such luminaries as Jim Kerr, George Woods, and Neil Nichol from TransCanada; Bill Daniels, CEO of Shell Canada;

Smiling Jack Gallagher of Dome; Gus Lott of Imperial Oil; and Stephen Roman of Denison Mines. I was called away to take a call from none other than Ludwig Jesselson, the chairman of Phibro.

"What can I do for you, Ludwig?" I asked.

"Dick, we've got this oil and gas property in the Beaufort Sea. We're worried that the Foreign Investment Review Act might keep us from developing it. Can you suggest the name of a good lawyer to help us get the approval we need?"

"Sure," I replied. "Call McCarthy & McCarthy." This was the Honorable Donald MacDonald's law firm. In due course, Phibro received its approval from FIRA.

I don't think I'd ever heard of the Beaufort Sea before this call, but I later discovered that I had a kind of personal connection with it. According to the recent book *Blind Man's Bluff*, a story of U.S. submarine espionage after World War II, the first U.S. submarine sent to the Beaufort Sea was my old vessel, the USS *Blackfin*.

Even more interesting is the story of how Phibro obtained this property in the Beaufort Sea—a tale with a curious connection to the fabled purchase of Manhattan island from the Indians.

In the late 1970s, Nelson Bunker Hunt and William Herbert Hunt—the Hunt brothers—together with a consortium of rich Arabs mounted a remarkable effort to corner the world market in silver. Once they were long over 200 million ounces of silver, the price rose some tenfold to $50 an ounce, and other speculators jumped aboard. However, the Comex metals market and the Federal Reserve Bank didn't allow the Hunt brothers' market manipulation to succeed. They intervened in January of 1980—Comex actually suspended silver trading for a time—and sent the market back to $10 an ounce, creating paper losses of over a billion dollars, including eight million dollars lost by a single trader for the Peruvian Government.

The brothers were now bankrupt, creating monumental problems for Merrill Lynch, Pru Bache, Phibro, and a number of banks, all of which had extended a large credit line to the Hunts. A hasty meeting was called by Fed chairman Paul Volcker, including Walter Wriston, chairman of Citibank, representatives of the three mentioned firms, and other bankers, scrambling to figure out what collateral the Hunts could put forth to cover their credit exposures. Late at night, as the group was scraping the bottom of the barrel, one of the Hunts mentioned a property in the Beaufort Sea, which thus became a $300 million marker late in the game. It was this Beaufort Sea asset, transferred to Phibro, that enabled Phibro to skate through the crisis induced by the Hunts' collapse.

What does all this have to do with the sale of Manhattan to the Indians? Just this: Later, after it turned out that there was really no oil to be had at an economically viable price in the Beaufort Sea, Salomon's oil and gas team, with the help of outside consultants, concluded a sale of the Beaufort properties for a grand total of $24.00—the same sum the Indians got for Manhattan.

Ultimately, after twenty-odd years of involvement with TransCanada Pipe Line, I turned the account over to Bill Farrell in our Canadian group when I moved on to running all of corporate finance. A few years later, in the midst of the collapse of the U.S. private bond market during the high-inflation days of the Carter administration, Bill did a $400 million dollar private placement for TransCanada in the U.S.—the largest such placement of that era.

That was a painful time to be doing business. I remember one time when President Carter summoned the heads of various financial institutions to the White House for a conference to show that his administration was serious about fighting inflation. John Gutfreund asked me to attend in his place.

The president's advisor Bob Strauss kicked off the meeting. The president was attending a political meeting in one of the southern states, he explained, but he wanted us to know that he took the meeting and the inflation issue very seriously. Bob then turned the meeting over to the secretary of the treasury, Mike Blumenthal, and left for another meeting. Secretary Blumenthal then introduced Herman Kahn, who had been appointed "inflation czar" for the administration. Then *he* left for another meeting.

"Well," someone remarked, "It's certainly obvious that the Carter administration takes inflation seriously!"

Fortunately, Paul Volcker eventually took command of the problem and got inflation under control—despite the ditherings of the politicians.

Shell USA provided another interesting chapter in the life of an investment banker. Shell UK, the majority shareholder, decided to make a bid for the shares of Shell USA they didn't own. This was not warmly received by John Bookout, Shell's president, a Canadian who had moved to Houston to run Shell USA. As a defensive move,

Shell USA decided to hire an investment banker to offer a "fairness opinion" on Shell UK's offering price. Ray Golden, who ran our Dallas office, directed our bid for this assignment.

Ray had grown up in the Bronx, attended James Monroe high school, and gone on to the Bernard M. Baruch School at City College. After earning at MBA at the Wharton School, he started his career in investment banking, working first on Canadian deals, then in the leasing and energy areas. Later he became financial vice president of Phibro, an executive with Texas real estate developer Trammell Crow, and COO of James Wolfensohn & Co. until its acquisition by Bankers Trust. Ray served on the board of the M. D. Anderson Hospital in Houston and serves on the board of Jewish Philanthropies in Palm Beach.

Salomon had to compete for the Shell job against teams from First Boston and Goldman Sachs. After flying from New York to Houston, we arrived at Shell and met with John Jacobson, vice president of finance and his team, to prepare for our presentation.

"Whatever you do," John warned us, "Play down your relationship with Shell. The less you've done in the past for Shell, the better your chances of getting this assignment."

"Who's making the decision?" I asked.

"The outside directors," John replied, and mentioned the name of the chairman. When I heard it, I groaned. He had been the chairman of a bank that First Chicago, a long-time client of Salomon, had taken over with our help—which cost him his job. Salomon would have an uphill battle to win this job.

After waiting some three hours, we were ushered into the conference room to make the third presentation. Ray Golden, Ron Freeman, and I were introduced. As soon as we sat down, one of the directors asked, "Do you have any relationship with Shell Canada?"

Under normal circumstances, I would have described us as "the manager for Shell Canada." Now, however, I decided to finesse the question with a more technically accurate response. "Well," I said, "Morgan Stanley is the lead manager for Shell Canada. However, we are a less important member of the management group."

"Thank you very much, gentlemen," said the director. "The meeting is over." We'd invested fourteen hours in what turned out to be a three-minute meeting.

On our way to the airport, Ray Golden said, "Do you know who is going to get this business? Goldman Sachs, because they've never been here before. First Boston and Salomon are out because of our relationships with Shell U.S. and Canada." Ray was right, of course.

I might add, however, that after the takeover was complete, our friends at Shell named First Boston and Salomon to do a huge debt offering for them, rewarding our years of service.

One of the great characters I met in my journeys through Canada was Stephen Roman, CEO of Denison Mines. Steve grew up in Velky Ruskov in eastern Czechoslovakia. In 1937, when his native country faced the threat of Soviet expansion, sixteen-year-old Steve and his older brother decided to migrate to Canada. They became farm workers in Southern Ontario. Steve served in the Canadian Army, went into the mining business, and eventually built Denison Mines, which in its prime proved to have 137 million tons of uranium, twice the reserves of the entire U.S.

I was introduced to Steve by a good friend of mine, John Coleman, then vice chairman of the Royal Bank of Canada. I often lunched with Steve in his private dining room with a group of his directors. Steve was such a dominant character that his directors seemed afraid to disagree with anything he said. I think Steve liked the fact that I spoke up, whether I agreed with him or not. We ended up having many lively debates, which we both enjoyed. Later I visited his large farm, Romandale, outside of Toronto, and met his wife Betty, daughter Helen, young Stephen, and the rest of the family.

Canadians will remember when Steve announced a deal to sell his company to Hudson Bay Oil and Gas, a subsidiary of Conoco. This would have made the Roman family unbelievably wealthy and the largest shareholders in Conoco. Unfortunately, Steve neglected to inform the Trudeau government of the impending sale. As I understand it, Prime Minister Trudeau was badly embarrassed and quashed the deal.

Another time, Steve, who owned slightly less than five percent of U.S. Steel, gave me an order to buy 500,000 shares of a new U.S. Steel issue that Salomon was co-managing—a gigantic order, We eventually cut him back to 250,000 shares, still not too shabby.

One day, I was playing tennis at the Palm Beach Polo Club in Wellington, Florida. I was serving match point when I was called to the phone. It was my wife Priscilla, sounding upset. "It's Helen, Steve Roman's daughter," Priscilla said. "I think something's happened to Steve."

Sure enough, Helen told me that her father had suddenly died. "Can you come to Toronto for the funeral mass?" she asked. "Steve asked that you do the eulogy."

I've never had much of a serve, but when I returned to my tennis game, I said, "This one's for you, Steve." I put in an ace to finish the match.

I left the next morning to arrive the night before the mass. It was attended by several thousand mourners, and thousands more came by to pay their respects. The ceremony resembled the funeral of a head of state rather than that of a private individual.

Even after his passing, Steve continues to do good. He devoted a great deal of energy, money, and fifty acres of his estate to build a Slovak Byzantine Catholic Cathedral in Markham. In gratitude, Pope John XXII had bestowed on him the Order of Knight Commander of St. Gregory the Great, one of the highest honors in the Catholic Church.

Steve liked to quote the gospel saying, "It is easier for a camel to go through a needle's eye than for a rich man to enter the Kingdom of God" (Matthew 19:24). With this in mind, I keep giving away money, but unfortunately the stocks I hold keep going up. Well, at least I am trying.

*　　*　　*

For over twenty years, I'd been contacting Imperial Oil, the large Canadian company of which Exxon owned approximately a seventy-percent share. Despite its U.S. ownership, Imperial was quite independent in many ways and fiercely Canadian. My first contact there was Don McGibbon, whose wife Paula was lieutenant governor of Ontario. They were among my early friends in Toronto, along with Bob Taylor, then vice president of finance at Steel Company of Canada (and later chairman of Hydro Quebec). Over time, I became friendly with Gus Lott, then the assistant treasurer, who had been a Spitfire pilot during the Battle of Britain, as well as three CEOs of Imperial: Bill Twaits (and his wife Fran), Jack Armstrong (and his wife June), and Don McIvor (and his wife Betty).

For many years, Imperial had never borrowed in the U.S. market. Jack Armstrong was the CEO when Imperial decided to take the plunge. Gus Lott informed me that Morgan Stanley was making a strong push through Exxon in New York to get the Imperial assignment, and that Exxon's Bill Young, was being transferred to Imperial to serve as the senior finance man and a key in the choice of a lead underwriter.

Immediately prior to the final decision, Jim MacKay, who headed our Canadian corporate finance group, and I were scheduled to have lunch with Gus and with Bill Young, whom we had never met. The schedule was tight: Gus warned me that Bill would have to be

A high-powered pow-wow about Canadian business, featuring Tony Fell (Dominion Securities), Jack Armstrong (Imperial Oil), Jim McKay (Salomon), and (from behind) Stephen Roman of Denison Mines.

back in Imperial's offices by two o'clock for the decisive meeting to choose the lead manager.

Trouble struck in the form of a snow storm in Toronto. Our plane was delayed. I called Gus and moved the restaurant reservation closer to Imperial's office. We finally arrived in Toronto. Traffic from the airport was agonizingly slow. We got onto St. Clair Street, where a particular traffic light proceeded to drive me mad. We'd crawl forward two or three car lengths and bang! The light would change again. The clock was ticking. It was one twenty. I remember saying to Jim MacKay, "Some day I'll be in a cab under the gun like this and I'm going to say, Screw it! I'll get out and walk away, and nobody will ever see me again."

We finally raced into the restaurant at 1:25, fifty-five minutes late. Our guests were already digesting their lunch. After apologizing, we plunged into our "Why Salomon?" presentation. At 1:50 sharp, Bill Young departed.

Yet there is a just God. Imperial Oil rewarded Salomon for its twenty years of attentions by choosing us, along with Wood Gundy, to market a $250 million U.S. offering.

Later, we and Wood Gundy were members of the management group (led by First Boston) for a Gulf Canada Equity offering in the U.S. At the same time, we were advising Imperial Oil on a rights offering. These two giants of the Canadian oil industry were on a collision course, but neither Wood Gundy nor Salomon broke the confidence of either firm. Finally, the companies announced their timetables one week apart.

Harold Hammer, CFO of Gulf, U.S.A., was very upset that Salomon and Wood Gundy hadn't informed him about the Imperial rights offering. He gave us both the boot. When I told Gus Lott, he suggested that if we *had* informed Gulf, Imperial would have kicked us out.

Gus and I have had some odd adventures together. We both attended Ted Medland's 60th birthday party at the Rosemont Club in Toronto. I'd been playing tennis with Bob McIntosh earlier, and when we arrived I left a bag containing my eyeglasses in Bob's car. During the evening, I got word that Gus Lott wasn't well. Sure enough, he was white as a ghost, and in a few minutes he fainted. Someone called an ambulance while a doctor who happened to be at the party bent over Gus, trying to revive him. Something about the doctor's grim demeanor suggested that Gus was dying. His wife began to sob.

The ambulance arrived, and I got in the back with Gus, while his wife followed in another car. The attendant administered oxygen, and shortly before we arrived at the hospital, his color improved. Soon Gus was feeling better. (It turned out that he'd collapsed due to the combined effects of a drink or two and some medication he'd been taking.)

When I returned to the party, Bob McIntosh and most of the other guests had left. Unfortunately, Bob's car contained my bag—including my eyeglasses. I was scheduled to take an early flight to New York where I would be introducing two Eastern-bloc diplomats at a seminar at the United Nations. Of course, I didn't have Bob's address or telephone number, and looking him up in the phone book was hopeless—the Toronto listing contains several pages of McIntoshes.

Early the next morning I lucked out. I got Bob's telephone number from a friend, and he brought me my bag and glasses in time for my flight to New York.

Harold Hammer ultimately forgave us for not breaking Imperial Oil's confidence. Some time later Hammer came into our offices to meet with Tom Marron and Ron Freeman. I took the opportunity to gave Hammer an overview of our depth in Canada, which resulted in him giving us the mandate to manage the sale of Gulf Canada.

Our relationship with Gulf was largely due to the efforts of one of the great salesmen in the history of Salomon, Charles Simon, who built the Gulf relationship (later maintained by Tom Marron).

Charlie had come into the firm as an office boy in the early 1930s. Years later, he would regale us with stories about the journeys—Charlie's word—that Herbert Salomon would send him on: "Deliver flowers to Miss So-and-So," "Get me a dozen vanilla eclairs—don't forget, no chocolate," and so on.

Charlie played a major role in Salomon's early development. He grew into Salomon's number one salesman, virtually owning New York State, while his contacts with the Mellon Bank, Gulf Oil, and other Pittsburgh accounts were second to none. He also brought Sidney Homer and Henry Kaufman to Salomon Brothers, and launched our Dallas office headed by Joe Graf.

Charlie was an exceptionally generous friend. If you happened to admire his suit, you'd be invited to see his tailor; if you praised his hat or tie, you'd receive a gift of three just like it. Outside of working hours, Charlie was a superb art collector and a member of the board at the Whitney Museum. He worked tirelessly to find a home for the Indian Museum as well.

Selling Gulf Canada proved to be a complicated matter. The Canadian government had introduced a highly nationalistic energy policy, which created Petro Canada and signaled that the government wanted more control of the industry. This policy was a disaster, and the oil industry signaled its displeasure by moving to sell their Canadian properties. Both Texaco and Superior Oil made it known that they were prepared to abandon Canada.

Soon signs of a shift in policy began to appear. A high-level official in Ottawa signaled to me that Imperial might be allowed to buy Gulf Canada. I relayed this to Cliff Garvin, the CEO of Exxon, whom I'd met at the Alfalfa Dinner in Washington. I'd suggested that Exxon might want to consider buying Gulf Canada. Now they began to take a serious look, and it was my impression that they were ready to make a bid. But suddenly, the same official in Ottawa called to say that policy had again hardened, and Gulf Canada and Superior were out of bounds for a U.S. multinational. Somewhat embarrassed, I informed Cliff Garvin of the shift, grateful that Exxon hadn't expressed its interest publicly.

The soap opera was far from over. Next the famous Texas oilman and corporate raider T. Boone Pickens appeared on the scene, announcing that he was going to buy Gulf Oil, Pittsburgh. Hammer retained Salomon to defend Gulf, and the sale of Gulf Canada was put on the back burner.

A few weeks later, while I was at a Salomon pulp and paper conference in Sea Isle, Georgia, I received a call from our New York office. Gulf wanted us to bring in a second investment bank. They mentioned one firm that we'd previously clashed with. I responded by suggesting Merrill Lynch, a good co-manager because they had a fine distribution network and didn't rock the boat. (We always used to say, "If Merrill ever gets its act together, they'll be awesome." Today they have fulfilled that prophecy.)

Our relationships with most other investment banks weren't so amicable. In the classic war movie *All Quiet On The Western Front*, there's a scene where a French regiment in a trench can hear the sound of digging close by. It's the Germans tunneling underground, preparing to dynamite the trench and blow the French soldiers to kingdom come. This is what many co-managing relationships feel like. Name any two firms from among the quartet of Goldman, Morgan, First Boston, and Salomon as co-managers, and immediately one or both will start digging a tunnel under the other in an effort to become the lead manager.

Pickens's attack signaled that Gulf was in play. After a prolonged period of uncertainty, Chevron, represented by Morgan Stanley, bought Gulf Oil. At the closing dinner in San Francisco, Jim Murdy, Gulf's vice president of finance, thanked Salomon and Merrill for the manner we conducted the defense. This was Murdy's idea, I'm sure; I doubt that Morgan had any desire to share the spotlight with Merrill or Salomon. But I grabbed Murdy's invitation and ran with it. I rose, thanked the Gulf people, wished them and Chevron well, and then introduced Hal Berry, who spoke on behalf of Merrill. Meanwhile, the Morgan people sat by, fuming.

Something weird happened a few months later. Having borrowed heavily from the banks, Chevron had to refinance their debt over a longer term. Accordingly, Chevron announced a huge debt offering to be headed by Salomon and co-managed by Dillon Read, a quality firm with a long-term advisory relationship with Chevron but little placing power in the bond market. I never knew how this came about (what happened to Morgan Stanley?), but we were delighted, as it strengthened our position as the number one debt underwriter—one of the five times during my six years as head of corporate finance that we led the pack. I suspected that the move by some of the Gulf financial people to Chevron played a role in our becoming the lead underwriter on this deal.

After the smoke cleared, we turned our attention back to selling Gulf Canada. It eventually went to the Reichmann brothers, those great real estate moguls from Toronto, who were riding high at the time.

We on Wall Street, our minds clouded by the huge fees involved, don't think much about the impact of mergers and acquisitions on communities. Gulf was a major contributor to the well being of Pittsburgh and the surrounding areas. When the company headquarters moved to San Francisco in the wake of the merger, the entire western Pennsylvania region was devastated. Several years later, I heard that none of the senior people who left Gulf were employed by other Pittsburgh corporations. Very sad if true.

Nonetheless, the drumbeat of deals continues.

One quiet day, I was at my beach club on Long Island with my wife Priscilla and Paul and Jan Dwyer, a couple from Colorado Springs we'd met on our honeymoon in Bora Bora in the Society Islands. We sat down in our beach chairs and had just started to relax when I was called to the phone. It was Tony Hampson, CEO of the Canadian Development Corporation. Tony had been talking to Ron Freeman and me about buying Texas Gulf Sulphur, and now he was ready to pull the trigger. I spoke with Tony and Ron for a while, then returned to my guests.

A few minutes later I was paged again. This time, it was Dick Brinkman, the financial vice president of Texaco. He was calling to see if we would represent them in bidding on Conoco. Smiling Jack Gallagher of Dome had bid on Hudson Bay, Conoco's subsidiary in Canada. Bill Farrell of the Canadian group covered Hudson Bay Oil and Gas, and we were hired by CEO Jerry Maher to represent Hudson Bay, which was finally gobbled up by Dome, the darling of Ottawa and the NEP. They finally stretched the rubber band too far and had to be liquidated.

So Conoco was now in play. They had told Texaco that they preferred to merge with someone outside the oil industry, as this would be less disruptive to the Conoco team. But if it was to be an industry player, Texaco was their first choice. I spent the day taking still more calls as Salomon teams were being assigned. Our friends from Colorado Springs watched bug-eyed as I dashed back and forth across the hot sand.

Texaco was another story. On July 4, 1981, I served as godfather for little Charlie Leonard, whose father Charles was a friend of mine. The party had just begun when I kissed my wife good-bye and headed for Texaco headquarters in Purchase, New York. (When Priscilla explained my absence to the other guests by saying, "He had to go to work," the usual reply was, "What are you talking about? No one goes to work on the Fourth of July." Well, sometimes investment bankers do.)

At the time of our Independence Day meeting, no outside player had yet surfaced. John Gutfreund, Jay Higgins, and I were there on behalf of Salomon. Texaco was represented by its chairman, John McKinley; by Jim Kinnear, who later succeeded John; by Al DeCrane; and by Dick Brinkman, the CFO. I believe Texaco's in-house attorney, Arthur Taylor, was also there. The understanding was that we were to receive a phone call that evening giving us the nod if no other non-industry player appeared.

At one point, Al DeCrane mentioned to Gutfreund that there were rumors that Phibro might bid on Conoco. Unbeknownst to the others in the room, we had been in merger talks with Phibro for the last couple of months. Gutfreund and I glanced at each other, kept straight faces, and said, "We don't think that's the case."

Then we heard a plane passing overhead. Little did we realize it was the DuPont corporate jet, spoiling the elaborate victory dinner John McKinley had planned. A short time later, John received the call notifying us that we were Secondhand Rose—that chemicals giant DuPont had indeed closed the deal. We all quietly left.

Many years later, one can only speculate what might have happened if Texaco had bought Conoco. They undoubtedly would not have been in a position to buy Getty when it came on the market and, therefore, would not have been involved in the suit with Pennzoil that cost them several billion dollars and sent them into bankruptcy.

As for Dome Petroleum, several of my Canadian friends advised me that Dome under Smiling Jack Gallagher was headed for trouble. At the same time, I heard through the grapevine that they wanted to talk to Salomon. We passed. Ironically, the American firm they picked made a great deal of money selling off Dome's assets when the company hit the rocks. There is more than one way to skin a cat on Wall Street.

Some time after that, Lazard approached Texaco to buy Monsanto Chemical. Brinkman called me and asked if we would take a look at Monsanto and give them our advice. We were cool on the idea. Brinkman told me, in effect, that if we had recommended the deal, it might have been our last deal with Texaco.

I just remembered we never sent Texaco a bill for our services then. I wonder if it's too late now.

At a later date, Ed Hennessy of Allied Chemical asked Gutfreund and me to arrange a meeting with McKinley to discuss a merger. We made the introductions at a suite in the Waldorf and withdrew. The deal never got off the floor, evidently because Hennessy wanted to be the CEO and McKinley had other ideas. (I met Hennessy recently in Florida and he confirmed this was the case.)

Our relations with Texaco were hurt on two occasions. The first time, a comment attributed to someone at Salomon appeared in the *Wall Street Journal* saying (in rough paraphrase), "In the Conoco race, everyone else was riding a horse, but we were riding a donkey." I had my suspicions as to who said it, but the partner I confronted denied everything.

133

After smoothing that over, our trading department caused us a little more grief by selling a large block of Texaco shares to the Bass brothers, forcing Texaco to pay those well-known cage rattlers a handsome premium to go away. Although we had an understanding with our equity trading desk that they wouldn't sell large blocks of stocks in response to potential greenmailing or cage rattling, we in corporate finance found ourselves having to mend fences after this kind of embarrassment more than once.

Over the years, we did a great deal of business with Texaco—bare boat charters, stock repurchases, sinking funds, debt for equity. We offered to raise several billion dollars for Texaco prior to their bankruptcy, and we also did the first bond underwriting for them when the emerged from bankruptcy.

One final word on the world of mergers and acquisitions. One night while chatting with a leading M&A attorney, I said to him, "In the world of Wall Street where I grew up, when you shook hands on a deal, it was done. You stood by your word, and your firm stood by you. In the world of mergers and acquisitions that rule doesn't apply. It's never over until it's over. And sometimes not even then."

My dear, departed friend Walter Wriston used to say that the three most important things in banking were character, character, character. It makes me sad to see some leading firms lower their character standards to pursue the almighty dollar Gordon Gekko-style. Although they may grab a few extra bucks in the short term, I can't believe they'll benefit in the long run. And I'm sure their customers won't.

Chapter 9
Deals, Deal-Makers, and Some That Got Away

When you spend a lifetime in a people business like investment banking, you end up having more than your share of memorable evenings. I've found that the most memorable by far are the ones when nothing goes according to plan.

On one occasion, I was scheduled to be a guest of honor at a luncheon hosted by the chairman of the Royal Bank, Earl McLaughlin. The other guest of honor would be Premier William Davis of Ontario.

The night before, I was hosting a dinner at the Inn on the Park for Len Farmer, the Treasurer of Hydro Quebec, and his finance team. I'd reserved a table in the hotel's dining room and was looking forward to an early night when Len arrived and shouted across the room, "We're not eating here—we're eating in your room and playing cards."

On the principle that the customer is always right, we retired to my room and set up a card table. Now, Len liked to play for really big money, while I liked to play for really small money. (As a member of Salomon's Executive Committee, I found that going to sleep each night with over $100 billion in inventories was enough gambling for me.) On this occasion, I prevailed—we played bridge for a penny a point until about three A.M., the biggest winner raking in some five bucks. I drank four or five bottles of beer—not too much for me in those days, though now it would represent my yearly consumption.

The next morning, I got up around seven A.M. and went down for breakfast. Suddenly, the general quarter BONG sounded in my head, and the elevator started going up and down in my stomach. I retired to my room and proceeded to down about a half dozen Bufferin and several Alka Seltzers. All my morning appointments were cancelled.

At 11:45, I gingerly got into a cab and headed for the Royal Bank luncheon, still uncertain whether I was up to the task. There was a bar in the dining room. I quietly slipped up to it and whispered, "Club soda, please."

Bev McGill, a senior officer of the bank, overheard me. "Did I hear you order a club soda? Give him a straight scotch, that's what he drinks." (I haven't had a scotch in decades.) Terror surged through my tortured body. Somehow I held myself together through the luncheon. How I did it should be a course taught at the Harvard Business School.

This confession may be mild compared to Seymour Hirsch's exposé about Kennedy and Marilyn Monroe, but I feel better now that I've let my Canadian friends know that I wasn't as perfect as they thought.

Another evening, I arranged a dinner at the Ritz in Montreal for the top brass of the Royal Bank of Canada. Salomon was to be represented by me; our chairman, John Gutfreund; our esteemed economist, Henry Kaufman; and our banking corporate finance partner, Craig Sterns. Rowlie Frazze, the chairman of the Royal Bank, had about six other senior executives with him.

At the last minute, fate played havoc with the schedule. Around five P.M., a member of Frazze's team called. "Rowlie had a late night yesterday," he explained. "He's really looking forward to an early evening. Is it possible to move our dinner from seven to six thirty?" Sure, no problem.

A few minutes later, I received a call from the Salomon team. "We're stuck in traffic."

"Where the heck are you?"

"On the Brooklyn Bridge—we missed our plane. We're trying to charter one to get to Montreal."

I was left with an embarrassing dilemma. For some three hours, I hosted the dinner on my own, playing chairman, economist, statesman, and bank analyst by turns. Mercifully, the Salomon team arrived around 9:45, and I was able to regain my voice. It was evenings like this that turned me prematurely gray, as a mere lad in my sixties.

Then there was the time I was coming back from Mexico. Having been on vacation, I was dressed casually in dungarees. I was scheduled to have dinner that night with Ron Freeman of Salomon and a group of financial people from Mobil Oil, but I figured I've have plenty of time to change.

You know what they say about the best-laid plans. We lost our connection because of a gate delay in Houston. I arrived at LaGuardia already late for dinner, grabbed a suit my chauffeur had brought, and dashed into the public men's room, where I proceeded to strip to my shorts and change into my suit as a group of strangers stared in puzzlement. I arrived at the restaurant just in time for dessert.

On another occasion, a plane delay made Priscilla and me late for a formal dinner hosted by Canadian Pacific. Priscilla was a little upset, but I pooh-poohed her concerns. "This kind of thing happens all the time," I said. "It won't be the first time I've changed on a plane."

Priscilla replied, "If you think I am going to change into a formal dress in the washroom of a jumbo jet, you are out of your mind."

I convinced her to at least put her evening makeup on, thereby saving us a few minutes. We arrived at our hotel, the Chateau Champlain, and when we reached our floor, I shouted to the elevator operator, "Hold that elevator here!" We dashed into our room, changed in record time, and made it to the restaurant in time for the second course.

On another occasion, I arrived at the Chateau Champlain on a hot summer day, soaked through and late for a seminar I was hosting. I grabbed a bellhop. "Take my clothing bag and follow me." I stripped to my shorts and bathed in the first floor john as the bellhop held my suit and shirt at the ready.

These experiences led to recurring dreams that would leave me either drained or headachy in the morning. In one dream, I found myself back in my high school gym with a tee shirt pulled down, try-ing to hide the fact that I'd forgotten my pants. In another dream, I found I'd come to work with no coat or tie; and in yet another, I was getting ready to go to work and couldn't find my wallet or car keys. This is what happens when you live with pressure, unrelenting pressure.

Sometimes we were victims of others' mistakes. One time, Salomon's Henry Kaufman accepted an invitation to speak at a dinner honoring Frank Miller, the conservative treasurer of Ontario. At the last minute—too late for Henry to back out—he discovered that it was a fund-raising dinner for the Conservative Party. Henry was extremely upset, as were Peter Gordon and I; it had always been our policy to avoid political entanglements. Frank had a brief stint as premier but was soundly defeated by David Peterson in the next election. The incoming Liberal treasurer, Robert Nixon, expressed his displeasure with Salomon for its involvement in the Miller dinner— and rightly so. We could only get down on our knees and beg for mercy.

I admired Bob MacIntosh, the Executive Vice President of the Bank of Nova Scotia. Bob and I were co-chairmen of the Canadian American Committee for several years in the seventies, and Bob later became the President of the Canadian Bankers Association. We played a lot of tennis over the years, and because I value his friendship highly, I will refrain from telling you what I thought of Bob's game. Incidentally, Bob's brother David MacIntosh wrote a great book called *Terror in the Starboard Seat* about his experiences as a navigator with the Royal Canadian Air Force in World War II. He flew with a Jewish pilot named Sid who would take crazy risks in his zeal to attack anything German. The only thing Sid feared was balloons. When things got too hot, David would claim he saw balloons to get Sid to back off.

Ted Avison was my first contact at Canadian Imperial and someone whose company I enjoyed on many occasions. On one occasion, Ted had one of the bank's cars pick me up at the Dorval airport for a meeting in Ottawa with Governor Rasminsky of the Bank of Canada. My plane arrived late and we were burning rubber to make up lost time. Suddenly, a mountie waved us down, our speed having been picked up by a helicopter. "Do you realize you were going eighty miles an hour?" the mountie asked our driver.

I jumped in: "Officer, it's my fault, not the driver's. I'm late for an appointment with the governor of the Bank of Canada, and I didn't want to keep such an important man waiting."

My name-dropping exercise didn't get me very far. "The sooner I give you the ticket," the mountie replied, "the sooner you'll be there."

I recalled a similar run-in with the law when I was playing basketball for the Kokomo Clowns. A state trooper hailed us for speeding on our way to Sauguerties, New York. I was appointed the spokesman for the group.

"Officer," I said in my most sincere voice, "I regret that we were speeding. You see, we're playing a charity basketball game in Sauguerties, and we are quite late. We didn't want to keep the crowd waiting.

"Very commendable," the trooper replied as he wrote the ticket. I was a pretty good investment banker, but I wasn't very good at getting out of traffic tickets.

At the peak of Salomon's power in Canada, we managed or co-managed ninety percent of the public offerings of U.S. pay Canadian issues. This business was important to Salomon in more ways than one. First, of course, there was the underwriting spread—pure revenue for us, varying from half a point to one and a half points. Second, the manager who runs the books sets aside a portion of the bond offering for institutional sales, known as "the pot." For example, suppose Ontario was doing a $250 million offering. $100 million might be retained in the pot. Now, if the John Hancock insurance company wanted $25 million worth of bonds, the Hancock manager would come to Salomon and say, "I would like you to have $10 million and designate other members of the underwriting group for the other $15 million." So if Salomon's original participation was $40 million, by controlling the pot and seeing all the designated orders, we might receive orders for another $30 million, putting us in a position to buy another ten million at a re-allowance from members of the syndicate who couldn't place their bonds. The end result would be that Salomon made a full commission of three quarters of a point on $40 million, three eighths of a point on $30 million and one eighth of a point re-allowance on another $10 million. On top of all this, we also earned a management fee. In short, a very lucrative deal for Salomon.

Our dominance of the market produced other benefits as well. When you are the manager or co-manager for Ontario, Quebec, Manitoba, British Columbia, Nova Scotia, New Brunswick, Saskatchewan, and the Commonwealth of Canada, plus various crown corporations, like Export Development Bank, Canadian

National Railway, and the Federal Development Bank, it gives you a great advantage trading between the various entities. We knew where the bonds were and had a pretty good idea when borrowers were coming to market, giving us the additional advantage of knowing who owned the various Canadian issues and the ability to swap Canadian issues against one another and against U.S. issues as well.

In my mind, two things propelled Salomon to the top as a bond underwriter. One was our huge volume of Canadian underwritings. The other was our lead role on the IBM financing, which came about when Morgan Stanley refused to co-manage with Salomon and got dropped in favor of Merrill Lynch.

In addition to my Canadian duties, I had senior responsibility for several corporations in the United States, including Exxon, Texaco, Borden, DuPont, Union Carbide, Uniroyal, Northern Natural Gas, and Metropolitan Life.

I also put together the corporate contact department under Bob Quinn, Jr. At one time, corporations were covered by various sales groups within the firm. For example, a particular salesman might cover Pittsburgh, including banks, insurance companies, pension funds, municipalities, and corporations. As a result, corporations got little attention from salesmen, who could write large tickets with a variety of the other accounts.

I originated the idea of putting all the eastern corporations under one roof instead. Bob Quinn headed this new unit with Tom Marron at his side, covering corporations on sinking funds, pension funds, commercial paper, treasury bills, bonds, and stock buybacks. They built relations that led to underwriting, mergers and acquisitions. It was no easy task getting strong partners to relinquish control over corporations under their jurisdiction. But we pushed the idea through, and it was so successful that it was eventually emulated by some of Salomon's strongest competitors, including Goldman Sachs.

After leaving Salomon, Bob ran as a Republican candidate for Congress from Long Island and was narrowly defeated. He also went back to college, earning a diploma from Notre Dame and becoming one of the oldest graduates in the history of the university.

Like many others from the great days at Salomon, Bob gave generously of his time and energy to many worthy causes. As I mentioned earlier, Bob was chairman of the Christening Committee for the magnificent aircraft carrier, the *U.S.S. Theodore Roosevelt.* For several years, Bob was chairman of St. Francis Hospital on Long Island. He also served as a board member of what was known as the Greenpoint Financial, now part of the North Fork Bank.

Mentioning the Metropolitan Life brings back one of the closest calls of my life. One Friday early in 1975, Jack Kugler, a partner at Salomon Brothers, had arranged a lunch for me, Bob Schwartz, president of the Metropolitan Life, and two financial people from the Met. Later, my cousin Dick Taffee called and invited me to lunch on the same day. Dick and I always lunched at the historic Fraunces Tavern in downtown Manhattan and sat in a table at the back near the Anglers Club.

I said to Dick, "Let me see if I can get out of Jack Kugler's luncheon—I'll call you back." But Jack was adamant: "I need you and want you at the luncheon." So I had to ask cousin Dick for a rain check.

That Friday, while Kugler, Schwartz, and I were sitting at lunch in Salomon's dining room, there was a loud explosion, and the building shook. Later, Cousin Dick called me with the news: A group of Puerto Rican terrorists known as the FALN had set off a bomb by the Anglers Club, killing one person and injuring several others. If Dick and I had been seated at our usual table, we might have become footnotes in history.

When Jim Wolfensohn was brought in to run corporate finance, he succeeded Dan Sargent, who became Salomon's man in charge of corporate quality control. Dan did an outstanding job keeping Salomon out of trouble. There were a number of bad apples running savings and loans, and Dan did a good job keeping corporate finance away from that crowd.

One of Salomon's near misses was the Drysdale affair. My cousin Dick Taffee had just become president of Drysdale Government Securities, which had been doing some very big government bond transactions with no involvement from Salomon. Craig Coats, one of the senior traders in Salomon's government department, asked me to set up a luncheon with the chairman of Drysdale and my cousin Dick. The meeting was duly arranged, and over lunch, Drysdale's chairman went on at length about the huge number of government bond trades he was doing. We liked the sound of this, and sent him the questionnaire we required accounts to complete before we did business with them.

A week or so later, Dan Sargent called me. "We never got the papers we need from Drysdale," he told me. "But I know your cousin's the president. Should we go ahead and open an account anyway?"

"Forget about my cousin," I said. "Treat them like any other account. And never forget my favorite rule: Shoot anyone who tries to get in the lifeboats before Salomon. The firm comes first."

Good thing I said this. Drysdale turned out to be a Ponzie scheme, victimizing (among others) Drysdale's bankers at Chase Manhattan. Some thirty banks and brokerages had lent government securities to Chase Manhattan in return for cash, and Chase in turn had lent the securities to Drysdale. Using its borrowed securities as leverage, Drysdale parlayed its roughly $30 million in capital into holdings estimated at as much as $4 billion. But when the semi-annual interest date came up and the original thirty holders were entitled to their interest, Drysdale could not come through.

Both Chase and Drysdale's parent firm, Drysdale Securities Corporation, disavowed all responsibility for the default and the resulting $300 million in losses. It also appeared that insiders had used prior information of the impending collapse to speculate against Chase's stock, which dropped by eight points in the immediate aftermath. Within twenty-four hours, Wall Street was panicky, the market for government securities was in turmoil, and several leading brokerage houses seemed in danger. The Fed found itself forced to choose between letting Chase welsh on its debts, risking a major Wall Street collapse, or bailing out banks whose predicament was the result of their own greed and stupidity. It chose the latter, announcing its willingness to act "as lender of last resort to assist the commercial banks in meeting unusual credit demands relating to market problems."

Chase eventually agreed to make good on Drysdale's debts, pending the inevitable lawsuits. As for my cousin, he had done one trade while at Drysdale—fifty million in treasury bills. The Chase people said they knew he was innocent, but their lawyers would not let them put it in print. His career was over.

The energetic Jim Wolfensohn was now in charge of corporate finance. Born in Australia in 1933, Jim holds B.A. and LLB degrees from the University of Sydney and an M.B.A. from Harvard. He spent his early business career with Darling & Co. in Australia. Jim then went on to Schroeders Limited in London and moved to New York as president of J. Henry Schroeders Banking Corporation before joining Salomon Brothers in 1976.

While Jim was in charge of corporate finance, the division had three executive partners, including Jim, me, and "Mr. Chicago," J. Ira Harris. (Eventually I stood guard alone after Jim left and Ira decided to step down.) Soon after Jim joined the firm, Bill Salomon mentioned him at an executive committee dinner as someone who could possibly run the firm. The internal wagons quickly began to circle, as long-time partners had a natural aversion to new guys on the block. The internal bickering soured Jim, and he left in 1981 to start his own firm.

As CEO of James D. Wolfensohn, Jim's true talent as an investment bankers was realized. He brought in Paul Volcker, former head of the Federal Reserve, to act as chairman of the firm, as well as Ray Golden, an ex-Salomon partner who acted as COO. Ray gave the firm balance while Jim and Paul pursued new business.

Jim went on the boards of CBS, The Rockefeller Foundation, and Daimler Benz AG, to name a few. He has also served on a great many cultural and educational boards. In 1995, he was made an honorary Knight of the British Empire by Queen Elizabeth II, and he has been decorated by many other countries as well. An accomplished cellist, he became a chairman of Carnegie Hall and later of the John F. Kennedy Center of Performing Arts, in Washington, D.C.

Jim left his highly successful company to become president of the World Bank in 1995, placing the firm in the able hands of Ray Golden until its acquisition by Bankers Trust. Jim truly is a man for all seasons whose great talents never quite fit into the Salomon machine.

When Jim left Salomon, I took over worldwide corporate finance, while Harold Tanner was in effect our chief operating officer. He and I had a Mr. Outside and Mr. Inside arrangement. New business took up about seventy percent of my time, but just about thirty percent of Harold's. He spent a great deal of time working on the quality of our underwritings and the internal operation of the department.

Harold had grown up in Glens Falls, New York, a small village best known for its insurance businesses and the traffic jams that stymied travelers to Lake George prior to the building of the New

York State Thruway. His parents were children of immigrants, and neither ever graduated from high school. Harold's mother was an ardent Zionist, founder of Hadassah in Glens Falls, and a leader in the League of Women Voters and the Parent Teacher Association. Harold's father, a traveling salesman, was very active during World War II, an avid volunteer and a lifelong leader in the American Legion.

Harold attended local high school and went on to graduate from Cornell and attend the Harvard Business School. Before joining Salomon, Harold worked at Blyth, at Eastman, Dillon, and at New Court Securities. After leaving Salomon (just a year or two after my departure), Harold started his own firm, Tanner & Co., Inc., and he has successfully advised many major clients across the United States.

Harold has been exceptionally generous with his time and talents. He and the late Steve Weiss of Weiss, Peck, Grier, headed an endowment campaign for their alma mater, Cornell, which brought in over one and a half billion to the little school high above Cayuga's waters. Harold has also served as chairman of the board of trustees at Cornell University and has been a very successful fundraiser for the Harvard Business School. In addition, he and his wife Nicki have raised large amounts for various Jewish causes. He also served as President of the American Jewish Committee, while Nicki has served on the board of Colonial Williamsburg and as vice chairman of the Wellesley College board.

Harold and I set out to do two things: to build strong units to do bond and stock offerings for our clients, and also to work more closely with our mergers and acquisition teams. We formed industry groups focused on banking, energy, utilities, technology, and telecommunications, as well as a general industrial group. Having these groups work with the M&A teams paid big dividends. For example, Ron Freeman, heading the energy group, worked effectively in the Gulf Oil transaction assisted by Tom Marron, as well as on the sale of Gulf Canada Texas Gulf Sulphur and other acquisitions.

Probably the most successful acquisition of a large company in the eighties was General Motors' acquisition of EDS from Ross Perot. It all started with a dinner in a private room at the 21 Club in New York, which was only arranged after a year of effort by Bob Quinn, who was responsible for General Motors. The participants included Roger Smith, CEO of General Motors, as well as his treasurer and his VP of finance, along with John Gutfreund, our senior partner; Bob Quinn; Bob Scully, who also had a strong relationship with General Motors; Denis Bovin, who headed our technology team, and me.

We had known that Perot wanted to sell EDS to diversify his fortune, and we'd already talked to General Electric and AT&T. At the dinner, Roger Smith did the bulk of the talking and gave us quite an insight into General Motors' strengths and weaknesses. Later, we arrived at the conclusion that EDS would be a good business fit for General Motors, although we realized that the chemistry might not be easy.

As we expected, the deal proved to be a complicated one, but in the end GM profited handsomely from the acquisition. Later, numerous people claimed credit for the deal. There's plenty of credit to go around, but I would point out that the bulk of the heavy work on the deal was shared by Bob Scully and Jerry Rosenfeld from our M&A group, while Bob Quinn was responsible for our overall relationship with GM.

DuPont was another relationship I pursued in the U.S. I had for a considerable period of time been in touch with DuPont of Canada, and Herb Lank the company's chairman, had been something of a mentor, introducing me to many financial people in Montreal and offering much valuable counsel. Later, DuPont Canada's CEO Bob Richardson and the financial VP Ken Place were good friends of mine. But in the U.S., Salomon could not rise above the assistant treasurer level at DuPont, and although we did a fair bit of business with their pension fund we couldn't get to first base on the corporate side.

Finally, Ken Place arranged a meeting between me, Hal MacCray who managed our Philadelphia office, and the treasurer and assistant treasurer of DuPont. It did not go well, to say the least.

The DuPont treasurer turned to the assistant treasurer (a man I'll call Tom), and asked him, "Do you know Salomon Brothers?"

"Yes," he replied, "And I've had some good dealings with Salomon and some bad dealings."

I inquired, "What do you mean by bad dealings?"

"Well," Tom replied, "Salomon reneged on a couple of transactions."

"I would like to hear about these incidents," I responded.

According to Tom, the first "renege" occurred when he had given Salomon an order to buy Aluminum Company of America bonds and we couldn't deliver. The second was on an equipment trust railroad issue.

I assured him I would look into his complaints and get back to him.

When I returned to the office, I asked our industrial traders about the Aluminum Company complaint. They informed me as follows. One of the New York banks had given us an order to sell the bonds. They left us the order for two hours. We, in turn, called DuPont and left the bonds firm with them for two hours. After two hours, the bank called back and cancelled the order. It was late in December, and the bank explained they were finished taking losses for the year and would renew their sell program early in January. DuPont called back some three and a half hours later to buy the bonds—when we no longer had an offering.

This kind of thing happens all the time, and Salomon had acted completely properly. In fact, a couple of weeks later, in January, we sold DuPont the bonds at a better price.

As for the second incident, it turned out that Tom was confusing us with someone else.

When I reported this to Ken Place, he offered his own theory. "DuPont has a caste system something like the military," he said. "The assistant treasurer probably had his nose out of joint because we went over his head."

Sometime after that, Bob Richardson went down to Wilmington to become treasurer of DuPont, and Irv Shapiro became chairman of the company. It was a great sign of changing times for DuPont to have a Jewish CEO, and Irv brought an end to the DuPont's rigidly hierarchical system.

The first time I met Irv Shapiro was with my partner and sales manager Morris Offit, a great person in his own right. Morris was a graduate from John Hopkins University in 1957. He then attended the Wharton School of the University of Pennsylvania and earned his MBA in 1960. Morris served as a general partner for ten years at the Mercantile Safe Deposit and Trust Company in Baltimore before joining Salomon in 1969. For several years, he was in charge of equity research and eventually became Salomon's partner in charge of worldwide equity and fixed income sales.

In 1983, Morris started Offit Associates, which eventually

became Offitbank, a highly successful, limited-purpose trust chartered in New York State. He succeeded Mike Bloomberg as Chairman of the Board of John Hopkins University and served in that capacity from 1990 to1996.

Morris has been extremely generous with his time and money, especially in service to Jewish causes. A well-known lecturer on international finance, he has received several honorary degrees and serves on a number of corporate boards. Morris sold his company to Wachovia Bank & Trust in 1999 and later founded Offit Hall Capital Management LLC, where he is currently co-chairman and co-CEO.

Morris was named 1998 Philanthropist of the Year by the greater New York Chapter of the National Society of Fund Raising Executives—another Son of Salomon of whom we can all be proud.

Anyway, when Morris and I met Irv Shapiro at DuPont, Morris was eager to discuss Jewish philanthropy with him. Irv recounted his earlier days in Minneapolis as a law school student and said that many people had advised him to change his name, since Jewish lawyers supposedly couldn't get ahead in that city. "But now that I'm the CEO of DuPont," he said, "practically every rabbi in the country is calling me to speak on behalf of various Jewish causes. And if I turn them down, I'm a bad Jew."

To which Morris Offit replied, "Well, maybe you should change your name *now*."

Up to that point, Morgan Stanley had been DuPont's sole banker. However, Shapiro decided to open up other relationships. Through my friend Bob Richardson, who'd advanced to financial vice president, Salomon was appointed to manage one of two industrial revenue bond issues along with Goldman Sachs—the first time DuPont had ever used anyone other than Morgan Stanley on a bond issue.

Our next assignment was to give a fair market value on a DuPont bid for the minority shares of Remington Rand. Morgan, which had an excellent veteran M&A team, represented DuPont. Our group decided DuPont's offering should be improved. I heard later that Shapiro was furious and threatened never to do business with us again.

Eventually we made a comeback. We were given a chance to compete against First Boston on a commercial paper program. Both firms were asked to estimate how large a program they could undertake. We came in with a limit of one billion. First Boston said they could do three billion to five billion. They were awarded the program and were as good as their word.

So Salomon's chance to become a co-manager for DuPont went down the drain.

I did visit Irv Shapiro on another occasion. Irv was chairman of the Howard Hughes Medical Foundation, located in California, so Bob Matschullat, then Salomon's west coast finance partner, and I planned a joint visit to Irv at DuPont's headquarters in Wilmington.

Bob and I were scheduled to travel to Delaware by train out of New York's Penn Station. Bob was already aboard the train while I was stuck in a horrendous traffic jam on a blistering summer day in the city. Realizing I would never make the train if I remained sitting in my cab, I decided to sprint the last eight blocks, briefcase in hand. The train was moving as I jumped aboard, soaked through.

Bob was so relieved he almost kissed me. He said, "Here I was, on my way to Wilmington all by myself, even though I don't know Shapiro and have no idea what to say when I get to the meeting."

When I could breath again, I said to Match, "I hope you realize I'm the only member of the executive committee fast enough to catch a moving train."

Chapter 10
Outside the Office:
Sunny Days and Bad Breaks

My career at Salomon Brothers demanded more than one hundred percent of any normal human being's time and energy. But somehow, as I built my career and youth gave way to middle age, I managed to have a life outside the office with more than its share of happiness and heartache.

In 1946, fresh out of the service, I married Betty Conaghan. We'd gone together before the war for a little more than a year. Like most of our friends, we married young, with more love in our hearts than money in our pockets.

Here's a story that epitomizes the circumstances of those times. My friend Frank Peters called me the night before his wedding to asked me if he could borrow a pair of blue shoes. Luckily, I had two pairs of shoes, and Frank happened to be a size 12, like me. Frank came over and borrowed my shoes. The next day, as Frank knelt before the altar of the church of St. Francis de Sales in Rockaway with his bride Ruth, I noticed that there were holes in the soles of both shoes.

After Betty and I lost our first child, she was heartbroken and eager to have another. We didn't waste any time. In order came Betty, Rickie, Marrie, Stephen, Virginia, Garry, and Michael. In the early days, we lived upstairs in my mother's two-family house. When our family was still small, we would move to a basement apartment next door during the summer so my mother could rent the whole house. Living this way created a tremendous incentive for me to do better on Wall Street.

In 1953, I bought my first house with a lending hand from Salomon Brothers. Life was fairly calm in those days—at least, as calm as it could be with a large family. We were near the ocean and the tennis club for the summer, and our kids' activities were centered around the school and the Catholic Youth Organization.

Life became a lot more complicated with a series of health emergencies that began when Garry was an infant. One Sunday after church, Betty went upstairs to check on Garry in his crib, where he'd been left in the care of our oldest daughter. Suddenly I heard a loud scream from my wife. Garry had gone into a convulsion, a terrible thing to behold. Betty thought he was dying.

Garry survived, but this was the start of a long struggle for him. Doctors explained that he had a condition such that, when a virus struck, his temperature would shoot up very quickly to 104 degrees or so. He had to be closely watched and checked frequently during the night, and he often slept wrapped in cold sheets. He was constantly on medication.

One time Betty flew home from Florida with Garry in the middle of March. I went to pick them up on a very windy night. As they got off the plane, I could literally see the fever burning him up. A ride home at breakneck speed, a cold bath, and wet sheets followed. It was a tremendous strain.

In 1966, my daughter Marrie fell ill. She pleaded with us to let her go to a CYO dance despite the fact that she was suffering from a bad cold. Betty and I made the wrong decision and let her go. Marrie came home with a terrible headache. We called a standby doctor who gave her some antibiotics. By the next morning, she was in intense pain and unable to move her head. When our own doctor arrived and said, "I think she has spinal meningitis," I felt as if my own head had split down the middle. I had a headache constantly for many months after that shock.

Meanwhile, our son Stephen began throwing up and complaining of a severe headache. My brother rushed over (he was always there for me), and he took Betty and daughter Marrie to the hospital while I tended to Stephen at home. Terrified of the contagion of meningitis, I threw all the bedding out and opened all the windows in the house.

In the hospital, Marrie nearly succumbed to a coma, but with the help of antibiotics she fought it off. Fortunately, Stephen just had a bad virus, and this crisis passed.

Two years later, Betty and I walking along the beach in Fort Lauderdale when she began complaining of shortness of breath and a pain in her side. When we returned home, she went in for a check-up and was found to have breast cancer. When they operated, they found it had entered the node gland. I remember my instinctive reaction: *This is fatal.*

Later in the same year (1968), our youngest son, Michael, had a very serious accident. Betty and I returned from a short vacation, having left my cousin Isabelle in charge of the family. As our car approached the house, we could see several neighbors congregated in front of our house. None of them were smiling.

Michael, we learned, had been playing ball in front of the house. The ball rolled into the street and he gave chase. A young girl with a learner's permit was driving down the street with her instructor. She said she never saw Michael until she hit him. A neighbor said he went ten or fifteen feet in the air.

Upon hearing the news, we immediately left for Peninsula General Hospital, where Michael's condition was very serious. He had a fractured skull, a broken leg, and they feared a ruptured spleen. For the first forty-eight hours they weren't sure he would make it. All this took place in the first year of my wife's diagnosis of cancer. Fortunately, the spleen was not ruptured, but he did have a fractured pelvis. Michael spent forty-some days in the hospital. (I visited every day except one, when I had to host a dinner for Premier Duff Roblin of Manitoba.)

When Michael finally came home, he had a cast on his right leg from the waist down. It weighed a ton, as these were the days before the modern light-weight casts. Some two months later when the cast was removed, he was so happy to be able take a bath again. He had to crawl around the house for a while until he was strong enough to walk.

Family troubles continued to multiply, though not without an occasional positive side. While vacationing in Paris with our two daughters, Betty suffered a heart attack and spent time recovering in the American Hospital in Paris, which turned out to be the finest hospital I've ever seen. Built during World War I to care for wounded

American servicemen, the hospital is spotless and graced with beautiful gardens. When I received the doctor's bill for three weeks of treatment, it was less than the cost of a fancy meal at one of the better bistros in Paris. I wrote a check for double the amount.

The trip home was a nightmare. I'd arranged a car to take us to the airport, and I'd called ahead to make sure the flight was on schedule. But after Betty (in her wheelchair) and I, along with all the other passengers, had boarded the plane, an electrical malfunction forced us all to disembark. We had to wait six hours before being transferred to another flight, which was immediately followed by an announcement of another hour's delay.

By this time, I was furious. I demanded to see the captain. "I don't want to be jerked around any longer," I said. "If you're expecting any more problems, tell me now and we'll go back to our hotel."

The captain was reassuring. "Oh, no, Mr. Schmeelk. We'll be on our way in an hour."

Sure enough, we took off as planned, but somewhere over the Atlantic yet another snafu occurred. "Due to head winds," came the announcement, "We'll have to make an unscheduled landing in Gander, Newfoundland, for refueling." In the end, the trip took over seventeen torturous hours.

During one of Betty's hospital stays back in Long Island, we had a fire in our house. Ricky came home late one night and decided to cook a steak in the oven. Unfortunately, the maid hadn't cleaned the oven in a while, and when Ricky opened the oven flames shot out and spread rapidly. He ran upstairs and shook me awake, yelling, "The kitchen's on fire!"

Thankfully, our two older girls who normally slept on the third floor were sleeping on the second floor with the two youngest boys. I ran from room to room, sounding the alarm. When the family had congregated in the living room, I said, "Is everyone here?"

"Stephen is missing!" someone yelled. I ran up the stairs, shouting, "Get out, the house is on fire!" By the time I got to the second floor, I was choking on the smoke—I seriously doubt I could have made the third floor. Finally, the door to one of the third-floor bedrooms opened, and I heard Stephen running down the stairs. Everyone was safe.

Our house, however, was quickly gutted. Stunned, frightened, but glad to be alive, my flock dispersed to the nearby houses of their grandmother house and my brother, dressed in bathrobes hastily provided by thoughtful neighbors.

Early the next morning, I was sitting across the street from my burned-out house on the porch of my neighbor Jimmy Gallagher. The newspaper deliveryman arrived. He got out of his car, examined the smoldering ruins, and carefully tucked the day's newspaper under a flowerpot.

Taking a cue from the newspaper man, I also tried to maintain a modicum of normality: After breakfast, I got my tennis gear from my car and went to hit a few balls at our club. After that, I made arrangements to clothe and house my flock among family and friends. I also called the hospital where Betty was staying and made sure no local papers would reached her. Gradually, over the next week, I broke the news little by little.

When the fire stopped smoldering, we gingerly reentered the house. The kitchen and dining room were so badly damaged it was hard to tell what kind of rooms they were. Betty had kept her jewelry in the dining room china closet. Amazingly, when a group of her girlfriends sifted through the charred remains, they were able to recover practically all her jewelry.

The insurance company adjuster arrived to assess the damage. He was standing in one of the third-floor bedrooms under a light fixture held up by a thin wire. "Maybe you ought to move," I suggested, "That wire looks as if it could break at any time."

Very bored, he responded, "I've been doing this for a long time and I don't need your help." Right on cue, plunk! The fixture came down on his head. I permitted myself a brief smile before we continued our tour of the house.

I experienced a fair amount of frustration in trying to buy a new home. I liked one that had been on the market for over a year. My wife was in Florida at the time, and I flew down there over the weekend to show her the plans. When I called the agent on Monday morning, I learned that the house had been sold over the weekend. Next, I bid ten thousand dollars over the asking price on another house, only to be told that the owner had decided not to sell.

Most irritating of all were my dealings with a justice from the New York State Supreme Court who lived facing the ocean in nearby Neponsit. The judge and I agreed on a price over a handshake and a drink. When the judge's lawyer failed to follow up with my lawyer, I called the judge. "I've been meaning to call. Someone walking along the beach saw my house and came in and topped your bid."

"Judge," I said, "in my business, a deal is a deal."

"Well, you know," he replied, "I have a great wine cellar and some very nice furniture. Maybe you would like to improve your bid."

"No, thanks," I answered.

"Or maybe you'd like to offer me a hot stock pick or two. You must get a lot of those in your work at Salomon."

"We don't work like that," I responded, and hung up.

Sometime later, the judge called me at the office. "I'm on Wall Street," he reported, "May I drop in?"

"Sorry, judge," I told him, "I don't have any free time." I think he got the message—that was our last contact.

In the meantime, I'd rented a house on the ocean in Neponsit about a mile from our home. Betty was in Florida—the climate seemed to ease her lung ailment—with my mother and our two oldest children, while Marrie, Virginia, Stephen, and Garry were with me. Michael, our youngest, was with my brother and sister-in-law.

It was the most exhausting year in my life. I had a housekeeper named Kelly who would put a plate of food in front of me as I arrived home, then run out the door. Mae Swan, an elderly "girlfriend" of my mother would drop in from time to time and help out.

One day I was getting dressed for a black-tie dinner in Toronto when I decided to call the house to check in. Kelly answered the phone. "I'm leaving, Mr. Schmeelk. No, I'm not giving you two weeks' notice or even two days' notice. Tonight's my last night." As you can imagine, I was fit to be tied. But Mae got on the phone immediately and said, "Don't worry, Dick. I'll take over until you can work it out."

Mae was a piece of work. When I got home, my mother said, "You know, Mae likes a drink before dinner. Make sure you take care of her."

Dutifully, when I came home from the office the next day, I greeted her with, "Mae, can I fix you a drink?"

She winked. "Thanks, but I've already had three."

Friends and neighbors pitched in to help. A family named McGoldrick lived on the block where I rented in Neponsit. One of the McGoldrick daughters would stop by to help get the kids off to school as I departed for Wall Street. It was so early in the morning that she made the trip in her nightgown and robe, which probably provoked a little gossip among the neighbors.

The house was the last one on the street, right on the beach. One of the problems I had was there was a no parking policy on ocean blocks. I would come home at night only to find someone had parked and blocked my driveway. I would have to go down to the beach and try to find the lovers and request they move their car. On one occasion, I received a parking ticket while searching the beach.

On Christmas Eve, 1972, Betty's younger brother Jack dropped dead from a heart attack. He was only in his forties. Betty never knew it happened. As her condition worsened, I'd removed the phone from her bedroom, and whenever she asked about Jack, I would say, "Oh, he called to see how you're doing."

The last five years of Betty's life were a downward spiral. One event after another increased her suffering. First a careless radiologist burned her lungs and caused her tremendous breathing discomfort. There followed ovary removal, a heart attack, and the loss of sight in one eye. Finally, in 1973, bone cancer took her from us forever.

Despite her long struggle against the illness, some in our family were still in denial. My son Garry ran away when he heard the news. One of our neighbors found him late in the evening several miles from home.

*   *   *

I decided to move to another area and make a fresh start. I put my house up for sale and eventually moved from Rockaway to Lawrence, about six miles away. But tragedy wasn't finished with our family. Early in September, 1974, my son Ricky was admitted to Peninsula Hospital with a high fever. He was diagnosed with hepatitis B and a bleeding ulcer. His condition deteriorated, the doctors were unable to stop the bleeding, and they decided to move him to Mount Sinai Hospital in New York. After a wild ambulance ride, he was being brought into his room at Mount Sinai when he went into cardiac arrest and died. Another devastating blow.

I stayed home for a few weeks, unable to go back to work. When I finally returned to the office, I realized that the only cure for tragedy is to stay occupied. It gives you less time to think.

Sometime in 1975. I began dating Priscilla Perasso, a young women who worked as an executive secretary for Bob Quinn, a partner at Salomon. What started out as a light-hearted friendship developed into a serious romance, and in 1978 we were married.

Priscilla introduced some light into my life, as well as a little order. She made me buy a headboard for my bed, for example, and she taught me to buy four or five well-made suits at a time rather than picking up clothes an item at a time in Florida, Newport, New York, or wherever I happened to be.

With my bride Priscilla, who gets lovelier with every passing year.

Priscilla and I settled down in Lawrence. I'd also had a home built on the beautiful island of Normans Cay in the Bahamas, completed in 1973. It came about when I visited my friend Alan Smith and his wife Mary in Miami. Alan founded the second oldest real estate investment trust in the U.S., and his company had lent money to the developers of Normans Cay. I'd always thought about building a vacation home, and Alan helped me make it happen. He showed me the layout of the island and helped me to pick a lot, a builder, and architect. My lot was on a cut between Normans and Saddle Cay to the north, with a small island in the midst of the emerald green water. On windy winter days, large waves would send up huge sprays as they hit the rocks.

Six houses were being built by the same builder, including one for Alan himself, and our architect gave us monthly progress reports and photos. My house had a master bedroom on the north end, a combined living room, dining room, and kitchen with cathedral ceiling, and three bedrooms on the south end. There was a large screened porch, a patio, and a generator house adjoining the driveway. A cistern held the only fresh water available, and the showering and washing were almost as stingy as in my submarine days.

Normans Cay was beautiful, some four miles long with a two-mile-long fish-hooked back. There were several lovely beaches, a club on the southern tip of the island with a public bar and restaurant, and a handful of rental huts on the beach. Sailboats lay at anchor in the harbor. The

The house at Norman Cay.

airport was about a quarter of a mile from the club house.

The club was managed by a Philadelphian named Alan Emblem, who, as my cousin Dick Taaffe once remarked, "drank so many martinis that the olives were growing out of his head."

There were strange happenings at the club from time to time. I was sitting in the club house one day when a plane landed. Soon a group of men with several girls in skimpy bathing suits were seen walking toward the club. That night after dinner, I was standing at the bar with my neighbor when a steel band suddenly showed up, along with the guys and gals from the plane. My neighbor spoke to one of the girls. "Are you all married couples?"

She replied, "The men are married, but we are all single."

The capper was the appearance of a young lady with a card asking the men whom they would like to be paired with for the night.

On another occasion, my son Garry introduced me to a couple of ladies named Goldie and Sheila, who knew some friends of mine in

View from the porch.

Toronto. Over drinks at the club, Sheila remarked, "I love this island so much that I'm thinking of buying a place here." Knowing that Alan Smith was interested in selling his place, I invited the two ladies over to my house for cocktails that evening. Alan would be there, and if he could close a deal I would charge him a special reduced commission.

The cocktail hour was in full swing with my usual crowd of older conservative friends when in walked the two ladies, both dressed in skin-tight jumpsuits with front zippers opened all the way down to here. What followed was one of the more embarrassing evenings of my life, with Goldie clinging to my side and remarking over and over, "Oh Dick, what a beautiful person you are."

When I arrived at the club for breakfast the next morning, I got the scoop on my two friends. Island gossip reported that Goldie was a hooker, Sheila her booker. The two had been caught servicing the natives and politely invited by the authorities to take the next flight and sin no more—at least not on Normans Cay.

The island also proved to offer some opportunities for espionage, deliberate or inadvertent. One day, I was sitting in the club having lunch with the radio on in the background. Lo and behold, a familiar voice suddenly filled the room—that of Paul Miller, then Chairman of First Boston. He was on a yacht negotiating an equity offering for the Aluminum Company of America, and due to some quirk in the ship-to-shore radio transmission his words were being piped through the Caribbean. I thought about leaving the room to avoid eavesdropping on a competitor, but finally figured, "Why should I inconvenience myself?" I finished my hamburger listening to Miller debate whether First Boston should cut the size of its offering.

My next trip to Normans Cay was scheduled in the midst of negotiations for deals involving DuPont Canada, the Bowery Savings Bank, and Bell Canada. I knew I would have to go over the details with a young fellow in our syndicate department nicknamed Rochey, so, recalling what had happened to Paul Miller, I decided to use code names to disguise our dealings.

"Remember, Rochey," I said, "no names. Instead of DuPont Canada, say Little D. Instead of Bowery, say The Bum. And instead of Bell Canada, say The Ding Dong. Got it?"

"I got it," Rochey promised. I was proud of my cleverness and figured that the master spy Intrepid of World War II fame had nothing on me.

I arrived in Normans Cay and called the syndicate department for an update.

"How are things going, Rochey?" I asked.

"It looks like the Bowery is going to buy all the five-year DuPont of Canada notes at ex rate."

"Rochey, I told you no names."

"Oh, I forgot. Sorry."

"What about The Ding Dong?"

"Well Aetna is in for five. The Travelers and Prudential are going to be big. They like Bell Canada."

"Rochey, I said no names!"

"Oh, I forgot."

When I saw Rochey at a Salomon reunion in 1995, I greeted him with, "Remember Rochey, no names!"

He laughed and said, "Okay, I got it this time!"

Life on the island also had its unique native side. One time a couple of tennis courts were built on the island, but before they could be used the nets disappeared. It seems that some of the local residents were using them to catch fish.

Another time one of the Bahamians approached me to ask for help in building a church on the island.

"How much do you need?" I asked.

"We can do the whole thing—chairs, prayer books, everything—for five hundred dollars. Best of all, if we ever leave the island, we'll deed the church to you."

I missed a good opportunity there. I could have set myself up as the Bishop of Normans Cay rather than knocking myself out at Salomon.

For a few years, my family and I enjoyed the island. We spent our days fishing, visiting the beaches, diving for crayfish, collecting conch, and admiring the peacocks at dusk. My son Michael used to build bonfires on the beach at night with his friend Tommy Rosen and drove around the island in our little Dodge at the age of fourteen.

Then times changed. The island was bought by a land company owned by Donaldson, Lufkin & Jenrette, then sold a few years later to a shoestring operator. The quality of our neighbors began to go downhill. Charlie Beckwith, the head of Sea World in Florida, who owned a nearby house overlooking the ocean, sold out to Carlos "Joe" Lehder, the son of a reputed ex-Nazi who had become one of the richest coffee growers in Columbia. Carlos himself was the largest exporter of cocaine from Columbia into the U.S. Lookout posts manned by German bodyguards were built around the island, and boats could be seen out on the horizon at night flashing signals to Lehder's cronies on shore. Priscilla found herself being followed and having planes buzzing her while she tried to sunbathe on the beach.

It got to where there was only one neighbor I trusted, Dr. Ray Dillon, who lived outside of Boston and owned a place on the island with his wife Dodie. Ray was the first Army doctor to attend to General George Patton after his fatal car accident in Germany in 1945, and he'd twice sailed around the world with the adventurer Irving Johnson on the yacht *America*. He was also a ham radio operator and a skilled mechanic who used to repair my generator and the motor of my boat as well as keeping an old World War I jeep in running order.

I believe the Lehder gang left Dillon and me alone to lend the island a veneer of respectability. On several occasions, the island was raided by police and Bahamian authorities—always an hour or two after Lehder and his entourage had departed.

Eventually, I stopped wanting to visit Normans Cay. Finally, Dillon and I headed down there together for the first time in two years, accompanied by my son Steve. We went to Dillon's house first, where we discovered that Lehders' Columbians had been living there. It was a pigsty.

Next we went to my house. As we entered, Steve remarked, "Well, everything looks in order here."

"Yes," I said, "except that we don't have a cat." There was a bowl of milk on the floor next to the refrigerator.

The appearance of normality vanished when I went into the master bedroom. There were several thousand dollars' worth of stereo equipment, a safe, strange pictures on the wall, and closets full of unfamiliar clothes, shoes, and cowboy boots. Priscilla's clothes and mine had evidently been thrown away. To top it all off, the squatter had gotten wind of my arrival and had used my plane to make his escape.

It turned out that the bad guy living in my house had been a Bahamian I knew by the name of Steve Francis. The police sergeant in charge of our case said to me, "I can't believe he knew it was your house."

I replied, "Oh, you can't, can't you? His father built my house, his uncle put a new roof on it, two years ago and you don't think he knew it was my house?"

Steve and I proceeded to rip up and throw away his extensive wardrobe, right down to the boots. The police left with the safe as well as some diaries and books that indicated a Cuban connection. Master swindler Robert Vesco was reported to be on Normans Cay island at times before fleeing to Cuba to avoid prosecution. My guess is that Vesco knows too much ever to be returned alive to the U.S.

That night, Steve and I stayed at Ray Dillon's. Around ten, I said, "Guess I'll turn in."

Steve said, "How can you sleep, knowing who might be out there?"

I replied, "Steve, when I was on the submarine, we were going through a minefield one night. I started to think about it, but then I said to myself, There's nothing I can do about it, so I'm going to sleep. Well, there isn't anything I can do about the bad guys tonight, so I am going to sleep."

I got a good night's sleep. When I woke up, there was Steve, sitting up in bed with a monkey wrench beside him.

"Have you been up all night?" I asked.

"Not only that. I heard a noise during the night. Good thing I had the wrench. I went outside, heard somebody moving around in the garage, and I quietly sneaked up on him."

"Wow. Who was it?"

"Dr. Dillon. He was working on that darn jeep of his."

Lehder's tentacles reached everywhere on Normans Cay. There was a young fellow on the island named Ed Ward who lived with his wife Lacie in an expensive home that sported several generators, a dock, and a fancy boat—plus he flew an expensive looking plane. I remarked one day to Priscilla, "You know, I made pretty good money when I was Ed's age, but couldn't afford his toys." That's because I picked the wrong profession. It turned out that Ed and his brother-in-law worked for Lehder.

One day back home in Lawrence, Long Island, a couple of men from the Treasury department showed up and asked to talk to me. The subject was Normans Cay. "How well do you know Ed Ward and his wife Lacie?" they asked.

I shrugged. "It's a small island. I've probably been in his house for drinks a couple of times, and he was in my house once."

Thereupon one of the feds reached into his pocket and pulled out a check. "Would you mind explaining why you paid Ed Ward $5,000?"

Luckily, I could. Ward had been doing some construction on the island, flying back and forth to Nassau to pick up materials frequently. On one of those trips, he offered to pick up a new generator for me. "See," I said, "It says 'new generator' right there on the memo line."

Once again I'd managed to avoid the slammer—more than some of my fellow financiers can say.

I went down to the island a few more times. On one occasion I was there with a few friends, having called some of my U.S. consulate friends in Nassau to inform them I was going over to the cay. "We'll look in on you over the weekend to make sure you're all right." Sure enough, we were sitting on the patio when suddenly a helicopter from the Bahamian American Team, a drug enforcement outfit, flew overhead with one Bahamian leaning out the window, machine gun in hand. The B.A.T. group landed on the road behind the house, strolled down for a warm beer, then flew away.

But life on Normans Cay was growing more and more chaotic. I got tired of having boats and engines stolen, and having my car hot-wired by the mob. Once the club shut down, Priscilla and I had to bring in all our supplies from outside, and we got tired of lugging fifteen boxes of stuff to the house every time we visited. As more and more houses were deserted, people started helping themselves to one another's furniture. On one of my last visits, I opened the front door of one of the abandoned houses and had a stampede of goats race past me.

It wasn't too hard for Priscilla to convince me to move our winter residence to Florida, where civilization still reigned.

Lehder was eventually apprehended in Columbia and brought back to Florida to stand trial. He was sentenced to life in prison. His number one deputy, Jack Reid, drew a long sentence of his own. Ed Ward and his wife testified against Lehder and, after a short prison term, went into the witness protection program.

Normans Cay wasn't my only diversion from working at Salomon. I got involved in supporting the United Nations Association (UNA), an organization devoted to supporting U.S. involvement in the UN and educating Americans about important global issues, from international trade to arms control to humanitarian relief efforts. I served as a vice chairman of UNA during the tenure of ambassadors Bill Scranton, Andrew Young, George W. Bush, Jeanne Kirkpatrick, and Thomas Pickering. It wasn't an easy time to be a defender of the UN, since the organization was not high on most Americans' list of their favorite institutions. For a while the credit of the UNA was so shaky I had to personally guarantee its commercial paper borrowings with Chemical Bank.

Another long-time commitment of mine was to the National Policy Association (NPA) in Washington, D.C.. Founded as the National Planning Association during World War II, the NPA included business, academic, and labor leaders. It provided valuable input into the Marshall Plan and the reconstruction of Europe and later addressed many vital issues affecting government, industry, and labor. I served as the U.S. chairman of the NPA's Canadian American Committee and later as the non-executive chair of the National Policy Committee. One of the studies I helped finance was *New*

Meeting Soviet Prime Minister Mikhail Gorbachev at the United Nations. On the left is John Whitehead of Goldman Sachs, then chairman of the United Nations Association.

Directions: African Americans in a Diversifying Nation, edited by Professor James S. Jackson of the University of Michigan, which eventually sold more copies than any other NPA publication.

My good friend Mooen Qureshi, formerly of the World Bank, later Prime Minister of Pakistan, and now head of the Emerging Market Fund, succeeded me at NPA until the organization's demise several years ago.

For about fifteen years I served on the board and investment committee of the Americas Society, chaired for many years by David Rockefeller, whose mission was to strengthen the hemispheric ties among the US, Canada, and the nations of Central and South America. Under David's leadership, the organization grew in strength, numbers, and financial strength.

For a number of years, I served on the board of Covenant House, which had originated as a small shelter for street kids in downtown New York run by a Franciscan priest named Bruce Ritter. By the time I got involved, it had become the largest private provider of shelter and job training for street kids in the country, with branches

Surrounded by a raucous group of residents from the Covenant House "Rites of Passage" program.

in Latin America and Canada as well, and Father Ritter was being toasted by presidents, senators, congressmen, and CEOs.

In 1989, the board was in the process of converting the operation from one-man rule into a more sustainable, self-perpetuating organization, when disaster struck. A former male prostitute accused Father Ritter of sexual misconduct with him. In time, a few other young men came forward with similar allegations, and evidence surfaced of a secret trust fund that Father Ritter had tapped to lend money to family and friends.

Father Ritter resigned, and the board came under tremendous pressure. It included quite a few luminaries from business and government, including the late Ralph Pfiffer, former president of IBM International; Denis Coleman from Bear Stearns; Ellen Levine of the Hearst magazine empire; the late Nancy Dickerson Whitehead, the famous Washington newscaster; Bill Finneran of Oppenheimer; former treasury secretary the late Bill Simon; and Frank Macchiarola, former superintendent of the New York City school system and now president of St. Francis College in Brooklyn.

Eventually, an internal investigation suggested that Father Ritter had engaged in sex with some of the young men at the shelter.

A White House meet-and-greet. From left: David Rockefeller, Vice President Dan Quayle, me, and George Landau, president of the Americas Society.

However, all of the trust fund monies were accounted for, and no criminal charges were ever filed. Father Ritter retired to upstate New York and died in 1999.

What happened to Father Ritter, who had once been a hero to many of us, was very sad. Sadder still was its impact on Covenant House, whose reputation was unfairly besmirched by the cloud of accusations that settled around its founder.

I served on the search committee charged with finding a new leader for Covenant House. We interviewed several candidates and finally came up with what turned out to be a brilliant choice—Sister Mary Rose McCready, who did a remarkable job of building the organization and expanding its reach and financial capacity, receiving twenty-odd honorary degrees from various colleges and universities. Upon her retirement, she was succeeded by Sister Patricia Cruise. I still support Covenant House financially and serve as an Honorary Director.

Today the organization is still active and provides services to thousands of homeless and runaway youth every year. It's nice that my success in business enabled me to give something back to a group that has done so much to help kids who are in desperate need of a break in life.

Chapter 11
Caught in the Crossfire

As Salomon rose to the top of the investment banking universe, during the late seventies and through the eighties, my colleagues and I were working very hard. The results were enormously gratifying. But with success comes responsibility, stress, and often conflict.

When I first ran corporate finance, it wasn't providing substantial profits to the firm, and there was a good bit of deserved criticism. There were, however, a number of contributions that the rest of the firm overlooked. For example, corporate finance did a lot of what I would consider research and development. It took time to build corporate relations. After we spent months or years building a solid investment banking relationship, we would open the door to other sales and trading people, leading to profitable deals involving pension funds, stock repurchases, sinking funds, currency swaps, hedging and short term investments. So the valuable time we invested ended up producing benefits for the firm that appeared on someone else's bottom line.

Texaco is a perfect example. I built a relationship there with Pete Whistle, the vice president of finance, followed by Dick Brinkman. We did several bareboat charters for them, which accrued to corporate finance. We also did several bond issues for Texaco and represented them in their failed bid for Conoco, as I mentioned earlier. Somewhere along the line, they called me to do a debt-for-equity transaction. Salomon made three million dollars on the transaction, divided between the industrial desk and the equity department. It was great business for the firm, and I didn't care about getting the credit, but unfortunately these kinds of deals often got overlooked when people wondered what corporate finance did for Salomon.

Another time, Texaco approached us about a debt-for-equity deal promising some three million in profit. There was only one thing wrong: Texaco had made the mistake of buying some bonds before-hand, which violated the rules requiring the whole deal to be done simultaneously. I discussed the problem with our in-house attorney Don Feuerstein and our outside consul Cleary Gottlieb. Both agreed that Texaco and Salomon could face criminal charges if we went through with the transaction, and I didn't care for the idea of becoming a jailbird. However, when I reported our legal advice to Texaco, I was chastised for speaking to outside lawyers without their permission. I got so ticked off that I wouldn't call the treasurer for a couple of months. We didn't really bury the hatchet until his retirement dinner.

Sometimes, we overlook the pressure from higher up on our clients. I believe there was a great deal of pressure on my friend at Texaco.

There were many other instances where corporate finance devoted time and energy to deals that mainly benefited other divisions of the firm. For example, we did a $50 million bond deal with one of our clients with little or no profit so that John Merriweather's group could do a hedge transaction worth two million dollars or so.

Another time, the municipal department implored us to bring in industrial revenue bond business, telling me they were earning a two and a half point spread on industrial revenue bonds. Accordingly, I made this a high priority, and did our first industrial revenue bond with the Borden Company. However, some time later the municipal people informed me they were losing money on their deals. I asked, "How can that be?"

The answer: "We had to overpay to get the business. We gave back our commission, and then some."

Thank God I was fired off the municipal desk at an early age. I didn't understand the business then, and I suppose I never will.

In an effort to get fairer treatment for corporate finance, Harold Tanner and I came up with a system we called "phantom credits on profits," where we listed transactions that we helped arrange that accrued to other departments. For some reason, this irritated the other departments. So be it.

I don't mean to imply that corporate finance went completely without glory. During my seven years running the division, we were number one in bond issues in the U.S. six times. We also moved up substantially in the equity tables, from seventh place to fourth, then third, then second.

Our efforts in the Euro dollar market fell short, however, partly because Salomon's traders made too many demands on our European corporate finance people to do Euro issues rather than build good corporate relationships. As a result, one year we grossed all of four thousand dollars on one hundred and forty odd issues we participated in—issues that took up hundreds of people hours that could have been spent pursuing more profitable business. Actually, if you look at the time spent, the number of traders and people from our syndicate, sales, and operations departments who were involved, and the huge number of trades where securities were delivered or received late, you realize that Salomon lost many millions pursuing Euro dollar offerings.

Some partners wanted to do away with corporate finance as a profit center. The effect would have been the same as putting us in the middle of the Sahara without a canteen at compensation time. I countered with this proposal: "Look, if you want to assign everyone to a profit center, let's do it this way. Take the Analyst, Sales Trading, and Operations people in different divisions—banking, utilities, and so on—and see what their return is overall. Then let's do the same with all the other groups." This idea generated strong opposition from the traders, who (rightly) feared the results. After I left the firm, Don Howard joined Salomon from Citigroup and instituted the system I'd proposed, with results that were rather shocking.

It so happened that I had breakfast with Howard the day after he accepted the position with Salomon. "Do you have any advice for me?" he asked.

"Just this," I replied, "If you ever have to step away from a meeting, be sure to ask what happened while you were out of the room."

I had good reason for making this recommendation. One time, I left a meeting early to begin a scheduled trip, having been told that the business was completed. When I returned, I learned that two of my executive partners had recommended abolishing corporate finance as a profit center in my absence.

I was furious and told Gutfreund, "This is the most insulting thing that has ever happened to me at Salomon." Both partners later apologized, and the matter was dropped.

On another occasion, when the executive committee had been naming managing directors and senior vice presidents, I asked whether they were done. I was assured that the books were closed, and I left for a business trip to California. The following morning, when I called in from the airport, I found out that two senior vice presidents had been added in another finance department, causing me and Harold Tanner a great deal of embarrassment. I guess, as the great philopher Yogi Berra used to say, "It ain't over till it's over," especially at Salomon Brothers.

$$* \quad * \quad *$$

Through it all, my grueling schedule of international travel continued unabated. Not that it was without compensations. One of my most enjoyable trips of the early eighties was my first visit to Australia since my days of submarine duty. Through Jim Wolfensohn, who had a wealth of contacts in his native land, Salomon did a huge lease transaction with the Eraring Power Station for the state of New South Wales Power Commission, and I visited Australia for the closing ceremony.

On the way down, I stopped in Tokyo to visit our office and meet some Japanese clients. I also squeezed in some tennis with my good friend the late Yo Korasawa, President of the Industrial Bank of Japan, who'd taken up the game late in life. Yo suggested doubles, saying he had the best player in the bank to be his partner. I teamed up with a young colleague named Neil Benedict, and we played five sets on a hard indoor surface. The results were pretty one-sided. On several occasions, after Benedict hammered one of his hard serves at Yo, I took him aside and pleaded, "Neil, let up. I can't keep dumping on my serve to make it interesting." Neil's competitive juices kept flowing, and the final results were USA 5, Japan 0.

We then went to dinner, sitting in cross-legged Japanese style on a hard wooden floor. A geisha "girl" who had seen better days entertained us, with Yo serving as translator. A typical exchange went like this.

Geisha: "You are very handsome."

Dick: "Tell her I am Clark Gable's younger brother, Irving. I own a haberdashery in Brooklyn."

When the evening ended, I limped back to my hotel. Everything hurt—back, knees, ankles, you name it. Fearing that I would be too crippled to attend any meetings in the morning, I called the front desk to arrange a massage. In a few minutes, a little old lady arrived in my room. Since I struggle to understand several languages, including English, I had no idea what kind of massage to expect. The next thing I knew, the little old lady was identifying sensitive pressure points and plunging needles into them—my first brush with acupuncture. By the morning, my pains had miraculously disappeared.

From Tokyo, it was on to Sydney, where the closing dinner was to be a formal affair. I'd been determined not to lug a tux halfway around the world, but when I attempted to rent a tux, they didn't have anything that fit a six foot two-and-a-half inch Yank. This explains my appearance in the ceremonial photo with the Australian bankers and Neville Rand, the Premier of New South Wales, in which three to four inches of white shirt sleeves protrude from the arms of my tux.

Wolfensohn had arranged for several of us to visit with Bob Hawke, the prime minister of Australia, and Paul Keating, the treasurer. Our group included Peter Gottsegen, Neil Benedict, and Trevor Rowe, who managed our Australian business and later joined our office in Sydney. Trevor's great grandfather had been one of the exiles that the British sent to Australia; his father was a bricklayer, and Trevor was built like one of those bricks. He liked to remind Neil Benedict, an Englishman, that his great grandfather used to say, "If you ever meet a pommy [a Brit], give him one for me." Neil would grin nervously and edge away.

It wasn't the only time Neil's nationality generated controversy. During the Falkland Islands war of 1982, Neil occupied an office in Salomon next to Eduardo Mestre, whose family had fled Castro's Cuba and settled in Argentina. Neil followed the news on his office radio and would come rushing out to enthusiastically announce British triumphs, drawing angry glares from Eduardo. We implored Neil to tone down the victory laps.

Soon after my return to America, I received a call from an Australian news reporter in Washington. He asked for my comments on the Australian dollar, saying, "I heard you're an expert on the Australian economy."

I said, "Well, I was in Australia forty years ago in my navy days, and I just returned from a one-week visit. If you think that makes me an expert, that's up to you." (I'll never understand how these things get started.) Then I offered my opinion on the Australian dollar— seriously overvalued.

Salomon had earned a large fee on the Eraring lease transaction, and since we had no office in the country, the New South Wales people were concerned that we were going to take the money and leave. This led to a huge amount of hedging in various currencies after the closing. Back in New York, Peter Gottsegen and I recommended that Salomon open an office in Sydney, the Executive Committee gave its okay, and Trevor Rowe was appointed manager.

We approached Australia much as we had Canada. Peter Gottsegen, John Brim, Roy Claus, and I made several trips down under, visiting with the governments of New South Wales and other states and renewing our relationships in Canberra with Paul Keating and Prime Minister Hawke. Hawke was a great tennis fan and spoke

Surrounded by tennis greats Rod Laver and Roy Emmerson.
Notice which of us looks tired.

glowingly of the great Australian players Rod Laver, Roy Emmerson, Ron Anderson, Fred Stole, and Ken Rosewall, all of whom beat me in grueling matches (grueling for me, that is). Thanks to Roy Claus, then a young man in corporate finance who generously let me win our matches, I remain undefeated in Australia and New Zealand.

Trevor quickly created a thriving business. We did underwritings for several states and became a co-manager for the Commonwealth of Australia alongside their traditional banker, Morgan Stanley.

On another occasion, I visited Europe with former ambassador Henry Owen, who had orchestrated two summit meetings for President Jimmy Carter. Of all the consultants we hired over the years, he was the best, an outsider with an excellent feel for the business who knew how to write a ticket.

Our trip started in Austria, where Henry scheduled meetings for us practically around the clock. One day, for example, we started off with a breakfast meeting around 7:00 a.m., followed by seven more meetings. We got back to the hotel around 7:00 p.m. I was planning to take a quick nap before our planned a dinner with the minister of finance at 8:45. I'd scarcely put my head down when the phone rang. It was Henry, letting me know he'd arranged an 8:00 p.m. meeting with a banker. General George S. Patton would have had trouble keeping up with Henry.

From Austria, we went on to Bonn, where we lunched with U.S. Ambassador Arthur Burns, previously head of the Federal Reserve Bank, and a contingent from Salomon. Burns, who always sounded to me like the old comic actor W.C. Fields, started the conversation by asking Henry who was going to speak for Salomon. Henry replied, "Mr. Schmeelk."

"Okay," Burns said, "You have three minutes."

I replied, "I only need two." Sure enough, I did our entire pitch in two minutes—with seconds to spare.

After Germany, we went on to Denmark and then back home through London via the Concorde. It was during the flight from Copenhagen to London that my stomach finally rebelled against three hectic days on the road. By the time we touched down at Kennedy Airport I was wiped out, physically and psychologically.

It was my last trip to Australia that convinced me to retire. After late-night receptions to celebrate office openings in Melbourne and

Sydney, we flew in a small rented plane to Canberra early in the morning, then back for a luncheon meeting in Sydney, and then back to Canberra for dinner. This was followed by a 5:45 a.m. flight to Sydney and another flight back to the U.S.A.

At a certain age, this kind of itinerary becomes a bit much.

* * *

Business and politics inevitably collide, nowhere more so than in the energy arena.

I've tracked American energy policy for three decades now. I recall President Nixon setting the goal of making the U.S. energy independent by the end of his second term. That goal didn't survive Nixon's second term—and, of course, neither did Nixon. President Jimmy Carter then launched an alternative energy program which did next to nothing. Now, thirty years later, literally nothing has been done to increase our self-sufficiency, a failure that I find incredible.

The underlying reason, of course, is the economic facts of life: It's inevitable that low-cost energy sources will always be developed first. Today, with oil at record high price levels, alternative energy sources are becoming increasingly attractive. I believe we'll see further large hydroelectric power plants developed by companies like Hydro Quebec. I also believe we will have to go back to building nuclear plants. Electric cars are on the horizon, as the success of the hybrid Prius indicates. Furthermore, we have to expand our capacity for refining oil, despite the protests of environmentalists and the not-in-my-backyard crowd; the fact that our country has not built a refinery since 1976 is a disgrace.

With continued political uncertainty in the Middle East, as well as the advent of Chavez, the Castro-like leader of oil producing Venezuela, I believe the time for a North American Energy Policy has come. Canada, Mexico and the United States should be coordinating their energy policies more closely, working to ensure that North America is not dependent on unreliable foreign powers for our energy needs.

The politics of oil was deeply involved in one of the most controversial episodes in my time at Salomon, our merger with Phibro, the large commodity trading firm.

Phibro had made a lot of money under Mark Rich, who later was forced to flee the country to avoid criminal prosecution. (President Bill Clinton later granted a controversial pardon to Rich, who currently resides in Israel and Switzerland.) When Phibro approached Salomon about a possible merger in 1981, its chairman was the well-respected Ludwick Jesselson, and its two chief operating officers were David Tendler and Hal Beritz.

Salomon's business was growing strongly at the time, and we knew we'd need an infusion of capital to keep up with our expansion capabilities. This made a merger an attractive possibility. However, we'd dismissed the idea of merging with a commercial bank or insurance company. This left Phibro, a trading company. I realized this would please our competitors, who liked to put us down as a firm already dominated by traders.

Unfortunately, Salomon's due diligence on Phibro left a lot to be desired. We were told Phibro had a strong project financing team, that they were skilled at trading currencies, and that they had great loyalty from their people and enjoyed low employee turnover. All of these assertions turned out to be false. After the merger, we found out that the only real money Phibro made was from trading oil.

We were also told that Phibro had been operating without problems in the Arab countries. This was important to us, since Saudi Arabia and especially Kuwait were clients of Salomon. Imagine our shock when Salomon was promptly blacklisted by the Arab nations as soon as the merger was announced.

It was very difficult to get a straight story out of Phibro as to why they were on the blacklist. Eventually we discovered that the reason was that Phibro was the largest American buyer of Israel war bonds.

In hopes of resolving this problem, I arranged a trip to Saudi Arabia with former Secretary of State Cyrus Vance and Dick Beattie of Simpson Thatcher. It was fascinating traveling with a former secretary of state. As soon as we landed in Jeddah, six Mercedes pulled up to escort us into the city, blocking off other traffic and roaring down the highway at speeds between 70 and 80 miles per hour. I referred to our escorts as the Saudi Blue Angels.

Our travels took us to Riyadh Tief, the summer capital, where we visited the foreign ministry and the U.S. consulate. Cy Vance received a grand welcome everywhere we went, with even ordinary Saudis in restaurants and hotels recognizing and greeting him. (I kidded Dick

Beattie: "Don't feel bad, Dick. They must not realize that you were a star in the backfield at Dartmouth.")

Saudi Arabia was in the midst of a tremendous building boom. "Our national bird," people joked, "is the crane." Signs of Saudi grandiosity were everywhere; on one avenue in Riyadh, for example, we passed a replica of the White House, just a little smaller than life-size, that one of the princes had built for himself.

On the diplomatic side, our trip was only partially successful. We bought a little time and managed to do a few more profitable deals, but we landed on the blacklist for good several months later. As a result, several international firms dropped Salomon from under-writing syndicates in order to solicit business from Arab countries. Whenever possible, we returned the favor. When Nomura, the Japanese powerhouse, excluded us from a World Bank offering, we arranged to give Nomura the bounce on the next large World Bank issue we brought to market in the U.S.

Thankfully, being on the blacklist didn't hurt Salomon too much. We continued to do business in Kuwait through intermediaries, and only had to lose out less-substantial Saudi Arabian business.

Cy Vance and I became good friends, and I have several favorite stories that show his human side.

One time, I was giving Cy and my partner Peter Gottsegen a ride uptown on a rainy night. As we approached the FDR Drive, we spotted a young woman lying on the road—an accident victim. We parked, and Cy rushed to help the young lady, covering her with his coat, while Peter went to call an ambulance and I directed traffic.

As the young woman was being lifted into the ambulance, I told her who had been taking care of her. She couldn't believe it.

On another occasion, my wife Priscilla and I were having dinner in a nice restaurant with Cy and his wife Gay. The service did not go smoothly. First, the waiter spilled a glass of wine on me. Then, after dinner, a young busboy clearing the table knocked over a glass of water, causing a flood that carried bits of food from my plate onto my shirt, necktie, and trousers. Of course, I mopped up the damage as best I could and laughed off the incident.

Later the maitre d' approached us. "I hope everything has been all right," he said.

"Just fine," I responded.

"That's a very unusual design on your tie, Mr. Schmeelk," the maitre d' remarked.

"Yes, it's spinach," Priscilla said with a laugh.

Now the maitre d' realized what had happened, and he asked if there was anything he could do. "Call over the busboy," I suggested. Understandably, he was cowering in the corner, avoiding us.

The busboy came over to our table. "Is this your first day on the job?" I asked him.

"Yes."

"I thought so. And what's your name?"

"Christian."

"Well, Christian, I think you should have a little memento from your first day."

At my suggestion, Cy Vance pulled out his pen and wrote a quick note: "To Christian—Good luck on your new job! Sincerely, Cyrus Vance." We all had a good laugh.

On another memorable occasion, Cy, Gay, Priscilla and I had dinner at the home of Jimmy the barber and his wife Rosa. Jimmy cut hair for the Salomon partners and knew Cy from their shared interest in the Boy's Club, a charitable organization they both supported. After dinner, we all went to the Westbury Music Fair to hear Perry Como, a long-time fellow victim of Jimmy's clippers. It made Jimmy very proud to introduce Perry to Cy Vance after the concert.

Jimmy was quite a character. While giving me a trim, he would recite the list of the nine partners at Salomon whose hair he colored, and then say, "Why don't you let me color your hair?"

I would reply, "Because, Jimmy, I would be number ten on the list."

He would answer, "No, you're family. I won't give out *your* name."

Jimmy sold jewelry and watches on the side. Our lives at Salomon were so busy that many of us forgot to shop for birthdays, anniversaries, and other occasions. A couple of times I bought something from Jimmy at the last minute. Somehow Priscilla could always tell. "I know where you got that—take it back to Jimmy."

Anyway, to get back to the Phibro story: Following the merger, we made an effort to uncover possible synergies between the two firms. I appointed Peter Gottsegen, who headed international corporate finance, to liaison with Phibro. Unfortunately, there were no synergies to be had. Salomon dealt at a high level with industrialist and government entities, Phibro dealt way down in the trenches, and their way of doing business made us uncomfortable. They had a bank in Zug, Switzerland, that at first blush we thought could be valuable to Salomon. On closer examination, we decided we didn't like the operation and quickly sold the bank.

There was one big positive from the merger—the access to capital that Salomon had been seeking. When Ronald Reagan lowered taxes, we were able to bring home some one billion dollars in oil trading profits that Phibro had been holding in Europe and pay a tax rate of around 11 percent. This money was useful, since Salomon was expanding rapidly—too rapidly, perhaps.

Walter Wriston, then chairman of Citibank, offered an astute comment on the merger: "We'll have to see what will happen now that the golden handcuffs are gone." Walter was referring to the restraints on capital that the Salomon partners labored under. It took years to get your capital out of the firm. Under the system at that time, we received an annual salary in the $50 thousand to $75 thousand range, our taxes were paid by the firm, and our earnings went back into the business. Every year, we were allowed to withdraw just five percent interest (as well as to give some $3,500 to each of our children).

This system made Salomon partners into what I called "Sunfish sailors." There were no yachts in the partnership. Most of our money was on the Salomon books.

Here's an example of the practical consequences. In 1973, after my first wife, Betty, died, I was in the process of selling my old house for $80,000 and buying a new house for $132,000. In order to get through the purchase and sale, I had to borrow $75,000 from Chemical Bank and another $75,000 from the firm, "to be returned at my earliest convenience." This after having been a partner since 1966.

Well, after the Phibro deal, the Sunfish sailors had their hands on a lot of capital.

This initially led to greater profits for the firm. But it also meant that the culture at Salomon began to change. Under the old system, there was a strong work ethic and sense of sharing—"all for one and one for all." When the golden handcuffs came off, the atmosphere changed, and several important partners left. Some saw the opportunity to do other things; others didn't like the direction management was going. For a combination of reasons, a wealth of talent departed Salomon.

Several partners who'd participated financially in the Phibro transaction were actually asked to leave. It was quite painful to hear about them being shown the door just after celebrating their new riches. Salomon was never accused of having a tender touch.

Perhaps the most notable departure was that of Mike Bloomberg. Everyone who was a member of the executive committee at the time claims credit—or blame—for casting the deciding vote against Mike. In fact, mine was the decisive vote, which means I'm responsible for his fabulous post-Salomon career. You'd think he might have shown me greater appreciation—I wouldn't mind being named Honorary Mayor of New York. (Truth be told, I didn't really cast the deciding vote. It was a unanimous decision.)

In any case, Mike's success since his departure from Salomon has become legendary. He grew up in Medford, Massachusetts, a blue-collar community near Boston, where his father was an accountant at the local dairy and his mother was a woman of "liberal views" (Mike's own phrase). Michael has a curious, inquisitive mind. After attending the local high school, he attended John Hopkins, then Harvard Business School. He joined Salomon and eventually became an equity trader under Jay Perry. Perry definitely lacked people skills, and during his rise to (short-lived) fame he made a number of enemies. Some of this was bound to rub off on a bright but brash trader named Bloomberg.

Mike also did battle with a bright, erratic young arbitrageur, named Dick Rosenthal, a high school dropout who eventually became a member of Salomon's executive committee. Inevitably, if you don't have a strong clear mandate, you end up in turf wars. Mike went from trading equities into operations, looking at Salomon's technology and systems. Unfortunately, when you're operating in someone else's back yard without a clear mandate, you become vulnerable. That's why Mike's head rolled the week of the Phibro takeover. (He describes all these struggles in his entertaining book *Bloomberg on Bloomberg,* which I strongly recommend.)

As for Dick Rosenthal, he later left Salomon and died flying his own plane returning from a board meeting at Syracuse University on a very stormy day.

Getting fired was the best thing that ever happened to Mike

Bloomberg. He used his money to start the Bloomberg financial information service, which he has since built into a billion-dollar business. Then he startled the political world by getting elected mayor of New York in 2001 and handily re-elected four years later. Mike's dedication to philanthropic causes is overwhelming, making it very costly to be a friend or a former partner of his. He loves to challenge the fat cats to donate their wealth *now* rather than waiting till they die. As chairman of the John Hopkins University Board of Trustees, he gave the school a gift of $50 million, just one of many generous donations he has made.

What's next for Mike Bloomberg? Few mayors of New York have risen to higher political office, but I would never bet against Mike any time he sets his sight on a goal.

In the months following the merger, it became apparent to the executive committee that Phibro was not performing well. It didn't help matters when Tom O'Malley, the only moneymaker at Phibro, decided to leave. (He continued to be a real money machine at Tosco and other companies.)

Some new ventures were tried, with little success. For example, Phibro board member Dwayne Andreas arranged for John Gutfreund and Phibro's top management to visit Moscow and meet with Premier Mikhail Gorbachev and other top Kremlin leaders. Gutfreund returned quite excited to report that Phibro had signed an exclusive contract to market Russia's nickel exports. Several months later, Phibro's management gave its quarterly report at a board meeting. They had lost $50 million dollars trading nickel! "How could you lose money on nickel, given your exclusive deal with the Russians?" I asked. The answer: Phibro had shorted nickel for physical delivery. The Russians couldn't make delivery, and Phibro had to go into the market to cover their position.

Losses like these led to friction between David Tendler and John Gutfreund, co-chairmen of the combined Phibro Salomon. Some newspapers and financial publications reported that Gutfreund initiated a move to oust Tendler. Actually, it was the executive team that proposed a "reverse takeover," with Phibro generating a steady stream of losses. Henry Kaufman and I approached several directors, including Dwayne Andreas; Bill May, chancellor of New York University and former chairman of American Can; and Hank Greenberg, chairman of A.I.G. and a key member of the Phibro-

Salomon board. Meanwhile, David Tendler and Hal Beritz attempted to put together a buyout plan. This failed, pretty much sealing their fate at Phibro.

Over time, Salomon continued to slim down the Phibro operation, and it became a very insignificant part of the company.

As the eighties wore on, Salomon, along with just about every other firm on Wall Street, expanded too rapidly, taking on extra costs. As the firm entered new lines of business, such as real estate, interest rate swaps, and currency swaps, strong partners strove to build up their empires. Personnel were drafted from other areas to man the new frontiers, in which, unfortunately, the profit potential was sometimes greatly exaggerated.

Meanwhile, the instability and the accelerating quest for ever-new businesses caused serious problems. I remember one senior investment officer at a major insurance company calling Salomon to say, "You people have changed the salesman following our company three times in the last year. It has to stop—we're no longer willing to train your people."

After the August, 1987, break in the stock market, a dramatic contraction became inevitable. Suddenly the firm became cost-conscious, a freeze was put on hiring, and a substantial number of jobs were cut, not only in Salomon, but in the industry in general.

That summer, Salomon was a manager of an underwriting group that had guaranteed a fixed price to market a large offering of British Petroleum stock in North America. In addition to the U.S. managers, there was a tranch in Canada for the major Canadian firms, including Dominion Securities, MacLeod Young, Weir Nesbitt Thompson, Burns Frey, and Wood Gundy.

When the market collapsed in August, it was apparent that the syndicate would lose a ton of money if the underwriting went ahead at the agreed price. After some deliberation, Mrs. Thatcher's government decided to hold the syndicate to the agreed price. It was pretty bloody. The U.S. lead underwriters stood to lose around $250 million each, which the Canadian lead underwriters stood to lose $75 million each. (They had much less capital to begin with.)

All the major firms in the U.S. market survived. Salomon cut its loses substantially by trading shares of British Petroleum actively in the after market. But the Canadian picture was quite different— those firms could not survive independently. Tony Fell of Dominion,

Ted Medland of Wood Gundy, and Jack Lawrence of Burns Fry all called me, looking for a partner. The continuing upheaval ultimately led to alliances between Royal Bank and Dominion Securities, Canadian Imperial Bank and Wood Gundy, Scotia Bank and McLeod, and Bank of Montreal and Nesbitt Thompson. The only major Canadian firm *not* to do a deal at that time was Burns Fry, later to become Burns Nesbitt.

Later in 1987, I addressed the Empire Club in Toronto, with my good friend Ted Medland from Wood Gundy sitting on the dais. Looking at Ted, I ad-libbed this opening line: "Recently some of my good friends and I donated blood to the British Red Cross. We're awaiting knighthood as thanks from Mrs. Thatcher's government." I got some puzzled looks from those who didn't know about the bloodbath we'd taken over the BP stock underwriting.

Chapter 12
Farewell to Salomon

As the years passed, life at Salomon got to be less and less fun. The culture was changing. Here is a small example. For many years, the partners had held a year-end stag dinner at New York's 21 Club. It was great fun and everyone looked forward to it. While we men were doing out thing, my wife Priscilla would have dinner with four or five of the other wives. Later we would meet up at the 21 Club's bar, have one or two drinks together, and then call it a night. But in the early eighties, this tradition was upended. The stag party was replaced with a fancy dinner at the Metropolitan Museum of Art, with spouses included. I love women and especially my wife, but I missed the camaraderie of the old days.

Much more distressing was the infighting, which got pretty heavy at times. In combination with my strenuous work schedule and my responsibilities on the home front, the stress produced some very nasty migraine headaches. I remember sitting in airport lounges, paralyzed by pain and seeking a little quiet; invariably, it seemed, a couple of people would sit near me and start a loud conversation, which would add to my misery. Priscilla often found me in the middle of the night, sitting in the bathtub with a warm face cloth on my temple, trying desperately to get relief from my pain.

The annual compensation time was the period when I was most vulnerable to these attacks. The executive committee would rent a suite at the Waldorf, and each department would start the battle to obtain compensation and win new partnerships. One year, our negotiations had to be postponed for two days as a massive headache rendered me unfit for action.

Meanwhile, the fortunes of the firm were in decline. Salomon was suffering from a bloated organization, overly-rapid expansion, and a slowing economy. The resulting poor performance of Salomon's stock led to the creation of a task force to look at various business options. The verdict: Salomon would cut personnel and clamp down on expenses in general. More significantly, it would abandon the commercial paper and municipal bond businesses.

I thought we should stay in both businesses, while revamping the two departments. In commercial paper, we should have concentrated on large accounts, reduced the cost structure of the department, and strengthen its leadership. In municipal finance, salaries needed to be trimmed so as to bring the size of the department in line with its potential profitability.

About this time, Anglo American, the big South African mining company, decided to sell its block of Salomon's stock. Anglo was feeling neglected. After some early courting, they'd received little or no attention from Salomon's management, and when they'd raised the idea of increasing the dividend, they'd gotten nowhere. Hence their decision to sell. They gave the order to First Boston's Bruce Wasserstein, who approached Ron Perelman, who in turn expressed an interest in buying Salomon.

At this point, I'd stepped down from the executive committee in preparation for my ultimate retirement, although I'd remained on the board as a favor to John Gutfreund. But I was out of the loop on the South African deal. In fact, neither Ira Harris nor I were consulted, although we probably had more connections in corporate America than anyone else in Salomon's finance operation.

Perelman requested a meeting with Gutfreund, but the irate Salomon partners turned him down flat, and a great deal of pressure was exerted on First Boston to call off the dogs. In the end, Salomon called in the legendary investor Warren Buffett to act as the "white knight" and keep Salomon out of the hands of Perelman. But it took a sweetheart deal to get Buffett involved: a nine-percent convertible preferred stock issue with a sinking fund that gave the preferred a seven-year average life.

None of this was necessary, in my judgment. No one from

Salomon ever approached Hank Greenberg, the chairman and CEO of AIG, who served on the Phibro board and later the Salomon board. If given the opportunity, I think he would have made a bid and probably would have offered a better deal. But Hank was feared by various leaders of Salomon, who felt he would be too tough a boss.

Roger Lowenstein's book, *Buffett: The Making of An American Capitalist* offers some fascinating tales about Salomon. In particular, Lowenstein recounts the government bond scandal and senior management's failure to deal with the rogue trader Paul Mozer, whose actions precipitated the near-demise of Salomon. Although Buffett's involvement saved the firm temporarily, his latter moves in curtailing bonuses brought on a mass exodus of talent and probably helped force the ultimate sale of Salomon to Citicorp.

I can sympathize with Buffett's bewilderment over the compensation system in Wall Street. Although members of the executive committee always claimed that bonuses would go down when results were bad, in reality this never happened. Instead, when profits were down, we were always told, "We have to pay so-and-so at least as much as last year, or else we'll lose him to another firm." It didn't make a lot of sense—but Buffett's attempt to change the culture single-handedly was doomed to failure from the beginning.

Meanwhile, with Salomon floundering, I had told Gutfreund to reduce my salary from some three million plus (including bonuses) to 250 thousand. "In view of the performance of the firm," I added, "it might be a good idea for you and the executive committee to do the same."

I also lost out on the value of my options, which by now were well out of the money. When I asked, I was told that the cost of my options would not be reduced because I had made it known that I intended to retire soon. Two other partners handled it differently: They simply waited until after the fiscal year had ended to make known they were resigning. By then, they'd had their options reduced to a level that let them exercise the options profitably. But hey, I'd only put in forty years at the firm. What price loyalty?

Let me say that, from a philosophical perspective, I *don't* believe in reducing the price of options. The idea is to reward performance—not set up a heads-I-win, tails-you-lose equation. Capitalism means that sometimes you *don't* win, and I'm a believer in playing by the rules, not changing them after the game is over.

*   *   *

So by 1987, I'd had enough. Priscilla and I had gone to Bermuda for a week and I'd had a headache every day. When I visited the doctor upon my return, he informed me that I'd developed high blood pressure and hospitalized me for three days. When I got back to the office, I told Harold Tanner, my good friend and co-partner in corporate finance, that I didn't want to go through the year-end compensation battle again.

I met with John Gutfreund and told him I was definitely on my way out the door. I also shared with John my many concerns about the future of the firm. I told him that I thought the way we had exited the municipal and commercial paper business was deplorable, especially when we failed to inform our clients directly but let them read about it in the newspaper instead.

"What's more," I said, "the reputation of the firm is suffering. It's not just our competitors knocking us. It's the clients, too. Since the merger with Phibro, some of our partners seem to have let their new-found wealth go to their heads. They seem more interested in impressing each other than in spending time with their clients. And when you get too big for the clients, it's time to get out of the business."

Gutfreund asked me if I would repeat my remarks to Tom Strauss and Bill Voute, which I later did. Then he asked me about my own plans.

"I don't know exactly what I'll do," I replied. "But whatever it is, I won't be competing with Salomon." After spending a lifetime helping to build Salomon, I wasn't about to start selling some new brand.

My last days with the firm were painful. People began to bombard me with their tales of woe, treating me as a cross between a Jewish rabbi and a Catholic priest hearing daily confession. I'd been saying for a long time that Harold Tanner was the logical choice to be my successor, but some other partners disagreed. Now a compromise was reached: Harold and Jay Higgins, the head of M&A, were named co-heads of corporate finance. Unfortunately, this arrangement didn't work out very well. Harold Tanner felt forced to resign, and some other good corporate people followed his lead.

Finally, I packed up my things and departed Salomon for good.

By this time, I was happy to be on my way out the door. But I needed somewhere to hang my hat, if only temporarily, while I made plans for the future. Ray Golden, a good friend and former Salomon partner, had joined the Trammell Crow real estate development firm, and he offered me space in his office until I got settled.

It didn't take long for the right opportunity to become clear. It involved Peter Gottsegen, another good friend and ex-partner who had run international corporate finance and had left Salomon several months before me.

Peter Gottsegen grew up in Huntington, Long Island. Peter's father came from a large Jewish family that had emigrated from Europe to Brooklyn, while his mother was an Irish Catholic.

Peter attended the local grammar school, went to boarding school in Massachusetts, then on to Georgetown and the Wharton School of the University of Pennsylvania, where he earned his MBA. (Peter spent two years at Wharton, which shows what a slacker he is—I learned everything I needed to rise in my banking career in six days there.)

Peter's tours of duty included time at Halsey Stuart and Kuhn Loeb. He denies any responsibility for the decline of those two great firms of yesteryear. While he ran international corporate finance for Salomon, the firm greatly expanded its business in Europe, Asia, and Latin America. Peter was also responsible for the World Bank, and he and John Rotenstrich engineered the first major currency swap in the international currency market for the World Bank and IBM.

In his spare time, Peter served for eight years as chairman of Caramoor, an internationally recognized music and arts organization located in Westchester County. In addition to supporting a variety of charities, he serves on the boards of the Toronto Symphony, the Milbank Foundation and the Nature Conservancy of New York, and is a member of the Council on Foreign Relations and the Institute of Internal Education.

Now, with our Salomon days behind us, Peter and I founded CAI Capital, a mid-sized buyout firm, with a few other partners, setting up shop in the General Motors Building in midtown Manhattan. Eventually, Les Daniels, a friend of Peter's, joined us. Les had come out of the Street and spent about a decade doing healthcare deals with Dick Burge out of Cigna.

We did a few small deals, then invested our time and effort in a bankrupt company called Zenith Laboratories. Our senior partner was the renowned investor Michael Price. We invested a total of twelve million dollars and after a series of tribulations straight out of *The Perils of Pauline* we sold the company to Ivax for some $559 million—not a bad return for all the gray hairs Zenith had given us. The struggles included a summer spent by Les Daniels in the (non-air-conditioned) bankruptcy court in Newark, all with no guarantee that we would get the award. Fortunately, the new management team that emerged backed us, and Les became chairman of the company.

Then the Food and Drug Administration threatened to close us down, claiming our facilities did not meet their standards. Our lawyer wanted to fight the FDA, but Les said, "No, we'll get a prominent outside consultant to intervene on our behalf and solve the problem." Les was right—his approach worked.

Finally, Bristol Myers sued us. Reason: We were trying to get approval on a generic version of cerfadroxilin, a drug produced by Bristol Myers. The battle pitted our lawyer (singular) versus their sixteen lawyers. We won round one. They got the verdict reversed. We then won the final decision. All this took about two years, while Bristol made several hundred million marketing the drug. When we finally prevailed, the supplier of the raw materials we needed decided that he wouldn't do business with us. One can only speculate as to his reasons.

We finally managed to market a generic version of the drug, and added several other generics to our product list as well. CEO John Klein did an outstanding job running the company, and we ended up making a handsome profit on the entire harrowing experience.

*   *   *

In the years that followed my departure from Salomon, more and more long-time partners left the firm. One of these was J. Ira Harris, the powerhouse in mergers and acquisitions we called "Mr. Chicago." Ira was born in the Bronx where he attended public high school, then went on to the University of Michigan.

Ira's contacts in Chicago include the Pritzkers of real estate fame; the Crown's Kelly of Esmark; Cooke at the *Tribune*; the Quaker Oats people, and many, many others. He was responsible for many large municipal transactions emanating out of Illinois. But

Ira's reach extended far from the Chicago office, with contacts on the east and west coasts and throughout middle America. Right after the Phibro merger, Ira created the idea of "phantom stock," a kind of bonus system to keep and reward people at Salomon who either had just become or were on the verge of becoming managing directors.

Ira served on the executive committee for a number of years, and John Gutfreund sought Ira's counsel on many issues. Eventually Ira decided to step down due to a combination of family reasons and friction with the committee, and he left Salomon shortly after I did. He joined Lazard Freres, where he did many important transactions over the years. Later he joined his close friends, the Pritzkers, and more recently started the very successful company, Alternative Investment Management.

Ira and his wife, Nicki, have made many grants to the University of Michigan, Northwestern Hospital, a host of Jewish charities, and other worthy causes. Since their recent move to Palm Beach, they have been strong supporters of that community as well. The list of Ira's civic and public service directorships, honors, and awards would run on for pages.

Henry Kaufman was another casualty of the late 1980s. Henry was the most esteemed economist on Wall Street, the head of bond and stock research, and an invaluable asset to Salomon's stock, bond, and investment banking businesses.

Henry was born in Weinings, Germany, in 1927. In his memoir *On Money and Markets*, he tells how his grandfather's savings were wiped out in the runaway inflation following World War I and how the middle-class destitution that resulted led to the German Jews becoming scapegoats of the Nazi party. When the family fled to America, Henry's father, who had been a decorated soldier in World War I became a laborer working twelve hours a day, six days a week. Henry's mother cleaned other people's homes to earn extra money while his grandparents took care of him. Henry's character can be traced to the hard times and sacrifices his family survived. After receiving his Master's degree from Columbia in 1949, Henry went to work for People's Industrial Bank (later absorbed by Manufacturers Hanover). Henry received his doctorate from New York University in 1956, the year he joined the Federal Reserve Bank in New York. He joined Salomon in 1962.

In time, Henry became the number one economist on Wall Street, his annual forecast on credit supply and demand as eagerly antici-pated and avidly scrutinized as the Super Bowl. Salomon's clients in the US, Europe, and Asia flocked to hear him speak at dinners and conferences, and his prestige gave added luster to our firm. For a few years in the late seventies and early eighties he was considered one of the ten most important people in the United States—an achieve-ment even more impressive than my being named to the Far Rockaway High School Basketball Hall of Fame in 1943.

Henry's views could move the bond market, which meant that he had to be very careful about how and when he issued public pro-nouncements. He was scrupulous about ensuring that his market comments were released simultaneously to our clients, traders, and sales people. I remember how upset he was the one time there was a foul-up and the traders got the comments a few minutes early.

Like Ira Harris, Henry left Salomon shortly after I did, and he started a very successful money management firm. Henry and his wife, Elaine, have contributed generously to education, the arts, music, and other fields. They've endowed the Elaine Kaufman Cultural Center in New York City, donated ten million dollars to the Institute of International Education, and given many gifts to Henry's alma mater, New York University. I think Henry still has a little walking-around money left.

Shortly after my departure, a palace coup was attempted at Salomon. It was led by four men: Bill Voute, a senior trader and executive committee member; Craig Coats, a senior government bond trader; John O'Grady, a senior salesman and systems manager; and Ron Stuart, a senior international bond trader. These four attempted to oust Tom Strauss as president of Salomon, but their effort failed when John Merriweather declined to participate.

If they'd been attempting to overthrow a South American gov-ernment, they might have been shot, but since this was Wall Street, they just resigned and started another firm.

Bill Voute had attended Fordham University, and with his gre-garious personality he played a major role in encouraging his fellow Catholics to become deeply involved in philanthropy. He and his wife, Mary Jane, did tremendous work on behalf of the Inner-City Scholarship Fund, the Catholic Youth Organization, and Boston College. Bill was also involved in the Papal Foundation and was a close advisor to the archdiocese of New York.

When the new firm that Bill and his colleagues launched failed to take off, he went on to a brief career at First Boston before suffering an untimely death as a result of bacterial virus. Cardinal John O'Connor officiated at Bill's funeral mass before a standing-room-only crowd in St. Patrick's Cathedral. Others in the group also fared badly. John O'Grady died from a heart attack while skiing on a bitterly cold day in Windham, New York. The others scattered to the wind.

Ken Lipper, who managed the accounts of Bowater, Inc., a large paper manufacturer based in South Carolina, was another Salomonite who joined the exodus. Among the other accounts he covered were Fiat, Ryder System, and American Can. He left in 1982 to become Deputy Mayor of New York in Ed Koch's administration. A man of unusual breadth, Ken had come to Salomon from Lehman Brothers. After public high school, Ken attended Columbia University, where he graduated Phi Beta Kappa, then Harvard Law School. After passing the New York State Bar in 1965, Ken earned the degree of Master of Civil Law from New York University School of Law in 1967.

When Ken returned to the private sector in 1985, he started Lipper & Co. But Ken has many other talents. He authored the novels *City Hall* and *Wall Street* (the latter based on the Oliver Stone movie starring Michael Douglas), produced the film *The Winter Guest* (1997), and co-produced (with Steven Spielberg) the Holocaust documentary *The Last Days* (1998), for which he received an Academy Award.

Today Ken is an executive vice president at Cushman and Wakefield. He serves on a host of important corporate and philanthropic boards. His former wife, Evelyn Gruss Lipper, is the distinguished director of the child development division of New York Hospital and an associate professor of pediatrics at Cornell Medical School.

*　　*　　*

Even as my time at Salomon was winding down, life away from the office continued to evolve. Priscilla and I had our first son, Matthew, in 1981. In 1984, our second son Christian was born prematurely; he never made it out of the hospital. Priscilla then became pregnant with Andrew, and on the advice of doctors spent ninety days in New York Hospital before he was delivered some two weeks early by caesarian section.

The years since then have flown by. Some of them have been bitter, none more so than 1993. A series of heart-rending deaths marred that year. First my sister-in-law Kay died of colon cancer. Then Garry, my only brother and my closest friend, died of the same

My brother Garry and I help our mom celebrate her ninetieth birthday. I miss Garry still.

ailment. Then his namesake, my son Garry, died of AIDS. Completing the sad litany, Priscilla's grandmother, Gigi, also passed away.

But there have been moments of joy and celebration as well. Matthew graduated from Villanova in 2003, and his brother Andrew started Villanova that same year.

I learned to ski at age 60 and soon realized I should have taken up the sport a lot earlier. In my youth I had back problems and later tore a cartilage in my right knee, both of which convinced me to stay away from skiing. Too bad—I missed out on one of the great fun experiences of life.

A different sort of adventure was going out to the *USS Theodore Roosevelt*, a brand-new aircraft carrier, shortly after it was commissioned. My partner, Bob Quinn, had been chairman of the ship's christening committee. Amazingly enough, after the Defense

Department spends two billion dollars on a new carrier, the officers are responsible for raising funds for their wardroom, to buy dishes, glassware, silverware, and so on. Bob asked me to host a luncheon at Salomon for the captain, executive officer and another senior officer, and in true Salomon tradition, we raised ten thousand dollars at the luncheon.

(Now a digression. One of my partners, Mike Epstein, had been out shooting quail, and he delivered the birds he bagged to the chef at Salomon to be prepared for lunch. Unfortunately for Mike, he never got to enjoy the quail, because they were all eaten at our Theodore Roosevelt luncheon. A bit miffed, Mike got his revenge by pressuring me into buying a raffle ticket for a Junior Diabetes benefit dinner. First prize: a 1980 Rolls Royce. Wouldn't you know it, I won the darn thing. Great news? Not really. Mike immediately hit me up for a ten grand donation to the Juvenile Diabetes Foundation. Then the government came calling for $48,000 in taxes, my insurance company demanded six thousand to insure it, and my skilled mechanic soaked up another thirty thousand keeping the car running while I traveled some thirty thousand miles in it. When I finally unloaded it to a doctor in New Jersey, I opened a celebratory bottle of champagne.)

Back to the *Theodore Roosevelt*: As a thank-you for our fundraising luncheon, ten of us were invited to spend two days aboard the carrier. What an experience! We roamed the ship from the bridge to a pit on the flight deck where we could watch the planes take off. Unlike on a submarine, where there are long hours of boredom, a carrier is a constant hum of activity.

I remember spending one evening in the fantail of the ship, watching planes coming in to land. Three planes were waved off—too high or too low on their approach—they circled again and came in as a helicopter circled in the air nearby in case any one had to ditch his plane. I likened the captain to the nervous father of teenagers anxiously waiting for them to get home after a date. Late the next day I was catapulted off the carrier, which beats any amusement park ride. I came away with a great appreciation for the pilots who guard our nation and the busy officers and men who support them.

Sometime after that I had another ride which I hadn't signed up for. I was vacationing in Wyoming with my wife, my youngest son Andrew, and our friends Freddie and Annagret Botur. Freddie had a house in Jackson Hole and was partner in a 75,000-acre cattle ranch in Big Piney, some eighty miles away, with the late Nick Forstmann.

One day we were driving on the dirt roads that criss-cross the ranch, with me behind the wheel of Freddie's Yukon. Andrew was in the back seat. Just as I reached the top of one of the many hills, I spotted a cow in the middle of the road. As I hit the brakes, Freddie shouted, "No, no, we'll skid on the pebbles!"

Here's what the car looked like after our unexpected downhill ride at Freddie Botur's ranch.

Skid we did. The car was out of control. We plunged over the top of the ridge and down a hundred and fifty foot drop, turning over five or six times. My last thought before blacking out was, "My God, if anything happens to Andrew!"

When I came to, I was aware of intense pain in my chest and neck. Then I heard Andrew crying, "I think my arm is broken!" I was relieved to hear his voice, although I couldn't turn to look in his direction. Freddie had been thrown out the window. He was bleeding and later found he had broken some ribs.

Thankfully, a group of cowboys saw the accident and called for an ambulance from the hospital in Big Piney. I lay and waited for help, drifting in and out of consciousness. I understand they had to cut me out of the car, although I remember nothing. I was fortunate that the car didn't catch fire (the gas tank had been recently filled), as it was impossible for me to move.

At the hospital, X-rays revealed some chips in my vertebrae and a possible broken neck. They put me in a neck brace and on a stretcher to transport me by ambulance to the larger hospital in Jackson Hole. Andrew comforted me during the ride, broken arm and all. I

Recovering from the accident—and able to smile about it.

remember that the nurse who accompanied us was born on the same day as me—although decades later.

Priscilla was horrified to see me covered with cuts and stitches and with a huge black-and-blue neck. (It had swollen from my normal sixteen and a half inches to twenty-one inches in girth.) My son Matthew refused to believe it was his father. Luckily, the chips in my vertebrae proved to be old and were not in vital spots. They probably came from my basketball days.

When I got out of the hospital many days later, I chartered a Gulfstream 3 to take me back to New York. It would have been impossible for me to fly commercial—even in the G3 I couldn't find a comfortable position.

What I experienced during these days wasn't pain. The only word is agony. For several nights, I just lay awake, praying for daylight to come.

Fortunately I had a swimming pool at home. After a couple of weeks, I was able to float on a mat and kick my way back and forth forty or fifty times. I never realized how internal contusions could affect you. I couldn't use one arm while swimming and had a lot of

Happier times: riding with son Matthew at Jackson Hole, trying my best not to look like an investment banker.

internal pain.

I thought I would be back playing tennis within two months. It took me around nine months, and then I could hardly serve, since I couldn't look up.

As for Andrew, he got better quickly. He wore a lightweight cast on his left arm, a far cry from the heavy cast Michael had had to wear after his accident. Andrew was soon able to compete in the tennis tournament at our club and swam in races at the beach club.

And though today I still have trouble chasing lobs and have lost a lot of neck motion, I never forget what a lucky guy I am just to be alive.

Chapter 13
A Backward Glance

One night, as men of a certain age are wont to do, I was reminiscing with Priscilla about the "old days." "What a great group of partners I had at Salomon," I said.

"You miss them, don't you?"

"Sure," I replied. "I still see some of them once in a while, but we never get together as a group any more."

"Why not?"

I shrugged. "You know how it is. It just doesn't happen."

"So make it happen," she said. "Have a dinner for your ex-partners. I bet they'd get as big a kick out of it as you."

As usual, Priscilla was right. In 1990, I hosted what we called the Sons of Salomon Dinner at the Knickerbocker Club in New York. The invitation said, "We are the ghosts of the past." To allay concerns that our goal was to criticize current management, we sent out a clear signal: No comments on the present firm. Some 60-odd partners attended (some odder than others), and we had a wonderful evening poking good-natured fun at one another and recalling the crazy days when we were building the world's greatest financial firm.

I've already named and spoken about many of the fellows who attended that dinner—men like Henry Kaufman, Ira Harris, Michael Bloomberg, Bob Bernhard, and Ken Lipper. But there were others I haven't had occasion to mention yet. Bill Salomon was there, along with two of the more venerable members of Bill's executive committee—Bob Quinn, Sr., and Charlie Simon. Another old-timer

Some of the gang assembled for the 1990 Sons of Salomon dinner.

was Dan Kelly, a salesman who covered the major insurance companies in Hartford and was also the ghostwriter for the first letter on the course of the government bond market issued to Salomon clients. (The letter was attributed to Gerry Spencer, who was in charge of the government bond trading department at that time.) Other younger members of Bill Salomon's executive committee were present, including Vince Murphy and Alan Fine.

Tully Friedman was at the dinner. Tully left Salomon in 1984 to start Hellman & Friedman, one of the earliest and most successful buyout funds in the country. His partner, Warren Hellman, had been a partner at Lehman Brothers. Over the years, they raised many billion dollars, which they invested in Levi Strauss, Young & Rubicam, and other very successful buyout deals.

Tully's father, Louis, had emigrated to the US from Russia when he was seven years old. Later he deserted his family, forcing Tully and his five siblings to go to work as children to support themselves. Tully put himself through Stanford and through Harvard Law School in six years, then spent four and a half years with a Chicago law firm before becoming an investment banker. In 1970 he joined Salomon Brothers, later starting Salomon's west coast investment banking operation.

Tully's outside activities included serving as president of the San Francisco Opera Association and Chairman of Mount Zion Hospital and Medical Center. He has served as a director for many important corporations and as treasurer of the prestigious American Enterprise Institute.

Then there was Joe Lombard. As Ira Harris was to Chicago, Joe Lombard was to Boston. He was regarded highly by the politicos who ran the state of Massachusetts, and Salomon did major financing for the state.

Joe later became an excellent venture capitalist. Lucky Salomonites, including me, were still getting checks from Joe's successful businesses twelve and fifteen years after we invested in them. Joe's quiet demeanor, soft smile, unassuming manner, and unfailing professionalism made him one of the finest of the Sons of Salomon.

I don't want to forget Miles A. Slater, whose post-Salomon story is one of the most fascinating. Born in Brooklyn, the only child of Marvin and Edith Slater, Miles attended Brooklyn Technical High School. Miles was a proud booster of Brooklyn and used to brag that Brooklyn once boasted more corporate presidents than any other city in the United States. Of course, as I used to point out, they also had Whitlow Wyatt, Duke Snider, Gil Hodges, Pee Wee Reese, and Jackie Robinson, and they still couldn't beat the New York Yankees. (The only exception was in 1955, when I attended the World Series, and the Dodgers finally won.)   Miles attended New York University's School of Commerce at night and earned a bachelors degree in finance before launching his career at Salomon.

After leaving the firm in 1988, Miles traveled to Russia and developed a fine collecting of work by Russian émigré artists. He kept his hand in Wall Street, serving as chairman of the New York advisory committee for Bank Julius Baer, the legendary private Swiss bank.

Most significant of all, he began to study sculpture, working several months a year in Pietrasanta, Italy, under the watchful eyes of some brilliant old world artisans. (The name of the town translates literally to "sacred stone.") In 1995, he did his first major piece, *Rescue*, a memorial to the victims of the bombing of the Murrah Federal Building in Oklahoma City. It is a beautiful work now on display in the Oklahoma state capital building. Miles continues to develop his artistic talents out of his home studio in Pound Ridge, New York.

Congratulations, Miles, on your remarkable success in your new field of endeavor. I would also like to ask your forgiveness for all the money I took from you on the tennis court, and for not allowing you to warm up on that cold day that ended your tennis career.

Finally, no account of the Sons of the Salomon would be complete without a tribute to Bill Simon. Bill graduated from Lafayette College with a bachelor's degree in government and law in 1953. He joined Weeden & Co. and came to Salomon Brothers in 1974, where he was first in charge of the municipal department and later of the government department. Bill left Salomon in 1973 to become deputy secretary of the Treasury, and when George Schultz become Secretary of State in May, 1974, Bill became secretary of the Treasury.

After government service, Bill became a pioneer in the leverage buyout business as chairman of Westray Corporation. He and his partner, Ray Chambers, hit the mother lode with their first investment, the Gibson Greeting Card Company. Westray continued as a successful buyout firm throughout the late seventies and early eighties. During this period, Bill served on the boards of several leading U.S. companies. In 1988, he and his sons Bill and Peter founded William E. Simon & Sons.

A leading conservative voice, Bill served as chairman of the John

200

Olin Foundation from 1977 until his death in the year 2000, and as president of the Richard Nixon Library. He made generous gifts to several schools and colleges, including the William E. Simon Graduate School of Business Administration at the University of Rochester and the William E. Simon Center for Strategic Studies at

the United States Air Force Academy. Bill also gave generously to various Catholic charities and sports organizations, and served as chairman of the U.S. Olympic Committee.

Bill's funeral mass at St. Patrick's Cathedral was attended by thousands, including ex-president Gerald Ford, several former secretaries of state, and other high government officials, along with representatives from charitable and academic organizations he had befriended.

Quite a group, those Sons of Salomon. Who wouldn't be proud to have been counted in that company?

*   *   *

Looking back on my career, there are two things that stand out as having been of lasting importance to me.

One was dealing fairly, keeping my word, and making sure I could back up whatever I said.

The other was always protecting my reputation and that of the firm, avoiding doing business with people of questionable integrity even when a quick and substantial profit was being promised.

Having tried my best to live up to both of these aspirations, I was able to retire with the respect of my peers and competitors, which is the greatest compliment I could ever ask for.

Perhaps you're wondering where the title "Mr. Canada" comes from. I would never be so presumptuous as to claim it on my own. Some time during my career, one of my competitors bestowed it upon me. I can't remember who came up with the moniker, or when, but it spread quickly through the Canadian halls of Bay Street, and even today my friends and former competitors refer to me this way. Am I proud of the title? You bet I am.

Along the way I met a host of exceptional people, many of whom I've talked about in the pages of this book. The list of business people I admire and like is a long one. In Canada, the two most outstanding bankers I met were Alan Lambert of the Toronto Dominion Bank and Peter Godsoe of Scotia Bank. In investment banking, three men stand out: Ted Medland of Wood Gundy, Tony Fell of RBC Dominion Securities, and Tom Kierans of Scotia McLeod.

In the United States, I would single out two people. One is John Whitehead of Goldman Sachs. His list of accomplishments, starting with his command of a group of landing craft on D-Day, is too long for me to recite here and could fill a book in itself. In fact, it *has* filled a book, John's own memoir, *A Life in Leadership,* which I highly recommend.

The other is my good friend Walter Wriston, one of the great minds and hearts I have ever known. Shortly before Walter's death from pancreatic cancer in 2005, he was awarded the Presidential Medal of Freedom by President George W. Bush. Unfortunately, Walter was unable to attend the White House ceremony—his wife Kathy and his daughter Catherine Quintal accepted the medal on his behalf—but Priscilla and I were honored to attend, along with a small group of Walter's other friends.

Of course, it isn't only the rich and successful who deserve our admiration. When I was a youngster growing up in the Rockaways, there was a fellow a little older than me named Ralph, who was born with serious birth defects. He limped badly, and the only word I ever heard him say was *Yankees.* I would pass Ralph on the street, give him a smile and a little baseball swing, and Ralph would smile back and say *Yankees.*

Despite his handicap, Ralph was a hard worker. He delivered laundry to people's homes, wheeling the clothes down the sidewalk in a baby carriage. To me, this is what life is all about—giving the best you can in whatever walk of life you are called to, whether it's exalted or humble.

When I see someone from a wealthy family who is living on the interest from a trust fund and doing nothing with his life, I think of Ralph.

If I had to choose my personal hero, I would offer two names. First, there was my brother Garry, my closest friend and one of the finest men who ever lived. Then there was General Douglas MacArthur, a brilliant commander whose strategy in the Pacific saved many lives, making good his promise to return in triumph to the Philippine Islands. He also did a masterful job of ruling Japan during the post-war occupation and transforming the nation into a modern democracy and one of America's closest allies. He wouldn't have made a good president, and his outsized ego was a definite flaw. But in my lifetime, no public figure was more admirable.

As for my own life, what I'm most proud of is having been a Fireman First Class on the *USS Blackfin*. The World War II submarine service lost one out of every five men who went on a war patrol. They remain on eternal patrol. I think of those brave men who contributed so much to the Allied victory constantly. On a dark night, whenever I smell the aroma of diesel fuel or hear the sound of a ship's engine, it takes me back to those black nights in the Pacific and Indian Ocean and the deep sense of dread that always came over me whenever we sailed into harm's way. How difficult it is to relate this experience to those of later generations who haven't known war and fear. Yet being a submariner—no hero, mind you, but just another sailor—was an experience I wouldn't trade for all the wealth on Wall Street.

* * *

People sometimes ask me if I have any regrets. The answer is, not many. Sometimes I used to wonder how successful I might have been if I'd covered more large U.S. corporations. However, I certainly can't complain about the track record I was able to achieve.

I do wish I could have gone to college. If I had, I might have scaled higher mountains—but having received honorary degrees from three colleges and universities in Canada, I have to say that I didn't do too badly for a high school graduate. Other honors have followed as well, including, in 2005, the Order of Quebec (the highest award granted to any non-Canadian) and, most recently, knighthood in the Order of Saint Gregory the Great, bestowed upon me by Pope Benedict XVI. I'm still debating whether to ask my friends to call me "Sir Dick" or just bow when I walk into the room.

I'm sorry that Salomon, the great firm so many of us worked so hard to build, is no more. Every Son (and Daughter) of Salomon was greatly saddened by the government bond scandal that struck the firm in 1991. It was the inevitable result of paying a few traders unheard-of compensation, which creates envy and a focus on achieving unlimited wealth by any means necessary—including practices that are unethical and illegal. Hence the recurring appearance of rogue traders in the currency, bonds, and equity markets.

Now as my work life winds down, I have more time to enjoy my family, my wife Priscilla, and my personal passions in life—reading (mainly military history), playing tennis, and my newest love, gardening. It's very therapeutic to work in the garden or stroll my nature walk with Priscilla and a couple of glasses of wine in the evening.

One of my special joys is a metasequoia tree that rises some one hundred feet from its special location on the lawn of the home where I've lived for the past thirty-one years. It looks like an evergreen in the summer but completely loses its leaves in the fall. The metasequoia is a rare breed that supposedly originated in central China; the story goes that an Air Force pilot carried a seedling home after World War Two, and today the species has survived on the east coast of the United States. Recently I was surprised to discover three small seedlings from this tree nearby on the lawn. Perhaps I'll live to see them established and well on their way to being great living presences in their own right.

I find I've become addicted to seeds—discovering new varieties, from cosmos, sunflowers, and zinnias to impatiens, marigolds, and hibiscus, and planting them in our garden or handing packets of them out to my friends. I'm fascinated by the complexities of growing wisteria, whose seeds require refrigeration followed by planting, soaking, and shielding under a plastic cover to keep in the heat.

After a lifetime of nurturing investments, companies, and industries, I am now taking delight in nurturing living things that are smaller, more tender, and in their own way just as rewarding. Not a bad note on which to end this chapter of my continuing story.

Afterword

By Tom Kierans

Before Salomon Brothers had achieved any real measure of corporate success in the United States, Dick Schmeelk had carved an unsurpassed swath through Canada in all sectors of the underwriting business—among federal and provincial governments, crown corporations and private sector corporations. Salomon and Dick Schmeelk had become Canada's leading foreign investment bankers; and, as I maintained throughout my own investment banking career, Dick Schmeelk's investment banking career and Canadian successes contributed immensely as a launching pad for Salomon's subsequent successes in the United States in corporate financing.

Dick rose to be a member of Salomon's senior management executive committee. During his last six years at Salomon, he was responsible for world wide corporate finance at the firm. Salomon was the lead U.S. syndicate debt manager in five of those years.

This was achieved because Dick was Dick. His ethics were of the highest order. His integrity was such that issuers and investors were treated with the utmost respect and fairness; in turn, they trusted him completely. His advice, rendered softly, was sought out avidly when I joined the industry in 1962—a time when that age-old saying, "My word is my bond," really meant something. Dick's career epitomized that saying.

Dick's book is both touching and instructive. In his career, he scaled the summits, without compromising his principles. He lived by standards which all today who are working in any of the financial professions would best strive to emulate.

Tom Kierans was president of McLeod Young Weir Ltd., chairman of Petro Canada, and chairman of the C. D. Howe Institute. He is currently a director of several leading corporate and financial institutions and chair of the Canadian Journalism Foundation.

Acknowledgments

You learn from a career in business that no significant success is achieved without teamwork. That's as true in the field of book authorship as in investment banking. I couldn't have completed and published this memoir without help and support from many people, and I don't want to conclude without thanking a few of the most significant.

A major role was played by my executive assistant, Cathy Corona. It would be difficult to catalog all the ways in which Cathy helped to create this book, from typing and retyping sections of the manuscript, to sending out early versions for review, to monitoring dozens of textual changes and other details. Her patience and steady hand helped keep the project on track, and I am very grateful to her.

Freelance writer and editor Karl Weber did a fine job of helping me to shape and organize the manuscript, as well as sharpening my literary style. His help has certainly made the book more enjoyable to read, and I am happy to acknowledge it. Karl also shepherded the book through the production and publication process, using the fine professional services of Katonah Publishing to create the handsome volume you hold in your hands.

Several of my colleagues from the business world did me the honor of reading early versions of the manuscript and helping me with their suggestions and, on occasion, with factual corrections. In particular, I'd like to thank Tom Kierans, former president of Scotia McLeod, and Ray Goldin and Henry Kaufman, former partners at Salomon Brothers. I am also very grateful to Henry for contributing the Foreword, written in his typically eloquent and generous style.

Finally, I want to express my gratitude to the many people who have shaped and inspired my life and work, and thereby have made this book possible. The list begins with my Mom and Dad, two wonderful people who helped forge my personality and taught me much about the meaning of life. It includes my family members, past and present, including my first wife, Betty, and my wonderful second wife, Priscilla. It also includes my fellow Sons of Salomon,

Most of our clan, gathered at the Lawrence Beach Club. Standing, from left to right: Staci, Isabella, Ali, Andrew, Matthew, Virginia, Elizabeth, me, Marrie, and Betty. Kneeling: Michael and Stephen.

our many clients, and all those who did so much to create a great financial firm that, sadly, no longer exists, but which those of us who built our careers there will always remember with pride and fondness. And finally, my former comrades at arms, some living and some resting below the sea on eternal patrol.

Richard J. Schmeelk

January, 2007